This book is my true experience of gamb
never write every single lie I told. Every single time I lost to the gambling
thoughts. I couldn't write every pay check I lost throughout my 10 year
battle, every harmful thought than ran through my head but the events I
share with you in this book are all my own.

I was a gambling addict for 10 years of my life. That addiction tore
everything good in my life away from me. I lost everything and I truly
believed that there was nothing that could help me. If you've picked up
this book and can resonate in anyway, to the horrific effects of gambling
addiction, or any addiction for the matter, then I want to get across to you
this message.

You can get better. You can break and beat the cycle. No matter how long
you have endured your addiction. It is never too late.

As the world faces a global pandemic, where we are forced to stare at our
TV screens, our phones and have adverts of gambling pushed in our faces
with every football match, every other advert, every offer that comes with
'Just a £20.00 deposit' I wanted to share the true advert for gambling. For
problem gambling. I decided to come out of the shadow I was living in,
cast by shame and guilt that I had carried for so many years, that I know
so many gambling addicts carry, and show the light.

It is believed, that 4 in every 10 women gamble. It's those 4 women, the
ones too ashamed to admit that, between their day to day jobs, between
the housework, between being a mum, they gamble. To those 4 women
who I say, you are not alone. Whether you've tried everything or you've
yet to try anything to help, there is help and it really can work.

I truly am gamble free now. And it took only 6 days of learning the
techniques that suited me best, that taught me that access to money,
people and environment can save me in any situation, that it's ok not to
have control of your own finances, those 6 days taught me the skills I
needed to change my life for the better.

Whilst I will forever consider myself a problem gambler, a person who gets sucked in by it's incorrectly advertised appeal and a tendency to lose control, I also consider myself a survivor. A survivor of what it did to me. A lifetime of recognising what could be a trigger, or what door I may have left open, but, the relief and quality of life that comes with it is worth every thought and moment.

From the bottom of my heart, I thank everyone who helped me. And with special thanks to a charity that, for no cost at all, gave me freedom from my gambling addiction. Thank you Gordon Moody.

GAMSTOP

www.gamstop.co.uk

Register with GAMSTOP and you will be prevented from accessing all gambling sites and apps run by companies licensed in Great Britain. It's quick, simple and free and you can sign up for 6 months, 1 year or 5 years to help you control your online gambling.

GAMBAN

www.gamban.com

GAMBAN is an easy to use application that blocks online gambling on all of your devices, offering you a secure, reliable and affordable option to stay away from gambling sites and apps, helping those with gambling problems fight the urge.

GORDON MOODY

www.gordonmoody.org.uk

Providing advice, education and high quality innovative therapeutic support to problem gamblers and those affected by gambling through residential, online and outreach services.

Chapter 1

This was it. She stared at the crumpled £20.00 note pulled from the back pocket of her unwashed jeans. She began to iron the note between her index and middle finger as she contemplated what she was about to do. Running the note through, over and over again until it was straight enough to fit into the slot. What would seemingly be a bad choice, the truth of the matter is, she had no choice. Although no one whispering in her ear, egging her to do the unthinkable, convincing her it would be fine and everything ok, she simply had no choice in what was about to happen. Knowing the consequence and the outcome already, she fed the now somewhat straightened note into the machine. A part of her begged the machine not to take it. To spit it out and refuse to take anymore from her money whilst the other part, the part that led her onto this cold leather stool, into the shop with that distinct fusty smell, filled with people double and triple her age, told her 'it will work this time'.

And there it was. The credit on the screen showing £20.00. She fidgeted on the stool, her hands sweating profusely. She was so hot but didn't feel comfortable enough to take off the damp, green parker on her back. A million thoughts run through her head 'Should I play on a £1 stake to have more spins? But maybe on a £2 stake I'll hit the bonus I need? It only takes 1 spin to get the jackpot. I'm due a pay out. It's ready to drop.' She raised her right hand and hit the button. No win. She thought 'Ok. £18.00 left. I can't change stake now, it knows. I'll only get the bonus on a £2 stake.' Her hand slightly shaking, she hits again. No win. £16.00 left. £14.00 left. £12.00 now. She fidgets again on the stool. Looking around the shop, she see's people at the counter with their betting slips. The old Labrador having a snooze as the punter is watching the virtual race on the big screen. People chatting and laughing. But she hears nothing. All she can hear is the noise from her machine as it draws her line of vision back to the flashing light on the screen telling her what the jackpot was at this point. She pressed the button again. One bonus symbol. And another! The last reel on the screen spinning for what seems like an age. She can't bear to stare directly at the screen. She slides her still sweating hand into the sleeve of her coat and crosses her fingers as she prays 'please god, please.' The last reel comes to a stop, just missing the bonus symbol. She feels her heart sink and the tears begin to fill her eyes. Hand still in her sleeve, fingers still crossed, she continues to press the button. Staring at the credit bar now, £2.00 left. She presses the button for the final time and back at £0.00. She frantically checks both back pockets again, just to make sure there wasn't another note she'd missed. Finally, she checks her coat pockets and, full only of cigarette tips, an empty bank card, a bus ticket, copper coins and an old door key, she gives in to the inevitable. She peels herself from that stool and makes her way to the door, avoiding eye contact with anyone in the shop. She pulls the creaky door towards her and steps out into the rain.

As the raindrops hit her face, camouflaging the tears she was failing to hold back, she lets out a sob. She tried to pull a cigarette paper from her pocket but the rain tears it. She screws up the paper and throws it on the floor, pulls the oversized hood over her head and makes her way down the road to the bus stop. As she gets there, eyes puffy and red from crying, she squints as she tries to read the timetable. The raindrops on the plastic covering the schedule, make it hard to see. The next bus was at 19.20pm. She pulls her phone from her pocket. The light shining on her face, she wipes the screen with the sleeve of her coat and reads 19.04pm. She begins to lift her feet up on the spot that she's stood to try and warm up her legs as she's freezing, hands dug as deep as they could possibly be in her fur lined pockets. The 16 minute wait seemed much longer whilst it was so cold and raining. Thoughts run through her mind 'I can't believe it. That machine was due to pay out. How am I going to pay my bills? I don't get paid for another 4 weeks. Why, why you fucking idiot have you done it!' She comes to an agreement with herself 'We will think about this when we get home. You cannot cry on the bus. Everything will be ok lets just get home and we will sort it then.' As the old woman next to her udges up on the steel bench under the shelter of the stop, she squeezes into the space that's left and rolls herself a cigarette. Her hands almost numb now, she steps out of the shelter to light the uneven, hand rolled cigarette. It feels almost, with that first drag, that she blows out some relief with that first cloud of smoke. She discards the browned cigarette end into the grate against the road. The old woman in the bus stop giving her a dirty look as she does so. She sits herself back on the bench and stares down the road for sight of the bus. 19.23pm now. 'Where is it!? This is a fucking joke' she thinks to herself as she becomes visibly more restless and irritable sat on that bench. Finally, some bright lights bounce off of the rain water on the road, filling the bus shelter with light. That familiar noise of the suspension creaking on the bus. She looks down the road and there it was, almost like a mirage, but a warm, dry bus coming to take her home.

The old woman next to her approaches the side of the road and sticks out her gloved hand into the rain to flag down the bus. As the bus comes to a halt, it opens its slow moving doors and she waits for the old woman to climb aboard. 'For fucks sake hurry up!' she thinks, as the woman grabs for the rails on the door and begins to look for her bus pass. The woman shuffles towards the front seat on the bus, going at what seemed to be the pace of a snail. It was finally her turn, she smiled as she showed the driver her bent bus ticket, covered in rain. The driver smiled and said thank you. She knew where the heaters were on the bus and immediately looked for a free seat next to one. She spotted the perfect seat, hurried over and placed her hands on the heater.

All the way into town, she held back her tears. Staring into the road wondering 'what the hell am I going to do?' And then telling herself off. 'You cannot cry on this bus. You'll look like an idiot. Just stop thinking about it for now and we will sort when we're home'. The bus pulled up at it's final destination in town, a 10 minute walk from her flat. She hurried to the front of the bus so she wouldn't have to wait behind the old woman. She smiled, thanked the driver and stepped back into rain.

Hood up and head down, she marched her way towards the long alleyway that led to the road her flat was on. It was really dark by now and the alley had always scared her a little. As she approached the metal pillars that were at the beginning of the alley. She looked up and around quickly, then head down again as she picked up pace to get through the alley as quickly as she could. She even held her breath as she walked through it to make sure she went as quickly as she could. She reached the metal pillars at the other end and took a deep breath. She stared up at the college on the left hand side, only a few lights on now and a couple of people outside. 'Maybe if I'd have gone to college I wouldn't be such a fuck up now' she thought as she continued to walk towards her flat.

As she reached the bottom floor door on the side of the sandwich shop her flat was above, she fumbled for her keys. Her fur lined hood now dripping, she opened the door and made her way up the two flights of stairs to her flat. She opened the door and shivered. She turned up the thermostat on the wall to her left and made her way into the living room. One tiny room filled with nothing but a small sofa, a rocking chair the landlord had let her use and a 16" TV her sister had given her. She threw her sodden coat onto the sofa and walked into the kitchen that was attached to the living room. An open planned space but the kitchen so tiny, she couldn't fit both a fridge and freezer in it. She picked up the little plastic kettle with her still numb hands, filled it with water and clicked the kettle to boil. She put both elbows on the side next to the kettle, head in her hands and began to sob.

She squeezed her fists, hair wrapped around her fingers, tighter and tighter until it hurt. The kettle clicked, pouring with steam. She held her hands over the steam for a second to try and warm them up. Then she reached into the cupboard above the sink and pulled out an old yellow mug her nan had given her. She made herself a strong coffee, placed it on the windowsill and rolled herself another cigarette. As she opened the window in the living room, she made sure there was no sign of her landlord on the street before she hung her head out of the window and smoked. When she'd finished, she sat in the old wooden rocking chair, hands wrapped around her hot mug and sipped her coffee.

She took a deep breath, put down her coffee and went into the cutlery drawer. She lifted the tray which held her 2 forks, 1 knife and 2 spoons and rustled through the unopened debt letters, pen tops and betting machine receipts in search of a pen and piece of paper she could use to try and write a plan for how she would deal with the consequences of what she'd just done. She pulled out an empty envelope and blue biro. She scribbled the biro until she could see it was working. She walked back over to her chair, took another sip of coffee then sat with the pen to her mouth. After a moment, she began to write.

Rent:£350.00

Gas & Electric: £150

Council tax: £70.00

Mum: £200

Debts: £450

She started to doodle little flowers all around the brown envelope in the absence of any brain wave coming to her as to how she would deal with this mess. Her bank balance at this time £7.25 having been paid just this morning. A tear fell and stained one of the flowers she'd drawn on the brown envelope. She stabbed her pen through the weakened spot and made a hole, followed by ripping it up into a pile of scrap on the floor. After another cigarette, she went to the pocket of her coat and pulled out her phone. She sat back in the chair and opened up the search engine. 'How to get money quick' she typed into the search bar. She reached for her now luke warm coffee as her phone presented her with a number of payday loan options. She'd had many payday loans in the past, never paid them back and now had a terrible credit rating. 'Payday loans for bad credit' she typed into the search bar again. She scrolled down as she had already had loans with most of the providers that showed. But there, at the bottom of the page, was a website she hadn't heard of before. She clicked onto the advert that proudly displayed 'we accept 98% of all applications!' Without looking at a single review or any terms and conditions, she filled out the application. The page asked for her date of birth. As the 24 year old filled it out she thought '24 years old and already in this much debt and an addict.' But her brain wouldn't allow her to feel sad in this moment. No, because right now, there was a possibility that she could fix what she'd done. She filled out the rest of the questions and clicked submit. 'Please wait whilst we review you application' her screen read. She paced up and down the tiny living room as she watched the wheel turn round and round on the screen of her phone. Her screen dimmed because it had been loading for so long. She quickly tapped to ensure her phone didn't lock and affect the loading of the results. 'Come on please, please. I beg you' she said as she continued to pace and pace. 'I swear I wont gamble it this time, I'll just pay what I need to, I promise'.

Her phone started vibrating and one email after another after another came through. A text came through but still the results hadn't loaded. She scrolled down on the notification bar of her phone to see an email : Your loan application. She clicked onto the email and prayed again. She skim read the email and there it was. Unfortunately. That's all she needed to see, she knew by now that somewhere, a declined loan application would have that word in it and that's all she needed to find. She threw her phone to the wall and screamed. She sat on the floor in the corner of the room with her head in her folded arms, rested on her bent knees. 'What am I going to do?' She sobbed.

She sat on the floor for a while, just thinking and crying. She felt the heat coming from the radiator so she got up and turned the heating off because she knew she couldn't afford to have it on anymore. She couldn't pay her arrears as it was. As she stood at the kettle, making another coffee, she heard her phone vibrating. She walked over and picked it up from where it landed after she threw it. The screen showed 'Mum'. After a deep breath , she answered in the most 'normal' voice she could 'Hi mum, you ok?' Her mother replied 'Yeah are you?' Fighting back her tears and trying to hide any tone in her voice that might have let her mum know she'd been crying she answered, 'Yeah I'm fine.' They continued to have their normal conversation, 'what have you been up to?...Not much you?...' She knew it was just her mum checking in. She also knew her mum had a sixth sense for when she'd gambled. Even if she'd not seen her for a while, her mum always seemed to get in touch with her just after. She made the decision to not tell her mum, she couldn't hurt her again. This had been going on for so long now, she already owed her money. She knew the conversation would have to happen if she couldn't find another way, but not tonight. She said goodnight to her mum and hung up the phone. 21:58 was the time her phone lit up her face with. She placed herself in her rocking chair with her hot coffee and just sat, for over an hour, rocking back and forth. She then had her final cigarette and went into the only bedroom next door. It was freezing in there. It had a large window at the front and one at the side. A single pane of glass in each made the room even colder. She climbed under the quilt in a tight a ball as she could, reached her arm out of the bed for the hairdryer, as she did every night, and warmed the bed up with the hairdryer until it cut out from overheating. When it did, she rolled over, pillow damp from her tears, and waited to fall asleep.

Chapter 2

'Steph Goodyear!' The teacher shouted. 'Stop chatting and face the front!' As she continued to talk, the teacher screamed 'Steph!' The school bell started ringing but it was a funny ring, a kind of ring tone. It lasted a couple more seconds before she woke up. She'd been dreaming and it was her phone that she'd dreamt was the school bell. She reached her arm out of the bed and hit snooze on her phone. She tucked back into a ball, protecting herself from the harsh cold she knew lay outside the safety of her quilt. And then she remembered. For just a moment she'd forgotten. Her stomach fell so far it felt like it was about to fall right out of her. She immediately felt sick and wished she could just fall back to sleep. Of course, that was never going to happen. Not now she'd remembered what she'd done.

Her alarm had gone off because she was due at work today. 'I can't do it' she thought. 'I can't go in, I need to sort something out.' She paced the shabby carpet of her living room as the kettle boiled. Phone to her ear as she rang the call centre she worked in, praying she would only need to leave a message. 'Hello?' a croaky voice said down the phone. It was her boss. 'Erm, hello' she replied, trying to make her voice sound as ill as she could, 'It's Steph. I wont be in today boss I'm sorry, I've got a terrible headache and a bad stomach, I'm really sorry.' A moment's pause got Steph's heart racing, did her boss somehow know she was lying? Did he know what she'd done? 'Ok Steph, no problem, I hope you feel better soon. Will you call me later and let me know how you are?' 'Of course!' She replied. 'I'm really sorry and I'll be in tomorrow for sure'. Her boss wished her well and told her to get some rest. She hung up the phone and exhaled a huge sigh of relief. He'd bought it. Right, she'd got 24 hours before her rent cheque was returned and her landlord knew.

It wouldn't be the first time Steph had not paid her rent. Last month in fact she missed it. She managed to think of a good excuse about being signed off of work. Luckily, her landlord hadn't asked for proof and was quite happy for her to make up the payments bit by bit, but he wouldn't accept it again. He would know this time and kick her out.

Cigarette lit and coffee in hand, her mind raced at a thousand thoughts a minute. Exploring every single avenue she could to get some money to pay what she needed to. Loans, family, friends, would someone take out a loan on her behalf, rob somewhere, steal from someone, could she draw money and make it look realistic? The most ridiculous thoughts entered her head about ways she could fix it but, in that moment, in that level of desperation, everything was an option.

Her absolute last resort would be her mum and telling her mum what she'd done. Steph already owed her mum money. Her mum was a cleaner and had her own bills to pay. She'd promised month after month to pay her mum back and yet, every payday, she found herself typing the message...'Mum, I've gambled.' She wouldn't do it this time. She would find a way to fix it. She would not hurt her mum again. As she sat staring at her phone, her battery already drained from the vast amount of searches she'd made on 'how to get money quick', her stomach grumbled. She looked at the time and it was 12:18! She thought back to the last time she'd eaten. It was well over 24 hours ago.

Throughout secondary school, Steph had suffered with anorexia. In an attempt to be as skinny as her friends, or skinner than them, she agreed to a challenge to see who could go the longest without eating. She of course was the only one who took it so seriously that it led to a severe weight drop and, after being dragged to doctors appointments by her mum, a diagnosis of anorexia. After many many appointments, counselling sessions, food diaries and coaching, she did manage to beat the disease and maintain a healthy weight. However, she knew her weight would be monitored closely now she was living alone. However right now, she did not have time to eat.

Her next search, prompted by her empty stomach, was 'I can't afford to eat'. She scrolled down the answers and came across a local community scheme which loaned 'emergency funds' to people. Steph did have a full time job and would, if she didn't gamble, be able to make the repayments. She read about the requirements and she was eligible! She hurriedly put the number in her phone and rang as she lit another cigarette. A recorded voice explained that the lines were recorded and there was a high volumes of calls. She didn't care, she needed to get through and would wait for as long as she needed to. After 25 minutes, a young man answered the phone and asked how he could help. Steph explained that she simply did not have enough money to feed herself, heat her house or eat this month and she didn't know what to do. The gentleman, who was very helpful, went through a list of questions with Steph. As she lied through each question, saying she had paid all of her debts and it left her with nothing, heart racing and the guilt flowing through her body, the man on the other end of the phone explained he needed to put her on hold and review the application and would she be happy to wait? She said yes of course, and listened to the monophonic hold tone over and over again. She had both her fingers crossed, pacing up and down her tiny living room. Finally, he came back to the phone 'Steph?' he asked 'Yes, yes I'm here' she replied, absolutely aching with anticipation. 'I'm pleased to tell you we can lend you £400'. She fell to her knees, crying as she thanked the stranger on the other end of the phone. 'No problem, you'll need to come into the office in downson Village, are you free today?' She couldn't believe it. Full of excitement and relief, she arranged to collect the money from town that day at 2.30pm. She ran to her bedroom, saying over and over again out loud, thank you, thank you. She didn't know who she was thanking, but she could not be more grateful. She put on the same unwashed jeans she'd worn the day before, a t-shirt from the wash basket, the still damp parker and ran out of the door.

As Steph sat on the bus into the village the where the office was, filled with such relief and happiness, she thought about how she had arrived in the position she had. It was only on her 17th birthday, Steph realised she was old enough to put on the lottery and buy a scratch card. She was waiting for the bus with her mum when she ran to the local shop and asked the cashier for a lucky dip and a £2 scratch card. She ran back to her mum, still at the bus stop, and scratched the card. She'd lost. Completely underwhelmed, she had absolutely no interest in buying another and said to her mum 'what a waste of money!'. She enjoyed the remainder of her day. She bought new clothes, a new phone with her birthday money and returned home to have tea with her 3 sisters. Two older, one younger.

Later that night, she checked her lucky dip, won nothing again and screwed up the ticket. Throughout all of that year, Steph never gambled another penny and never even thought about it. It was a year later, that Steph needed a new job. She'd been working in a call centre but had just been made redundant. As she walked through the town centre, after meeting her father for a coffee as they did on a Thursday, Steph saw the sign. 'Cashier required, 16 hours per week, must be 18+ years old ' sat in the window of the bookmakers. It was that sign. That tatty, hand written sign in the window with the fingerprint stains, that would start the downward spiral into addiction.

Chapter 3

The bus pulled into it's usual stop in and Steph hurried to the front to get off and get to the office of the lender as quickly as possible. She was always in a rush. Everything had to be done there and then. Growing up, she had a world of patience. She would wait for anything and anyone. She was a huge worrier and always thought about her family and friends. As she got older, and fell further into her addiction, her patience seemed to allude her. She thought about nothing other than gambling. Even when she was making a conscious effort not to think about gambling, she was thinking about not gambling which meant she still had gambling on her mind. But right now was an emergency. She needed to get to this office so that she could get the money and fix the problem she'd made for herself.

She staggered off of the bus and towards the old building she needed to be in. She was vaguely familiar with it although she hadn't actually been in it before. As she reached it, she looked at its large concrete steps and felt quite nervous. She checked the time and still had 20 minutes to spare. She sat down on the step and rolled a cigarette, picking the very last bit of dried up tobacco out of the bottom of the packet. As she waited, her thoughts went back again to that tatty sign in the window. If only she'd never seen it, if only she'd never gone in and asked for an application form, she wouldn't be here today.

She was successful in getting the job in the bookmakers. She couldn't believe it! 18 years old with no cashier experience and barely passed her Maths GCSE. She got given her shifts later that week and was asked to start on the Saturday. She thought it an odd day to start but didn't mind, she was just thankful she had a job. On her first day, she walked nervously into the shop. A few punters stood around the shop and a young man on the machine who looked angry. She walked towards the cashier desk and said in a shaky voice 'Hi, I'm Steph, I start here today.' A man, who looked in mid thirties, and a woman in her late twenties looked back at her. The woman immediately smiled and in the most welcoming voice said 'Oh my god, Hello! I'm Naomi! Come on round here and I'll let you behind the desk!' The blonde woman got up from her seat and walked to the back of the counter. She opened a blue door and beckoned Steph in. Steph stepped in and the man said ' Do you want a drink or anything?' Steph replied 'No thank you.' And smiled. The excited woman took Steph's coat and got her a chair. She explained who she and the man were, their roles and asked Steph about her life. She explained her recent redundancy and that she was excited to get to work. 'Fab! And the most important question of all...' the woman stated, 'Do you smoke?' Steph was worried that yes would be the wrong answer at this point, and that they might judge her however, she couldn't do a full shift without a cigarette! 'Yes.' Naomi replied with her head down. 'Good lass!' replied Naomi and took Steph out the front doors for a cigarette. Naomi was amazing. She made Steph feel so much better and relaxed, she was going to enjoy working here, she could tell. As they chatted, Naomi pointed to an oldish guy in the store. He wore a torn woolly hat and his clothes looked quite dirty. 'That's Matt, he's in every morning when we open until we close.

Everyday. I mean everyday. He has a real issue with gambling but he's a lovely guy and we always offer him help but he really does like it here. It's really sad. He lost his wife and kids and everything through it.' Steph felt sorry the guy and wondered how anyone could become that bad and lose everything through a bet!

Still sat on the concrete step, Steph dropped her cigarette and stubbed it out on the floor with her worn out trainer. She looked again into the office and climbed the steps to the automatic doors. As she walked in, there were rails everywhere for people to queue. She looked around for signs to see if she could recognise which queue she needed to be in. She finally saw, embedded on a silver sign, 'emergency funding department'. She guessed this was where she needed to go. She joined the queue of about 5 people. There was a woman in front of her with a baby in a pushchair. The baby was crying and the mum was rocking the pushchair back and forth. The woman couldn't have been older than 18. Steph thought to herself 'I'm so thankful I don't have a kid, it must be so hard.' The baby continued to cry and the woman stuck a pink dummy in the babies mouth. The baby stopped crying then and seemed to sleep. It was a pretty little thing and Steph felt some peace as she watched the baby nod off. She must not have realised how long she'd been watching for as the cashier called next and the woman and baby moved to the free cubicle. Steph felt a tad embarrassed however, there was no room for embarrassment right now. She had to fix what she'd done and she would put herself through anything so that she wouldn't have to tell her mum and hurt her again. As a pale looking man walked out of a cubicle, next was called and it was Steph's turn. She sat in the stained chair in front of the glass panel where she was met by a middle aged woman wearing really thick glasses. The woman, quite abruptly, said 'Name?' Steph gave her name and answered the questions asked of her by the woman behind the glass. The woman then stood up and walked to a door behind her. She inputted a code into the lock on the door. Steph tried to work out what it was. She couldn't make it out fully but knew it had a 2 in it. As the woman was in the room through the door, Steph's foot was tapping on the floor the whole time, her leg shaking, she couldn't stop it. She needed the cash in her hand now! 'Does it really take this long?' she thought to herself.

Then, she saw the woman walking back to the door through the small pane of glass that was in it. She saw the lock flash green and the small, fat woman holding £20 notes. She shuffled herself on the chair. Through the post office style vent in the desk, the woman asked Steph to sign the agreement. She didn't even read it, she just signed and handed back to the woman as quickly as she could. A few moments later, the cash was handed to Steph. She thanked the woman, even though she thought her quite rude, and walked away from the desk £400 better off than when she'd walked in. As she walked out, she heard the next being shouted for the next person.

She stuffed the wad of £20's into her pocket as she headed for the bank. 'Thank you, thank you, thank you' she thought as she made her way there. Even though £400 was not enough to cover everything she needed to pay, it was at least a start. As she marched, she remembered that she'd needed to buy some tobacco as she'd smoked the last remaining bits of dust from her packet before she went in to collect her money. She passed a shop she knew well and joined the queue of two people to be served. As she looked at the tobacco behind the desk, the huge tower of scratch cards caught her eye. Like a rainbow, every colour you could imagine displayed right at the front of the desk, begging to be an impulse buy as you get to the counter. 'If I get my tobacco, and a ten pound scratch card, I'll still have enough to pay my rent' she thought as she moved one closer to the front of the queue. 'But if I get 2 £10 scratch cards, my chances of winning double really don't they?' she asked herself. And just like that, she'd convinced herself that two £10 scratch cards, plus a £12 packet of tobacco was the purchase she would make from this store. '30 grams of tobacco and two number one scratch cards please' she asked politely. The man behind the counter granted her request, pulled the scratch cards from long reel and handed them over. She left the shop and saw a bench on the other side of the road. She headed towards it and dipped her hand into her pocket, rummaging for the copper coins she'd remembered were in there yesterday. She unfolded the bright blue pieces of card and began to scratch. 'no,no,no' she said to herself and she scratched away the silver paint to reveal she had no winners. The first card being a complete loss. She then began on the second. 'Oh!' she thought, as she revealed one winning symbol. 'Oh again!' as she revealed another winner. 'Get in! £50!

I knew my luck had to change!' was what ran through her mind as she revealed her winnings. So at this point, she'd got the two scratch cards and the tobacco she needed and an extra £20. 'Well if I get 2 more I could win again and if I lose, I'll just be left with what I had before.' This was how Steph justified her next purchase. She went into the shop and bought another 2 scratch cards and kept £30. She sat herself on the bench again, full of anticipation and a real belief that she would win. As her already dirty jeans became covered in the silver paint, she revealed two losing cards. 'At least I'm not down on money' she fooled herself with.

Steph continued her journey to the bank and deposited the £400, ready for her cheque to clear for her rent tomorrow. She would sort the other bills out later and buy herself some more time but for now, it was important her rent was paid. Feeling relieved, Steph jumped on the bus towards home. Her stomach growled again as she sat there. She remembered she had £7.25 in her account left from yesterday and so, decided to treat herself to a bag of chips from the local chippy at the end of her street. The bus stopped with a creak of it suspension and Steph jumped off. She made her way to the chippy and got herself a small bag of chips. Unable to wait until she got home, she opened the bag and began to eat.

She reached the bottom stairway of her flat and made her way up. With a full belly and a sense of relief that at least her rent was sorted, she sat back in her rocking chair and tried to relax. Her mind again went to how she'd ever ended up in a such a situation. A young girl with a good wage, unable to afford to feed herself and pay all of her bills. Her mind drifted back to that tatty sign, and the start of her job in the bookmakers.

Weeks and months passed at her new job. She became very good friends with Naomi. They went out together most nights and Steph practically lived at Naomi's house now. They were inseparable. As Steph continued to learn the systems, she watched the behaviours of the punters. Mainly older men would come into the shop, place their bets for no more than a couple of pounds and watch the races. It would be the same faces everyday but they seemed to enjoy being there. She grew closer to Matt and felt sorry for him. He had nothing. He'd spend all of his benefits money in the shop on just 50p bets that were never going to get him a good return. Matt knew this and yet, still, every day he spent in the shop. There was the odd customer who would come onto the machines. They would sit there hours, feeding hundreds and hundreds of pounds into the machine. You could see them getting angrier and angrier. You did however, get the 'lucky ones' and she'd named them. The people that would come in, put £10 in the machine and walk up to the desk checking in a ticket for hundreds of pounds! Still, it wasn't enough to convince Steph it would be a good idea. 'I'd never, ever put my money in one of them!' she explained to Naomi.

All of the bookmakers in town, no matter what company, worked closely together. They would go in each others shops to place bets, get change and everyone knew each other really well. One day, when Naomi was due to finish work, Steph met her in town just before she was due to finish her shift. They were going to go for some lunch. 'I just need to nip to the other shop Steph to get some change then I'm done, want to come for the walk?' Steph agreed and they made their way to bookmakers a few streets down. Steph didn't like this shop. It was tiny, always full and smelt like urine. She couldn't understand why. They had such strict cleaning rituals in their shop so how could this shop get away with it being this dirty? Naomi walked to the counter, happy as always. 'I need some change Pete.' She exclaimed to the grey haired man on the other side of the counter. 'Oh yeah, never come just to see me do you, always wants something from me' he replied jokingly. 'I just need to open the safe, it'll take a few minutes, you ok to wait?' asked Pete. Naomi nodded politely and turned to Steph. To the left of where they were stood was an empty betting terminal. Lights flashing and the £500 jackpot sign seemed to draw Naomi's attention. 'Shall we give it a try?' asked Naomi to Steph. Steph didn't really want to but, she trusted Naomi infinitely. She was her best friend and she'd taught Steph all she knew. 'Yeah go on then,' Steph replied 'Only a fiver though'. Naomi took the five pound note from Steph and fed it into the machine. All of a sudden, the screen lit even more and presented them with a £5.00 credit. 'We'll try roulette' Naomi said. Steph hadn't done this before so she let Naomi take the lead. She clicked on the black and red numbers until the credit was £1.00. '0 is my lucky number. Always put a pound on 0' Naomi told Steph. And so, with two last taps on 0 and a credit bar reaching £0.00, Naomi hit the big play button. 'Eeek, I'm excited.' Said Naomi. Steph was intently watching the roulette wheel spin and spin. As it slowed, the ball jumping from number to number, the girls were silent. 'You jammy bugger!' a deep voice shouted from over the counter. It had landed on 0! 'Oh my god!' the two girls hugged each other and we're giddy at the credit screen now showing £36.00 credit. 'That'll pay for dinner!' cried Naomi. She tapped excessively on the collect button on the screen and handed it over the counter to Pete. He returned to them a fresh £20 note, a crumpled £10 note and six pound coins. Naomi thanked him and turned to Steph to walk out of the door, waving the notes in front of her. 'Erm, your change Naomi!' Shouted Pete over the small shop. 'Oh yeah!' laughed Naomi as she jogged back towards the counter. She picked up the bag of change and the girls made their way back to their own shop. Steph was stunned, £5 into £36 just like that. She couldn't believe how easy it was!

Steph must have nodded off in the rocking chair she was in, thinking about her past as she was woken by the sound of her phone vibrating on the windowsill. The screen read once again, 'Mum'. Steph was nervous this time as she knew she should have transferred her mum what she owed her today and her mum would be asking for it. 'Shit' she said to herself as she let the phone ring until she'd missed the call. 'Fuck, what can I say?' she thought to herself. Steph was a master of lies and excuses by this point. Some of her lies so detailed, so far fetched she couldn't believe herself she'd gotten away with most of them. The truth was, she hadn't. Her mum knew when she was lying. Whether it be mothers instinct, or the fact Steph really wasn't that good at lying, her mum always knew. Steph knew she needed to think of something quick. If she didn't answer, her mum would know she was gambling, especially around payday. 'Shit, shit' she said, as she began again to pace the living room carpet.

She'd had to tell her mum last month what she'd done, so the truth wasn't an option. Not after she'd promised her for the one millionth time she wouldn't do it again. Excuse after excuse ran through her mind as to why she could say she hadn't transferred her the money. 'My card! I'll say my card is blocked!' She thought, convincing her self that this was a perfectly good reason as to why she hadn't given her the money she owed her this month. She hurriedly rolled a cigarette and called her mum. 'Hi mum, you ok?' she asked. The conversation followed it's normal pattern. 'Sorry I didn't answer I was in the shower.' Lie number one Steph thought to herself. 'I had to nip to the bank today mum, because I tried to transfer you your money but it said I needed to contact them.' Lie number two. 'They've had to send me a new card and I can't transfer any money until I get it. I promise as soon as it comes I'll send you your money' Lie number three. 'Ok Steph don't worry, are you ok though?' Her mum replied. Both Steph and her mum knew what that meant. It didn't mean are you ok, it meant you haven't gambled have you. And so followed lie number four. 'Honestly mum I'm fine, I'm much better now and I wont let you down.' Her mum, suspecting that something more sinister had happened, and that Steph actually wasn't 'ok', spared Steph the embarrassment of questioning her further. 'Ok Love, well let me know if you need anything.' They ended the call and an overwhelming sense of guilt filled Steph. Although the lies and excuses came to her so easily, she actually hated doing it. She hated lying and betraying the people she loved, but, believing that was easier than hurting them with the truth, she had no choice but to continue.

All the sense of relief she'd felt that day, through getting enough money to pay her rent had now gone. She was now filled with guilt and worry again because, how was she going to pay her mum? She'd already put her mum through so much, she couldn't do it again. 'Should I transfer her the money now and do something else about my rent? Would the landlord accept it late? I need to ring about my other debts' were the thoughts that filled her head in that moment. She needed to make a choice. She was still down by hundreds of pounds, with not enough money to live on and £350.00 leaving her bank tomorrow morning. 'Maybe I could win enough to pay everything?' That thought. That word, maybe. There it had creeped again. No matter the devastation the act of gambling had caused her not 24 hours earlier, not to mention over the past 6 years, it still entered her mind as a potential solution. 'No I can't' she argued with herself. 'But maybe just a tenner and it could turn into hundreds, like the lucky ones? You've seen it happen to people! It can be done!'. 'No, please no!' she shouted to herself. 'I don't want to!'

Now, to anyone watching Steph, she was talking to herself. She was arguing with herself but, to Steph, she was arguing with someone else. She was arguing with her conjoined twin. The twin was the addiction that lived inside of her. Another person who made these bad choices, who pushed her into doing these terrible things. It was the twin who lied to her mum and her family. The twin who had taken over the loving, caring, sensible Steph who would do anything for anyone. Every now and again, the twin would come and take over. She'd manifest in Steph's body, make her do these awful things and then leave, leaving all the mess for Steph to fix. Steph hated it. All she wanted was for the twin to leave her but she wouldn't. Sometimes, it would take over completely. On occasion, Steph genuinely had no conscious memory of what she'd done. Going into an almost autopilot mode, her bank would drain, her cash disappear, and the next thing she knew, Steph was back in her rocking chair with a cigarette, thinking up excuses to explain why she'd had done what she'd done.

'Look, you have £50 spare in your account. You could just use that £50, and even if you lose it, you can still pay your rent. Then we have a bit of time to think about the other stuff and get some more money but we might not have to! It might get us that few hundred we need!.' The twin had convinced her. Steph was sat in her chair, blanket over her frozen legs, phone in hand, typing in that website. She clicked deposit. As she typed in £50 to the amount box, her heart racing faster, her hands shaking. Was she really going to do this?

As her payment showed as processing, she felt sick. Suddenly, she could taste her chips again and wish she'd never eaten them. The screen on her phone flashed, 'Payment successful!' This was it. Could she spin her way out of her problems this time? Surely, it was her turn for a win. She clicked on the game that was her go to game. She liked it because of the colours and the bonus on this game usually paid out a lot. 'I'll start on a £2 spin and build my way up from there' she thought. Hands still shaking, she reached £14.00 left. Full of anger, anticipation and upset she pressed spin again. There it was! She'd hit the bonus! She knew it, she knew this would work this time! The bonus round on her phone lit up her face, spinning as it did with that most magnificent noise, her favourite noise on earth. The reels continued to spin and her balance going up, and up, and up! £350! 'I fucking knew it!' she screamed as she jumped out of her chair, 'I knew it was my time!'. The screen went back to the normal reels. She stared, and stared and stared and she discussed with herself. '£350.00 means I can pay my mum and my rent!' Steph thought. 'But imagine' a voice said in her head, 'if you hit the bonus on a £5 spin. Imagine how much you would have then. You could pay everything...' Steph rolled another cigarette as she contemplated. She could take the money and be ok at this point, she'd still have some other debts to deal with but she could pay what was most important to her. 'But what if...' And with that, Steph lost all control.

Spinning and spinning on a £5 stake. As she reached £300.00 credit remaining a voice told her 'Do a £10 stake – you're much more likely to hit the bonus on that and it will pay even more.' And so, with no conscious thought about what she was doing anymore, she pressed that little red button on her phone, the one that brought her so much pain and misery until she reached £0.00 credit. Without a single thought in her head she could remember, she deposited another £50, and then another £50 then £100. She rolled them all away. She attempted to deposit another £100 but her card declined. 'What?' she thought at this point. 'No, I have £300!!!' As she seemed to shift out of her auto pilot state and checked her online banking, reality hit. She had £50.00 in her account. She began to scream and shout uncontrollably, struggling to breath between sobs.

She couldn't even pay her rent now, let alone her mum. 'Fuck it' she screamed as she went to the website again and deposited the last £50.00. 'I can't pay anything whether I have £50.00 or not so I might as well try it.' She often used this justification. She called it her, 'fuck it' button. When she was in such a mess that it wouldn't matter what she did anyway, she would still be destitute. Her last £50.00 rolled away with not a single win.

It was absolutely silent as Steph sat, completely still, in her chair. Unsure as to how much time had passed, or what time it was at this point, she just stared at the wall. Not moving, not making a sound, not even thinking. Just sitting with a feeling of complete numbness and emptiness.

She wasn't crying, wailing or even thinking. She was completely empty. Hours and hours passed as she sat there. Eventually, the bitter cold seemed to bring Steph around. Again, without any conscious thought, she climbed into bed, still wearing her clothes. She didn't even turn on the hairdryer tonight, she just rolled over and fell to sleep.

Chapter 4

'Mum, I've done it again. I'm so sorry.' That was the message typed out on her phone. She stared and stared at the message with her thumb hovering over the send button. She knew she had no other option at this point.

Steph's mum was amazing. The love Steph had for her mum was completely contradicted by her repeated actions. Even though she continued to hurt her and lie to her, Steph loved her mum more than anyone on the planet and genuinely did hate what she continued to do her. Steph's mum hadn't had an easy life either. She was beaten as a child. She had 4 children to bring up single handed since her husband had an affair with her sister. She worked a full time job whilst trying to arrange childcare for her 4 children and each of them brought Steph's mum more issues to her life. Between drugs, addiction, mental health issues and early pregnancy, Steph's mum never did anything but the absolute best she could for her children.

Steph hit send. Her heart sank and a tear rolled down her face. She continued to stare at the screen, looking for the little tick to appear to show Steph her mum had read the message. After a minute or so, she sat in front of the broken mirror in her bedroom and scraped the last bit of foundation out of the bottle. She applied it to her face, focusing on the bags under her eyes. She didn't have the energy to go to work but she'd rather be there than wait in the flat for the knock on the door from her landlord. As she was applying the mascara to her still damp eyelashes, she heard her phone vibrate. That short little vibration that let her know her mum had replied.

'Oh Steph. Not again. I really don't have any money to help you this time. Are you ok? Xxx' read the reply from her mum. The three kisses let Steph know her mum didn't hate her. That she was still there and she loved her. Three little X's meant more to Steph than any money in the world. It let her know she wasn't alone.

'I know mum. I'm OK I just don't know what I'm going to do. I'm so sorry mum, I'm so so sorry. I just want to get better. Xxx'

Steph put down her phone and finished getting ready for work. Grabbing her keys, her phone and her bus ticket, she walked out of the door. She pulled up her hood and walked quickly towards that long alleyway she hated, being sure not be caught or seen by her landlord.

'Steph! Where the hell we're you yesterday you bitch!' The familiar and comforting sound of her work mate bellowed across the contact centre. Steph looked up and saw Charlene beckoning her to the seat next to her. They always saved each other a seat. When you're taking 100 calls a day, mainly from angry customers who want to scream at you, it's vital to have someone near you, you can talk to! 'Hahaha, Sorry mate. I wasn't well I had a right bad stomach!' Steph lied.

Steph didn't tell anyone about her addiction. The embarrassment of it all was just too much. She'd become a master of pretending she was ok to everyone around her. Steph continued with her shift, taking call after call as if nothing had happened whilst in her mind ran the same question as everyday. 'What am I going to do ?'

As lunchtime came, Steph, who had no money for any lunch and didn't even feel capable of eating at this moment in time, went out to the smoking shelter. A two minute walk from the main building. She lit a cigarette and checked her phone. 3 missed calls from mum. She quickly messaged her to say 'I'm at work mum, I'll ring you after xxx' This gave her the chance to sit quietly for the 45 minutes she had on her lunch break. As she sat there, she thought about the fact she had no other messages from anyone. Not one from her sisters, no friends and how she no longer ever heard from Naomi. Her thoughts drifted back to how they had been so close and how now, she felt so alone.

When Steph worked in the bookies, she was sent to shops all over. Sometimes over an hours drive away. It would be midnight some nights before Steph would get home, even though her shift finished at 10. She would have to wait hours for the slow busses to pick her up and then make the connections to the next busses to get her into town for the 10 minute walk home through that scary alley. It became too much. Even though she didn't want to leave, because of Naomi, she knew she couldn't sustain it forever. It was also only a part time job. It wasn't enough to cover all of her bills and the nights out her and Naomi loved to go on. And so, Steph started to look for a full time job. After a few weeks of searching, she found a local call centre looking for full time employees. It was perfect for her! Close to home and a good wage. Steph had experience of working in call centres before and so she knew she was in a good position. She filled out the application and waited to see if she would be invited for interview. When she told Naomi she'd applied, they made a promise. They promised that they'd still be best friends, no matter where they worked or where they lived. It gave Steph some comfort as Naomi was Steph's best friend and she never wanted to lose her.

'Hey Steph, you feeling better?' The same croaky voice she'd spoken to yesterday asked as it brought Steph back from her daydream. 'You still don't look well' it continued.

'Yeah I'm much better thank you, I'm just tired. I best head back in anyway because my lunch is over, I don't want to be late or my boss will sack me!' Joked Steph as she stubbed out the cigarette that had burned away. She walked back into the office, put on her headset and continued to take the same calls as everyday.

The end of Steph's shift approached and her stomach began to swirl with the thought of what she needed to face when she got home. Her landlord stood at her door looking for his money which she simply didn't have. She ended the last call of the day and put down her headset. She said bye to Charlene and made her way to the exit. 'Steph, do you have 5 minutes?' Asked a voice as she approached the door. It was her boss. 'Erm, yeah of course, is everything ok?' she replied. 'Shall we go into the office?' Her boss asked. At this point, she knew she was in some sort of trouble. With a fake smile painted on her face, she followed her boss down the corridor. She looked at his trousers as she followed him. They were clearly too small for him, riding up his backside with every step and his belt squeezing his hips so tight they spilled over the top in his off-white shirt. She didn't like her boss too much. He'd made inappropriate comments to her on more than one occasion and he only ever seemed to hire women. She armed herself with the things he'd ever said to her in readiness for what he was about to tell her off for, in case she needed to retaliate.

He opened the door and invited Steph to sit on the ridiculously over sized purple sofa that was in there. A feeble attempt of the company to create a comfortable environment. A 'chill out' office as they called it, renamed the 'kill out office' by the employees there, as more than one employee had been sacked in this office.

As she sat, hunched over and clearly uncomfortable, her boss sat next to her, legs crossed which made his trousers ride even further up his legs exposing his clearly odd black socks.

'Steph I need to make sure you're ok. Your levels of absence have increased lately and they seem to be forming somewhat of a pattern. Is there anything you need to make me aware of?' Her boss asked.

'Fuck!' Thought Steph as her hands again began to sweat and she was rapidly thinking of an excuse.

'No' She replied. 'I don't think so.'

'Ok Steph, well we need to monitor this closely. It appears to be at the end of the month you're a having a day or two off. This has been repeated 4 times in the last 7 months Steph and we really need to get to the bottom of it.' Her boss continued to probe.

'My periods!' Steph exclaimed. 'It's my periods Jamie, I'm really struggling with them. They make me feel really ill and I'm in so much pain with them.' Steph was so proud of herself. What a fantastic excuse! It fitted perfectly with the pattern of absence and she knew it would make Jamie hugely uncomfortable. Her boss began to fidget in his seat. He attempted to pull his trousers down to cover those weird socks but of course they wouldn't move due to the strangulation of his hips caused by his belt. 'Ah, erm, Ok Steph. I understand. I suggest Steph you make an appointment with your doctor and see if they can help you in anyway as we can't continue to sustain this level of absence but we want to help you.'

'Of course Jamie, I'll ring them tomorrow. Thank you.'

Steph, feeling relieved and strangely proud of herself, walked towards door. She thanked Jamie and began the journey out of the office and onto the main road.

'I've been so worried about you! Are you ok!?' A raised and concerned voice echoed down the phone. 'I'm alright mum I've been at work. I don't know what I'm going to do Mum, I'm pretty sure my rent cheque will be declined today and I'm already in arrears. I'm so scared mum what the hell am I going to do?'

'Has he been in touch with you?' Her mum asked. 'No, not yet.' Replied Steph.

'Where are you?' Her mum asked worriedly.

'I'm just outside work, I don't want to go home Mum.'

'Right, come here. Don't go there tonight, please just come here.'

Steph thought about the offer for a moment. She wasn't on shift tomorrow so she could stay at her mums and put off seeing her landlord for one more night. 'Ok mum, I'll start walking now.' She hung up the phone and began the 45 minute walk to her mums house. The bus ticket she had didn't cover her for the journey to her mums but Steph didn't mind walking anyway. It gave her time to think and to look around and seemed generally to calm her down.

Her mum lived in a tiny one bed flat. Steph knew when she went there to stay, she had to share a bed with her mum. She didn't generally. It wasn't ideal however, today, that was the least of her worries.

She reached the front door of her mums ground floor flat and walked in. 'Auntie Steph!' cried the voice of a little girl. It was Steph's niece. She was the most adorable little girl who Steph loved so much. 'Amelie!' Steph cried as she reached out her arms and picked up the tiny human. She squeezed her tightly but being sure not to hurt Amelie. She took a huge breath in with her face buried into the neck of Amelie.

'Oh Steph.' Her mum sighed as she moved towards her with opened arms. 'You'll be ok.' She said, as she gave Steph the warmest most loving hug ever. 'I'm so sorry mum' Whispered Steph as she held back her tears so as not to let little Amelie know she was sad.

'Right, tea time Amelie!' shouted Steph's mum as she put the tiny Winnie the pooh bowl on the coffee table. 'Eat it all up!' she said.

She handed Steph a plate. On it was a chicken wrap and chips. 'You better eat it all too.' Steph's mum said, winking at Steph.

As they all sat in that tiny living room, eating the food handmade by Steph's mum, a feeling of love, peace and gratitude filled Steph for a moment. No matter how bad a situation she put herself in, she had these two amazing human beings who reminded her that not all was bad.

After a warm shower and the latest episode of Coronation street, it was time to put Amelie to bed. 'Come on princess, bed time.' Said Steph as she scooped the little unicorn onesie clad girl up. She laid her in bed, brushed back the fine blonde baby hair from Amelie's face and kissed her goodnight. She walked back into the living room where her mum was knitting in the corner of the sofa.

'Oh mum, what the hell am I going to do?' Steph asked, now not being in the presence of the innocent little girl. 'I've fucked up again, so badly.'

Her mum, not replying at all stood up and went to the kitchen drawer. She took out a pen and piece of paper and told Steph to write down all that she owed. 'Don't lie to me Steph' Said her Mum. 'You need to tell me truth.'

Steph went on and wrote down the money she needed this month. Her mum stared at the paper. 'I just don't have it Steph. I don't mind that you can't pay me back but I really don't have anything else I can give you.'

'I know mum, I will pay you back I promise I will, I swear' Steph said, knowing full well there was no way she could.

'Right, this is what we're going to do.' Her mum said sternly. 'You go back to the doctors tomorrow. I'll come with you.' 'I've been before mum, it doesn't work' Steph interrupted.

Steph had been to the doctors before about her addiction. She'd been to gamblers anonymous too but didn't find it helpful. She didn't like the group session and when she went to the 121 sessions, it was a woman who Steph had no respect for since she'd told her she'd never had a gambling addiction and offered Steph a page from a colouring book that she suggest she use if she gets the urge to gamble. She didn't attend another session after that but she never told her mum that.

'There must be more they can do Steph. I mean it, either you ring them tomorrow or I will.'

Steph conceded.

'And what the fuck do you suggest I do about the fact I'm going to be evicted tomorrow?' Steph Asked. 'We will speak to your landlord tomorrow. We will explain.' Replied Steph's mum.

'No! I am not telling him I have an addiction mum. Why do you want everyone to know!? Why do you think it will it better for everyone to know I'm a fucking addict? So all my mates can find out and the people I work with. No!' The suggestion of telling anyone always scared the life out of Steph and it made her angry every time her mum suggested it. She put on her shoes and had a cigarette outside of the tiny flat.

Deep down, Steph knew her mum was right. And she felt bad for snapping at her. Here she was, at her mums house, owing her hundreds of pounds, eating her food and using her water and all Steph could do was scream at her when she was trying to help. The front door opened and her mum joined her for a cigarette. 'I'm sorry mum' Sobbed Steph. Without saying a word, Steph's mum put her arm around her and together they smoked. They both went inside and joined the tiny little girl in bed. Crammed in like sardines and being careful not to disturb Amelie, Steph went to sleep.

Chapter 5

'Stop tapping.' Steph's mum said as she placed her hand on Steph's knee to stop her leg from shaking up and down. She looked over at Amelie playing in the corner with a plastic telephone, pretending to call her mum. 'Steph Goodyear?' a voice called over the waiting room. 'Come on Amelie' Steph heard as her mum tried to peel the plastic phone from Amelie's hand. As Steph walked down the corridor, following the smartly dressed doctor into a small dark room, she thought to herself 'this is so pointless.'

'How can I help you?' asked the Doctor politely. 'Her gambling is so out of control doctor. I am so worried about her. She isn't eating, she isn't sleeping you can see. Look how pale she is. She really needs help because I'm so worried about her.' Steph's mum replied before Steph could. She hung her head and looked at the floor in complete despair and disgust with herself, tears filling her eyes.

'Ok, and how long have you had this addiction Steph?' Asked the Doctor.

'6 years! It's just getting worse' said Steph's mum.

'Ok.' Said the doctor and she looked at her screen and began to scroll down the reels of notes. It was quiet for a moment apart from Amelie fidgeting to get down and Steph's mum telling her to stop.

'I can see Steph that you attended some sessions with gamblers anonymous. Did they not help at all?'

'No' replied Steph.

'And have you tried the group sessions?'

'Yeah. But it was full of old men and I didn't like it.'

'Ok.' The doctor said addressing them both, 'As I'm sure you know, the best and most proven treatment for this type of addiction is talking about it. I really think that we need to get you back in with a counsellor to talk some of these issues through. That's the best thing to help you overcome this. Now I understand that Gamblers anonymous wasn't for you however, they do specialise in this type of addiction. What I'm going to do is refer you to our mental health counsellor here at the surgery. He's a lovely man and he does specialise in addiction. I really think it may help you to have some one on one sessions with him. What do you think Steph?'

'Yeah, I'll try it' replied Steph, unconvincingly.

'Ok. And in terms of the physical affects it's having on you Steph. Are you eating and sleeping ok? How are you coping?'

'I just really don't feel hungry a lot of the time. And I don't sleep well. I wake up all the time but it's my own fault because of what I've done. I'm about to lose my house and I can't afford gas or electric.' Steph said this with some hope that the doctor would be able to suggest something she hadn't thought of to get money to pay her bills. She didn't, she instead replied 'Ok. I'm not prepared, at the moment Steph, to prescribe you anything to help you sleep as there's a very real risk of addiction and becoming reliant on them. Instead, I'm arranging an appointment for you for Monday with Gary. That's the first appointment available. He will be able to support you with some coping mechanisms and handy tools to help stop your gambling. These should then help you eat and sleep better.' At this point, Steph stopped listening. The same advice as all the other times before and so it'll be the same result. She uncooperatively continued to say yes until she could leave the office.

'See!' Her mum said optimistically as they made their way back to the flat. 'You need to talk about it Steph.'

'Mum it doesn't help, how many times have I talked about it to professionals. All they do is give me a fucking colouring book. That isn't going to pay my fucking rent is it!' Her mum didn't reply. She held Amelie's hand and continued to walk.

They reached the flat and Amelie ran over to her bundle of toys and began to play. 'Where's Belle anyway?' Asked Steph. Belle was Amelie's mum, Steph's sister.

'She's working today she's picking her up later.' Replied Steph's mum.

Steph looked at her phone and still, nothing from her landlord. The bank must be really delayed. As she sat and thought about what the doctor had said, what problems she had this month and how she could possibly fix them, she turned to her mum and said 'Mum, can I move in here for a while?'

Steph used to live with her mum anyway. Before the sandwich shop flat, Steph lived with her mum in a beautiful flat they had together. It was a new build and Steph loved it there. She was happy. She had a lot of debts but she was controlling it as best she could. Steph and her mum made an agreement when they took on the flat that Steph would pay the rent and Steph's mum would cover the utility bills and food. Things were going really well. The rent was paid every month and Steph's life was getting back on track.

Steph's oldest sister had recently moved to Spain but it didn't work out and so, Natasha, her partner and 3 kids needed somewhere to stay whilst they found a house back in the UK. They arranged to stay with Steph and her mum. A few days before they arrived, Steph's mum told Steph she had found a 1 bed flat, close to her Nan. It came completely out of the blue. Steph was shocked as she thought her mum was as happy as her and, she knew it would be really cramped for a while with Natasha and the kids but it wouldn't be forever. Before she knew it, Steph's mum had moved into the one bed flat, leaving Steph with all of the bills. A few weeks passed and Steph received a letter. It was from the council. Steph opened it to see she had been summoned to court for unpaid council tax for a lengthy amount of time. Her mum had not been paying the bills. Because it had Steph's name on it, it meant she was responsible and they were demanding £300 a month. Steph was completely shocked and heartbroken. Is this why her mum had left her? How could she do this to her? How was she going to afford it?

Steph confronted her mum who sobbed and apologised over and over again. She told Steph just how much trouble she was really in and that she was going to try and fix it. Realistically, her mum couldn't fix it. Steph knew she had to pay the £300 a month which she did. As the bills mounted up, and her wages disappeared, she heard a familiar voice. 'Maybe we could win it and pay it off?' and with that, her gambling got worse.

'Of course you can stay here. But what about your flat and your job?' Asked Steph's mum.

'I'm just going to have to leave. I'll keep my job still.' Replied Steph. 'Are you sure mum?'

'Of course I'm sure, I just want to help you Steph.'

With that, Steph created a plan in her head as to what she would do. The bank wouldn't delay the bounce of the cheque much further so she convinced herself she only had tonight to leave.

'Dad? Are you free tonight please? I need to leave my flat Dad. I don't have the money to pay my rent and I really need to go before they force me. Mum said I can stay with her for a while until I get things sorted.' explained Steph to her Dad.

She wasn't particularly close to her Dad, after him marrying her Auntie. It caused Steph some real mental health issues when she was a kid as well as what it did to her mum. She was always secretly angry but he was her Dad and she knew, he would always help her when he could.

'Yes. Be ready at 8.' Her Dad bluntly replied. 'Thank you Dad, see you then.'

This was it. Steph would just leave the flat and not have to face her Landlord. Her mum would let her stay there with her. She hurriedly asked her mum for some money for the bus into town so she could pack her stuff and leave before her landlord noticed.

Back at her flat, it didn't take long to pack her things. She didn't really own anything. As she rummaged through the bag she kept under her bed, full of miscellaneous items she didn't want to throw away, she came across a photo of her and Naomi on one of their nights out. She thought about how much she missed Naomi and her mind went back to that night.

It was weeks after she applied for the job that Steph got offered the job. She didn't think she'd got it because it took so long but when they called, she was at work in the bookies. They didn't even offer an interview just offered her the job! She couldn't believe it. Her first call after accepting of course was to her best friend Naomi. 'Noooo!' Cried Naomi down the phone. 'Well done baby girl but I'm going to hate working without you!' They chatted for another 10 minutes about the job until Steph explained she needed to go back in and she would speak to Naomi, as they always did, when she finished work.

The end of her shift came and she waited for the bus back into town. She had Naomi on the phone the whole ride home. 'Oh my god!' said Naomi

'That lad from the other bookies came in today. He's so nice!' Recently, a guy from another brand of bookmakers had been coming into the shop. Naomi clearly had a crush on him and they flirted back and forth for weeks. 'Anyway' she continued, 'He's invited us out tomorrow!' The girls giggled and talked about what they would wear the next night.

The next night, they met the boys at the shop and made their way into town. Naomi and the lad were flirting all night. As Steph went to get another drink, she turned and saw Naomi kissing him. She smiled to herself as she was proud of her friend. The end of the night came to a close and they made their way to the taxi rank. Steph always stayed at Naomi's after a night out, it was basically her home. As Naomi walked hand in hand, completely smitten with her crush, she beckoned Steph over. 'I'm taking him home! She squealed excitedly!' Steph, proud yet a little hurt that for the first time ever, she would have to go to her actual home after night out, replied 'Oh my god! Go, go! Enjoy it!' as they hugged, Steph watched her friend and the new boy climb into a taxi. She giggled and got in a taxi of her own to her own house.

It was 2pm the next day before Steph heard from Naomi. This was hugely unlike them. They spoke every single day they had known each other. Naomi told Steph all about how the night had gone and how he was still there and how much she liked him! They were both on shift the next day and so they agreed to speak then.

In the shop the next day, the girls talked, giggled and worked as they always did however, today Naomi said she would be going out to meet Pat for dinner. Steph watched the shop floor and noticed, on Naomi's return, she had lip gloss around her mouth. 'Have you been kissing?' Asked Steph. 'Shhhhh' Naomi giggled. The end of the shift came and Steph asked if Naomi fancied a drink. They often went to a cheeky Rose after work. As she said it, she noticed Pat in the distance, walking towards the shop. 'Oh' said Steph. 'Have fun!'

She gave Naomi a hug and went for the bus home.

A few weeks passed and the girls talked less and less. Steph started the new job in the call centre and the girls drifted further apart. One night, at 11.49pm Steph stared at her phone. She watched it until 00:00 and thought, 'That's it. The first day I've ever not spoken to Naomi.' And with that, the relationship ended completely. There was no big fight, no arguments, they simply drifted apart and went down completely separate paths to the rest of their lives.

Pulling herself out of the daydream she'd been in once again, Steph shoved the photo's back in the bag and had her pathetic pile of belongings ready for her Dad to pick her up and take her back to live with her mum. She grabbed another empty envelope and that same pen she'd used to write her debts and wrote:

'I am so sorry I have had to do this but I cannot stay here anymore. I have

Posted the door keys through the letter box of the sandwich shop. Thank you

And I'm sorry again'

As she stared out of the living room window with a cigarette, she recognised the slightly dimmed drivers side headlight come down the road and knew it was her dad. She threw her cigarette to the ground and opened the door. As they filled the car with the few belongings she had, she posted the hand written letter and flat key through the letterbox of the shop. She hurried back to the car and made the journey back to the little one bed flat where she would be staying for the foreseeable.

Chapter 6

'So, I've read your notes and the first thing to say is yes, you are an idiot.' She smiled at Gary in the doctors office. Steph was able to get along with humour and liked the way Gary had opened up the conversation. He was a good looking guy. He had a really friendly face and she felt comfortable in his company. 'However, you are also one of a million idiots Steph. There are 3 major potholes in life. Gambling, Drugs and Alcohol. If you can avoid all three you are very lucky however, if you fall in one, there are ways to get you out and that's what we're going to do for you.' She liked this guy and the way he explained things. For the first time in a long time, she felt like she really did have someone she could talk to.

He would ask her questions that would make her think.

'What do you want Steph?' was the hardest to answer.

The immediate answer, you would think, for any gambling addict would be money. I promise you, this is not the case. Strangely enough, money actually meant very little to Steph. On the few occasions that she did win, she wouldn't buy anything for herself. She wouldn't use the money to improve her life in anyway. Instead, she would give it her sister, or her mum, or buy that sofa her mum wanted or find someone, somewhere to give it too. You see, that's what made her happy. If she looked deep inside herself, helping others is what made her happy. The irony made her chuckle to herself. The fact that all she wanted to do was help people when actually, all she ever did was lie to people.

'I just want to be happy, and for my family to be happy.' Was the response she gave. Gary smiled. Not in the way that showed he felt pity for Steph or felt sorry for her, just in a way that showed her he understood. It comforted Steph.

'Steph, one of the most important things to understand, is why you gamble. The answer isn't something we will find today but we can start the process. If we know why, then we can start working on how you react a little differently.'

The question that always ran through her head was why. Why did she do this to herself time after time? Why was gambling constantly on her brain? Why, when she knew the outcome before she even loaded the gambling website, was her brain so adamant that she needed to gamble? The thought of getting an answer to this question, even though she didn't believe in talking therapy, intrigued her.

'And so we need to go back through your life Steph, we need to understand what's happened and why you believe gambling is an answer to it. Tell me about your childhood Steph.'

'I had a happy childhood.' was Steph's immediate response, knowing yet again she was lying. Gary knew she was lying, she could see in his face the immediate disbelief at her statement.

'Ok Steph' he replied. 'Tell me about it. Tell me about when you were a child. 'Tell me about your family.'

Steph grew up with her three sisters. Two older, one younger. She only shared the same parents with her younger sister. The older two had different dads but they all lived together with Steph's mum. Truth be told, Steph had a lot more brothers and sisters from her dad but she never saw them and didn't know them and so, whenever anyone asked, her response was 'I have three sisters.'

'I lived with my mum and my three sisters.' Told Steph.

'Ok, and what about your dad? Was he around?'

Steph hated this part. She always hated telling people about the situation with her family. To Steph it was embarrassing and incestuous almost. Growing up, she learned to tell people as a joke. That way, it wasn't as hurtful when other people made jokes about it, because she'd done it first.

'He married my auntie' she said. 'That must have been hard for you?' asked Gary.

She knew what he was doing. He was trying to break down her short, closed answers to his questions to reveal some kind of daddy issues that were the route of all Steph's problems. She felt it so cliché and hated the notion. The truth though was, it was hard. Steph took her mind back to what she could remember of the situation. She couldn't remember much but she could remember her mum being ill and sad. And no matter what her and her sisters did, they couldn't cheer her up. She remembered her mums friend being there, and her mum being laid in bed very poorly having just come out of hospital. She couldn't remember what had happened, she was only 5. But she could remember being scared for her mum and having the feeling something bad had happened.

One thing she could remember though was going to stay with her granddad at the weekends. She loved her granddad. He would take her and Belle on walks in a morning to see the Jacob sheep and then take them to a caravan site where the was a donkey and an Emu. A strange pair but they were always there together. Her granddad would put an imperial mint in the tiny hands of Belle and Steph and show them how to hold it out. The donkey would gently take the mint from their hands and they would listen for the crunch it made when enjoying the sweet. He'd take them back to his house and there would always be lots of writing books and maths books to help them learn. Steph loved the time with her grandfather and remembered feeling how lucky she was that he would always buy her these lovely gifts. Only recently, Steph had found out it was actually her dad buying the books and he was leaving them at her grandfathers. She hadn't seeing her dad for quite a while, after the affair he had with her Auntie – Her mums sister.

She remembered her mum taking her to sessions to talk a man. Steph didn't know who he was but she remembered a big mirror, as big as the room. She knew now that it was a counsellors office, and the mirror was one of them two way ones where people were watching her on the other side.

Another memory that was clear in Steph's mind was when she did decide to start seeing her dad again. Her mum never tried to stop her. She let Steph make her own decision and she wanted to see him again. At 7 years old she remembered being on the park with her dad and asking him 'What do I call you now? Is it dad or is it uncle?' This memory often made Steph sad. How could a little girl be so confused about who her dad was?

'Maybe, sometimes' she responded to Gary, in an attempt to shut down the conversation and block the thoughts racing through head 'He didn't make me gamble though' she stated.

'I understand. And what about your sisters you said you lived with? What was your relationship like with them?'

Once more, Steph's mind was taken back to her childhood. To the small 3 bed council house she shared with her mum and her sisters. Natasha and Lilly were Steph's older sisters and Belle was the youngest. Steph loved all of her sisters. She couldn't remember much of Natasha and Lilly because they moved out at quite a young age. She did remember visiting Lilly in a hospital with her mum. She didn't know why her sister had been taken there but she knew she missed her. She knew now that Lilly struggled with her mental health as a child. She also knew that a root cause for it was her dad. He was a violent man and a drunk. He'd often smash the house up and Lilly and Natasha would be caught in the crossfire as her mum did her best to fight him off and keep the 4 girls safe. After visiting her in the hospital, her next memory of Lilly was when she'd moved out and had her first child, Baden. Steph remembered that she was quite young still when Baden was born but she loved him so much. She remembered going to Lilly's flat to see them. She also remembered Lilly being sad. She was in a toxic relationship. She struggled a lot with money and one time, she was in the living room playing with Baden when saw

her mum give Lilly a huge hug and Lilly saying 'Thank you so much mum'
She knew now that Steph's mum had paid a number of bills off for her to
make sure she was safe and could keep her flat. Steph always got along
with Lilly. They weren't as close anymore but she had a huge amount of
respect for her. She was a nurse now, married to a lovely man and had
two more children, Emma and Osmond. Lilly seemed happy which made
Steph happy. She wished she saw her a bit more but knew she was there
if she ever needed anything.

Natasha was the oldest. Natasha had a lot of issues when she was
younger. She took drugs and got in with the wrong crowd. Steph
remembered going home one night and her PlayStation being missing.
She searched and searched for it, it was her pride and joy but it was gone.
Her mum quickly realised that Natasha had stolen it. Steph was absolutely
heart broken. Natasha would often go missing and Steph remembered her
mum being hugely worried and upset and constantly on the phone. There
would often be police at the house and they were always talking about
Natasha. Steph's remembered walking miles and miles to see Natasha and
couldn't understand why she lived with another lady. She knew now that
Natasha had to be put into foster care. Another memory was Steph, Belle
and her mum getting 2 trains to visit Natasha. She remembered going to a
building that looked like a jail. They went through the doors and all three
would be searched and sent into a room where Natasha was sat. She
remembered very clearly buying Natasha some shampoo and the prison
guard telling us we weren't allowed to give it her. The truth was that
Natasha had been put into a secure unit. It was for her own safety.
Natasha had come very close to death and suffered a huge stroke when in
her teens through drugs. It was after this Steph recollected that Natasha
went away. Natasha and Steph got on well now. Steph would help
Natasha whenever she could with babysitting or shopping and got on
really well with her Niece Olive. Natasha had 3 children. Rhydian, Olive
and Loxie. She was living in a house now, separated from her partner but
she seemed happy and they would sometimes message each other and
see each other. Not often but it was enough for Steph to know she was
alright.

And then there was Belle. There was only 18 months between Belle and Steph so they went through things at similar times. Steph always felt second best to Belle. She was prettier and smarter and more confident however, she had a vile temper and a poison tongue. Everyone stepped on eggshells around Belle to avoid 'setting her off'. Steph remembered when they were kids and they shared a bedroom. They had these weird bunk beds which had a mesh frame and a thin sponge mattress. Steph often believed they'd come from a prison. One night, Belle had wet the bed. It was too late to wash the sheets and Belle screamed and screamed that she wouldn't sleep on the floor. Steph remembered having to sleep on the floor in a pile of teddy bears so that Belle could have her bed. As they grew up, things didn't get any better. In fact they got worse. When Steph lived in that beautiful flat with her mum, she remembered babysitting Amelie one night. She was happy in bed, cuddling Amelie when Belle came in the early hours of the morning. She walked in Steph's bedroom and screamed at her until Steph got out of her own bed so that Belle could sleep in it. She often wondered why her mum let her get away with all she did but she knew that it was easier to give her what she wanted than it was to listen to the screaming. Steph often felt like Belle was treated better than anyone else, especially her. Another thought came flooding into her mind. Belle from a very young age wanted to have a baby. Steph went with her to the clinic to have her implant removed so that she could get pregnant. Belle was only 17 but it was what she wanted and what Belle wanted, she got. It was on her 18th Birthday that Belle found out she was pregnant. She remembered her mum letting Belle off with her rent, buying her prams and clothes and presents whilst her mum shouted at Steph for not being able to pay the rent. 'Why doesn't Belle have to pay it?' She thought. And every time Belle and Steph had an argument, Belle would scream the same old thing. 'you're a gambling addict! All you do is lie and steal from people. You're killing your own mum because you take everything. You'll never get better you're just an addict!'

It wasn't all bad though, Steph was closer to Belle than any of her other sisters. She remembered growing up how they would play hospitals and Belle would walk into A&E and ask for a boob job. This was her favourite memory. Steph went everywhere with Belle. She remembered going to the doctors in the early hours of the morning when Amelie was poorly to make sure she wasn't alone. She would take her shopping, give her money if ever she did manage to win at gambling. She'd babysit whenever she needed her to and help her clean her house. When Belle took an overdose, Steph remembered being in the car with her and crying, being so scared she would lose her little sister. When Belle was in school she was bullied and Steph remembered sticking up for her. A girl had accused Belle of stealing money and, even though Belle knew it was true, she laid into the accuser to make sure Belle wouldn't get any trouble. She'd do anything for Belle, it was important to Steph that she was happy. And Belle was there for Steph too. Belle was one of the only people that knew about her gambling. Steph would often tell Belle what she'd done and go to her house. Belle would help Steph whenever she could too. Although they fought, they really were close and Steph felt lucky to have Belle.

'Yeah I get on with them fine. I don't see what any of this has to do with my gambling though?' Said Steph, slightly annoyed that they'd gone off topic. She genuinely didn't believe that talking about how she grew up would help her with the fact she didn't have a penny to her name and was now sharing a bed with her mum.

'I know why I started gambling. It was because I worked in a bookies. I saw people winning everyday and I thought, I want a piece of that. I saw how easy it was and I thought I could do the same as the lucky one's.'

'Ok Steph, Well I think that's enough for the first session but I'd like to keep meeting with you. I have a free slot next Thursday, is that ok?'

'Yeah that's fine' replied Steph, knowing full well she'd be at work and would cancel the upcoming appointment.

Chapter 7

3am. Steph had made her way out of the bed where her mother lay asleep, quietly manoeuvring her way to the door of the tiny bathroom, not big enough to house a bath, just a shower, toilet and basin. She very slowly pushed down on the cold metal handle, trying her hardest to avoid the high pitched squeak she knew it often made. She slid her way around the door, that was open just enough to allow her to fit through, locked it quietly and sat, as she so often did in the early hours of payday, on the hard plastic toilet seat.

It was strange. Her body seemed to know now when payday was. Even if it came early. Like an alarm clock, she would wake up between 2am – 3am and before she even opened her eyes, the thought 'I've been paid' came into her head. Of course, as soon as her brain had made her aware of this fact, there was absolutely no chance she'd be able to go back to sleep. Because there it was, the conjoined twin again, screaming at her in the loudest pitch known to man and there was only one way to shut it up.

Sat in her pyjamas on that toilet sheet, she squinted at her phone as her eyes still weren't working properly in the full light of the bathroom. She clicked on the little blue app on her phone. The app that made her so happy at the same time as making her more depressed than anyone thought humanly possible. That app that for one single day of each month, solved all her problems. Her banking app.

She keyed in the passcode that was the same for everything she had. Amelie's date of birth. The little wheel turned and turned and her stomach seemed to follow the same motion. She knew exactly how this worked. She knew what the twin was telling her to do and wouldn't shut up until she'd done. And even though she knew it was inevitable, she really didn't want to do it.

£1250.00 – Available balance.

She ran the usual calculation through her head about what she'd be left over with.

£300 to mum for debts

£200 to mum for rent

£450 for her debts

£150 for food

£50 for bus tickets to work

£1150 in total. 'I can spend £100 and I'll still be fine' she told herself.

Stomach swirling, palms sweating, heart racing, she typed in the website that was about to either make or break her. She logged in, listening intently for any stir her mother may make in the room next door. 'Deposit now' stared her in the face. 'Steph no, come on no don't do this. Just click the little cross in the corner and go back to bed.'

For a few seconds, her eyes flicked between the big blue 'deposit now' and the little cross in the corner. 'Your stronger now. You can't afford it. You can do it this time come on!' She lifted her thumb and clicked…

It was 11am before she climbed out of bed again. Her mum had already woken up and taken herself off to work. Steph, having no tobacco left, stole one of the cigarettes her mum had left behind in her coat pocket. She stood outside and smoked, staring at the couple across the road walking towards the country park. As she stood outside in her dressing gown, she could hear the buzz of her phone through the slightly ajar door. She threw her cigarette end over the little wall in front of the front door and turned back inside.

'Morning beautiful, are you ok?' read the text on her phone. It was from Adrian. She'd recently started seeing the boy that she'd known for a long time. He worked with her mum as a cleaner but they were friends before that. They'd had a cheeky kiss before on one of Steph and Naomi's regular nights out. She never really thought any more of it than that but recently, they'd been messaging more and meeting up and she really liked him. He wasn't a particularly good looking guy but looks were never important to Steph. She always liked kindness and Adrian was very kind. He of course, had no idea about Steph's addiction or how bad it was. She'd become level expert in hiding it by now.

Steph was able to attract people. She was fairly pretty and looking at her, you would never ever assume that she had the problem she did. Addicts are often thought of as people who wear torn clothes, have dirty faces, cuts everywhere and no teeth. It couldn't be further from the truth in a lot of cases. Steph made an effort most days to brush her hair, put make up on and did wash her clothes regularly. Smelling nice was important to Steph. She couldn't bear the thought of someone thinking she smelt bad. Steph's whole life was built on hiding this secret. This secret that consumed her entire life. Hiding from the world that she was an addict, sucked in so deep to her addiction, that nothing else mattered. But nobody knew or could tell. The fact she was a young girl was also a big difference from the perception people have of gambling addicts. They imagine the older men in the betting shops. Steph was a young girl who held down a job and tried, most of the time, to look presentable. She was the girl gambler.

She replied to Adrian 'Morninggggg, I'm good thank you, how are you?'.

Adrian, completely oblivious to the battle Steph had with herself earlier that morning, asked if they could meet. He loved spending time with Steph and wanted to spend all of the time he could with her. Steph agreed and the pair were to meet later that day.

'Mum, I've transferred you your money.' Was the next message Steph sent. Completely and utterly elated that she'd clicked the cross instead of the deposit button earlier that day. She'd sent her mum the £500 she owed her for the month and could not be more proud of herself. 'This is it' she thought 'I'm getting better!' Absolutely beaming with pride, Steph thought about what she would do with her new found happiness and her day off. She'd decided she would go into town and get herself a new top with her £100 spare, ready for meeting Adrian later that day.

After putting her favourite playlist on her phone and putting on her mums make up, she made the short walk around the corner to the local shop. She'd needed some tobacco. '30 grams of Sterling and 2 number 1 scratch cards please' she asked the guy at the till. He knew her well by now and knew what cards she liked. He probably knew she had a bit of a problem but Steph would strategically hit shops for scratch cards and where she'd cash them in so it seemed, to the people working in the shop, that she just did it occasionally.

It never even entered Steph's head that she'd undone the battle she'd had this morning whilst scratching away the paint on the cards to reveal no wins at all. 'Ahh well' she thought. 'At least I haven't lost hundreds like normal!'. Headphones in, still beaming with happiness, she stepped onto the bus and found her usual seat. At the next stop, a guy got onto the bus. He had a jacket that clearly hadn't been washed for months, trainers which had a hole in them and a pair of threadbare jeans. Steph liked to imagine what the lives of the people she passed were like. She imagined the guy addicted to drugs. She imagined the conjoined twin attached to him, telling him where he could get his next fix from. She felt empathy for the man and hoped things got better for him.

As the bus pulled into town, she hopped off, and headed towards the clothes store she'd decided she was going to buy her new top from. Before she did, she stopped at the cash point to draw the money out to buy her top with. She checked the available balance again and was delighted to see that, at 2pm on payday, she still had money in her account! This never ever happened. Ever. She drew out £300. 'If it's not in my bank, I wont spend it. This is my food and shopping money for the month and for what I need to meet Adrian tonight' she thought. She pulled the brand new bank notes from the rusty slot in the cash machine, placed them in her coat pocket and made her way to the store.

Steph never liked clothes shopping much. Her relationship with money was a very strange one. She wouldn't dream of spending £20.00 on a top she liked yet £200 in a betting machine was nothing at all. She looked through the rails, checking the price tags and rejecting anything over £15.00. In the sale rail, she saw a sticker that said £7.50. The top was her size and it wasn't bad. It wasn't the nicest thing in the shop but it was cheap and it would do. She dragged the mauve coloured top over the top of the counter where the woman on the other side scanned it. Steph always found it awkward, stood across from someone staring at them waiting for them to give you your item so you can leave. She never knew where to look. It made her anxious and fidgety and she always wanted to leave as quickly as she could.

The woman bagged her top and handed it over to Steph, who had paid with one of the shiny new notes she'd withdrawn earlier.

Steph went in a few more shops, just browsing and had no intention of buying anything at all. She never did. The only things she ever purchased were bus tickets, tobacco and gambling credits. Her brain would not justify her spending money on anything else at all.

Steph, still feeling happy and proud made her way back to the bus stop. 'What a lovely day!' she thought to herself.

As she walked toward the bus stop, she passed the little shop she remembered she had her first win. That first time she put that £5 in and turned it in £36 with Naomi. That smell. She began to itch as she tried to walk past, her steps getting slower and slower, her hands becoming restless. As she put her hand in her pocket, she felt the £2.50 change rattling that she'd got back from the awkward encounter with the woman who served her. 'I'll just put this in! I'll only use these and then I'll come straight back out. I turned a fiver into £36 before so even if I just win the money back for my top I'll be happy. If I lose then I've only lost £2.50 so it's ok.' Still absolutely beaming with pride at the fact she was now in control of her gambling, she walked into that little shop where it all started.

She didn't look at the counter because she didn't want Pete to know it was her going onto the machine. As she pulled out the two pound coins and the 50 pence piece and dropped them into the grubby coin slot, that feeling of excitement flowed through her. That anticipation of watching the wheel spin and being in a world of her own whilst it happened.

She loaded up the roulette game. She never did forget the trick Naomi had taught her as she placed a virtual £1 chip on 0. She randomly selected 7 other numbers all which had meaning to her in some way. And that was it. She hit spin. She found herself in that mental state again as she watched the wheel spin. Where she couldn't hear anything, she had no thoughts in her mind, no thought of sadness or happiness just completely numb and 100% concentrated on the wheel spinning in front of her. As the wheel slowed and that little white ball jumped around, her fingers were crossed. 'Black.Even.10' yelled out the machine. Her credit now at £0.00. She stared and stared. She knew she needed to leave now but her body had become cemented to the stool. She was so proud still of the decision she had made this morning to change the payday pattern. 'Just £20. That's still better than what I usually do.' She pulled a £20.00 from the bundle of notes in her pocket and fed it into that slot. That slot she'd fed for so many years. She came off the roulette wheel and chose a slot game that she'd won the jackpot on before. She immediately went for the £2 stake because she believed, given that the machine told her, there was a better chance of hitting the jackpot. 'Just one more £20.00. Just one more' was the sentence that kept going through her brain. 'This really is the last one now.' She thought as she reached to the bundle of notes in her pocket. Her hand fumbling around, there were no notes left. She frantically searched all pockets 'I haven't done £290.00. I haven't!' she thought. The notes had gone. All fed into that greedy machine. As her body filled with anger and upset, she tried to remain calm whilst she was in the shop. She took the few steps to the door and tensed all of her muscles and let out a tiny scream, not so much that could be noticed by any passer by. 'No! it's not fair! How can I have spent all of that and not hit the bonus once!' Absolutely convinced she'd been treated unfairly, she began to speed walk to the closest cash machine. 'It's not fair! It wont beat me' were the words she said out loud to herself, still full of rage as she fed her bank card into the machine. She chose not to view her available balance this time, she didn't want to see it. £400 was the amount she chose to withdraw, telling herself she had more than enough as she'd just been paid. All that time she'd spent calculating her bills that morning meant nothing now. No money was allocated to debts or to food or bills. Any money she was able to get her hands on now was destined for that machine, no matter what the cost.

'Fucking hurry up!' she shouted at the machine as it made that rolling noise it does before it spits out your cash. She snatched the notes from the machine and marched back to that shop. She walked back through the door and was relieved that her machine was still free, still loaded on the game she'd previously been playing. She sat on that stool and fell into that place again. No sounds, no thoughts, no smells. Nothing. Just her and the machine. This was a war she was determined to win. She would get her money back.

Spin after spin after spin. Note after note after note. Lose after lose after lose. She was at a credit balance of £2.00 when she came back to earth. When that feeling of despair, regret and fear entered her body. She pressed spin and watched her final loss. She quickly got off the stool and headed for the door, being sure there was no time for anyone to try to speak to her. Quietly sobbing, she sat on a bench and rolled a cigarette from the crisp new packet she had just purchased. Inwardly sobbing, she sucked on that dirty cigarette tip. She tried to compose herself, unsuccessfully. Looking up to the sky to try and hide her tears and then looking to her left, she noticed the shop she used to work in at the end of the street. Filled with anger again, she thought about her time there.

After the first day Steph didn't hear from Naomi, she knew their friendship had come to an end. She didn't know how or why, she just knew it had. She would often miss Naomi and send her a message if she was in a pub they used to go in or on a night out but it never opened up to much conversation anymore. It was before Steph received her first wage from her new job she started to struggle for cash. She had a 6 week wait for her wage because of the cut off date of payroll when she started. She needed to get herself something to eat and wanted to go on a night out but only had £5. It was when Steph was waiting for the bus one day she saw the betting shop across the street her and Naomi had won in that time. Steph thought 'If I could do it again with this fiver, I could get what I need.' Not truly believing this would happen, she walked into the betting shop. She felt strange going in there on her own, surrounded by the old men staring at her. Pete wasn't on so she felt a little better. She chose not to sit on the stool as she knew some of the states of people who sat in them! Instead, she stood at the front of the machine and inserted her £5 note. She decided against roulette this time as all the 'lucky ones' she'd seen in her shop always won on the slots. She picked a game she was familiar with and chose to go for a 50 pence stake.

A few spins in, she hit a bonus round. She liked the way it looked and started to feel excited about the result. As she watched the cartoon dogs in police outfits run around the screen, the machine told her she'd won £70. She couldn't believe it!

'Your lucky day' Said a voice from the man sat next to her. 'I know yeah!' replied Steph. She exited the game to the home screen and hit the collect button. As she walked over to the counter, there was the machine her and Naomi used last time and it was free. Steph knew that you could insert the credit note into another machine and use the credit there. She thought about it for a moment and slid her FOBT ticket into the machine. She chose the same game as the previous machine but this time, chose a £1 spin. 'No way!' she said excitedly as the three bonus symbols once again landed on the reels. She watched those cartoon dogs run around the screen once more, now winning her £375.00. She was absolutely elated and it shock. £5 she'd turned into £375! She was now a lucky one! She printed the ticket for the value on screen and handed it to the woman on the other side of the counter. The woman scanned the ticket and congratulated Steph. 'Thank you' she replied 'I really can't believe it!' Steph, absolutely over joyed, took the notes from the woman and left the shop.

Steph peeled herself from the bench she was slumped into, dragging the plastic carrier bag that held her new top across the steel bars and began to walk to the bus stop. Unable now, to paint the smile on her face as she usually did, she kept looking to the floor as she presented her bus ticket to the driver. All the way home she prayed that the bus would crash. Or it would blow up, or something would happen that would kill her on her journey home. It didn't.

She got off at her usual stop and walked to her mums flat, all the way wishing she was dead, all the way calling herself a selfish bitch who didn't deserve family or friends and who's only option now was death. She walked through the front door and to her surprise, saw her mum stood there. 'Steph! I am so proud! ' she yelled and she headed towards Steph arms wide open. 'I knew you could do it. And what is this? You've even bought yourself something! Oh I am so so proud Steph, well done!'

Steph's heart sank. 'I thought you we're at Belle's?' were the only words that she could force out. 'Yeah I'm going in a minute. Are you going out?' Shit. She'd forgotten about Adrian. 'Yeah, he's picking me up later' said Steph. 'Well I'm proud of you my girl. I have to go or I'm going to miss this bus but enjoy your evening.' Steph's mum kissed her on the cheek, picked up her handbag up and left out of the front door. Steph put down the sad, cheap sale item she'd purchased, picked up her phone and typed 'Babe, I feel really ill. I've got a massive migraine. I'm so sorry but I'm going to have to cancel. I'm going to try and go to sleep for a bit.' She sent the lie to Adrian.

Now she was alone, she sat and cried.

She lifted her head from the pool of tears that were sat on the brown leather arm of the tiny sofa she was sat on. She looked up at the ceiling, wondering if the light fitting was strong enough to hang herself from. Being in a ground floor flat ruled out the option of hanging. She looked in the kitchen drawer at the knives. She was too scared to slit her wrists. If she was going to do this, she wanted it to be as painless and mess free as possible. It was 6 years now she'd been trapped in her addiction. Trapped in the same cycle. She wasn't living anymore, she was existing. Existing in a lie where no one knew who she really was, even she didn't anymore. All she knew for certain is that she couldn't do this anymore. She found a box of unopened paracetamol and an unopened box of Ibuprofen. She'd decided, this is how it was going to happen.

Tears still rolling down her face, she popped the small pink pills from the blister packet. She lined up the pills on the kitchen side. Here they were, the 30 pills that would release Steph from the trap she'd found herself in for so many years. The pills that would enable her to fall asleep and not wake up as she'd prayed would happen naturally every night for as long as she could remember. The 30 pills that would mean she could stop hurting people and lying to them. She grabbed a glass from cupboard above the cooker and turned on the tap. She let it run for a while before filling the glass. She started with the pink pills. Lined up like soldiers getting ready for their mission. Their mission, to finally separate Steph from her conjoined twin. One pill down. Two pills down. It was on the 8th pill that Steph's phone vibrated. She wiped the tear from her cheek and picked up her phone. The screen showed a picture message from her mum. 'We love you auntie Steph' read the comment attached to a photo of Amelie, smiling from ear to ear with her mum. Steph's heart melted. 'I don't want to miss them.' She thought to herself. Suddenly filled with a glimmer of hope and determination, she scooped the rest of the tablets, lined up on the kitchen counter and put them in the bin. 'I wont let this kill me. I choose to get better.'

Chapter 8

Steph, in that moment, had made a decision. Enough was enough. Sure, she was an addict and she knew it would be hard, but she was determined to get better. She'd decided she would really try this time. She'd work on her relationship with Adrian and she would take steps to get better and she would have a life. She was going to free herself from her conjoined twin. The first thing she needed to do was to be honest. This was more difficult than you might think because, being completely honest meant showing herself, something she now instinctively hid from the world without even trying. She didn't feel it was the right time to tell Adrian, but she would start with her mum. Another message of hurt, another message on payday telling her she'd got no money. The thought of it turned her stomach. But at least she had paid her mum back this time. She did make the transfer and do it which was progress on it's own, wasn't it?

'Mum, you have no reason to be proud of me. I gambled again today. All my wages as usual. But mum I'm going to get better I promise. I want to see all of my nieces and nephews grow up. I want to have a happy life and I want to have good memories. I know I can't carry on like this anymore. xxx' After reading back the message to herself hundreds of times, she hit the send button. And, as every month when she sent the message, her stomach gave a swirl. She felt sick as she always did, waiting for the sign her mum had read the message. But then, something new. A pain which had her bent over holding her stomach, as though somebody was squeezing her stomach as tightly as they possibly could. She let out a cry in agony as she fell onto that tiny leather sofa. She always felt sick and nervous after she'd gambled but she'd never experienced this pain before. 'The tablets' she thought. Oh god, had the pill soldiers started work? Had they begun the process of making Steph ill enough to release her from her addiction? 'Surely 8 wont do anything' she moaned to herself, bent over in pain. As the pains got worse, she wondered what on earth she was going to do. She couldn't call her mum, not after the message she'd just sent and she was with Amelie anyway. She didn't want Adrian to know! He'd think her an idiot and end the relationship before it had even properly started! Her anxieties heightening now, at the realisation that this could be the work of the pink pills she'd hoped would allow her the escape she so desperately dreamed off. She tried to calm herself down. 'Come on Steph, it's just indigestion. Belle took more than this and she was fine. It's just panic an indigestion. You need to calm down.' As she attempted to take a deep breath, she was interrupted by a stabbing pain straight through her chest and let out another cry. She crawled over the open planned floor back to the cupboard she'd previously gotten the pills from. She managed to pull her self into an almost standing position, the cupboard handle holding all of her weight, and pulled out the old Tupperware box her mum kept all the medicine in. She found a bottle of Gaviscon and drank until the bottle was empty. The strong aniseed taste staining her tongue and that chalk like feeling all over her teeth. Steph, feeling as though she had no other choice, crawled into bed and hoped that the cocktail of drugs now in her stomach would pass through her system, leaving no long term damage. The absolute opposite of her intention when popping the pills from the blister packs. 'Please god, don't let me die' she pleaded as she tried her best to fall asleep.

Reaching her arm out of the safety of the duvet, onto the bedside cabinet, she checked the time on her phone. 3:17 am it read. She'd not died! The pain had subsided and she was ok. She felt a little dizzy but she didn't mind that. At least she wasn't dead! She peeled herself from the blankets and made her way to the bathroom. After having, what seemed to be the longest wee in the world, she hurried back to the warmth of her bed. 'Thank you' she said out loud as she looked to the ceiling. Picking her phone up once more, she saw only one message on her phone. It was from Adrian. 'Ok babe, I hope you're ok. Get some rest and I'll give you a call tomorrow.' But nothing from her mum? She quickly opened the app she'd sent the message from. 'Read at 20:43' the screen displayed. She'd read it and not responded? Once again, Steph's stomach fell to the floor. This was it. She'd finally done it. After years and years of the same message on the same day, she'd finally broken her mum. She'd finally hurt her so much that her mum couldn't do it anymore. 'Mum I'm sorry. Please, please talk to me, please. I'm sorry.' She typed frantically into the chat with her mum. She could see her mum hadn't been active on the chat for hours now and so didn't realistically expect a reply although that's all she desperately wanted. Nothing mattered now. 'I don't want money, I don't want anything I just want my mum. I need those three kisses' Tears once again rolling down her face, she put the phone back on the bedside table, screen down, submerging Steph into complete darkness. She slid her body down into the bed and sobbed into her pillow shouting, over and over again, 'I'm sorry'. Her thoughts returned again to how she had ever got here. How she had messed things so badly, even her mum had had enough.

Steph had never felt a buzz like this before. £5 into £375.00 just like that. And it was so easy! She understood now why people loved it in the shop. If that's the kind of feeling it gave you, why wouldn't you want to be there! Steph messaged her best friend Leanne ' Still up for tonight???' She excitedly typed. Leanne and Steph had been friends since school. Recently, they'd grown apart but after bumping into each other in the popular night club in town the other week, they'd started chatting more again and it was like they'd never stopped talking. 'OMG yes!' Was the reply that made Steph's phone do that high pitched ding noise. And so Steph, with a newly filled purse, went home to get ready for the night out she'd just won for free.

Steph enjoyed her night out. She bought her friend Leanne some drinks as she had done for her so many times previously, with the winnings she'd got earlier that day. She'd found, on her night out, she couldn't stop thinking about what had happened earlier that day. She was so lucky and it felt so good! The next morning, Steph, with a weary head from the hangover she'd got from the tequila, vodka and copious amounts of shots, rolled out of bed and searched for all the food she could. 2 packets of crisps, a twirl and a bowl of coco pops later, she didn't feel satisfied she'd eaten enough to begin to start to feel normal. 'McDonalds' she said to herself. As she imagined the Big Mac and fries calling her from town, like an angel from heaven, she slipped on some comfortable clothes, wiped off last nights mascara that was underneath her eyes and made her way towards the heavenly call of the burger.

BigMac in hand and special sauce around her lips, Steph sat on a bench to devour the food that had been calling her. Once she'd eaten it all, and began to feel sick from the vast amount of food she'd consumed that morning, she lit a cigarette and sat back, enjoying the warm sunshine on her face. As her thoughts took her back to the night before and how much fun she'd had, she wondered 'how much did I spend?' She reached for her purse out of the pocket of the coat she wished she hadn't worn as it was so warm. She'd managed to drink her way through £200 last night. With £150 left in her purse, after buying her feast and a few other bits and bobs she told herself she needed, a thought popped into her head. 'Maybe I could win some more?' And that, Steph believed, is where her conjoined twin was born. That one thought on that sunny day, she'd manifested a monster.

Steph must have managed to nod off again after wailing into her pillow. She stretched and reached for her phone. Still no message from mum, however, she'd also not read the one she'd sent in the early hours. 'She must not be up yet' She tried to tell herself. She tried to justify a time that would be long enough to leave before she sent another message. She didn't want to wake her or Amelie but she needed to know if her mum hated her. 'Please mum.' Was the next message she sent just a few minutes after deciding it was too early. Almost immediately, the little tick appeared to say her mum had read both of the messages Steph sent her that day so far. Her heart skipped. She stared at the screen with such intent, like she did at the gambling machine screen when she was waiting for that third bonus symbol to hit. The three little dots appeared to let her know her mum was typing. Then they disappeared. They appeared again. And then went. Steph was confused. Her mum always knew the right thing to say to her, why was it taking her so long this time? Finally, that little vibration shook her hand and the message was there. 'I don't know what to say anymore Steph. It's every single payday. I don't have the money to help you and I'm sorry but I wont give you anymore money. It's just feeding your addiction.' No kisses. No 'oh Steph'. No I love you. Nothing. Steph always knew this day would come, the day where other people would give up on her, as she had given up on herself years ago but it didn't make this message hurt any less. 'I know mum. I don't want to be like this I really don't. I'll prove to you I will get better and I promise, I wont ask for a penny. I really have hit rock bottom and there's only one way out now.' Steph replied.

Steph had so many emotions running through her in that moment. She had despair, anger, upset, hurt but also a streak of determination. A determination that this time would be different. She would prove to her mum that she could do it and she would get it sorted this time. And with that, Steph made a plan.

As Steph walked to work, she was rehearsing the whole way how she would explain why she needed her wages transferring into her mums account going forward. She couldn't tell them the whole truth but what could she say to make them do it? She ran through a million scenarios in her head as to what reason she could give. Her account had been frozen. She'd had money stolen from her account. She needed to move to an overseas bank and it was taking time. Aliens has abducted her and stolen her identity. Every weird, wonderful and down right ridiculous idea popped into her head. As she approached the building that housed 150 employees, all working like ants, a horn sounded next to her. It scared Steph and made her jump, almost making her fall. She looked over to the black focus driving along side her now and shouted 'Twat! I nearly had a heart attack!' It was Adrian. 'Hahaha, you feeling better?' He shouted through the window and he pulled up on the bend that her work office was on. She opened the creaky passengers side door and sat in the cigarette burned seat. She reached over and gave him a kiss. 'Yeah I'm loads better thank you, I'm so sorry Adrian about last night. How are you ?' 'I'm fine I just wanted to make sure you were ok. What time do you finish? Fancy some food?' Knowing she had only £50 in her account at this point, she was reluctant to agree but felt bad as she'd already blown him off once this week. 'Yeah ok' she replied smiling, hiding behind that smile, the worry about how she would pay. 'Fab, I'll pick you up at 5' Replied Adrian. He lent over the centre console once again, gave her a kiss and Steph got out of the car. 'And don't get another headache!' Adrian shouted as he drove off. Steph quickly rolled a cigarette and ran through the options she'd been through all the way here again in her head. She'd decided on telling work that she'd had money stolen from her account and that's why the wages needed to be paid into her mums account.

She walked through the contact centre as she always did. She didn't feel up to talking today though. She needed to be on her own so she could write the email to HR. She didn't want Charlene seeing it. And so, she scanned the room carefully for the perfect place to sit, where Charlene wouldn't be able to join her. She found a seat in the corner next to the window. Next to her was a team leader but he was always out of his seat walking up and down so it was perfect really. She sat down, threw her coat over the back of her seat and set up her computer.

Dear HR, I have recently had money stolen from my account that

Has left me in a real mess. The bank are currently investigating it

But could I ask in the meantime please, that my wages are paid into

My mothers account.

She'd been working all day on this email. Deleting and re-writing it to make it sound as believable as possible. She'd decided not to go into too much detail about it as it's easy to get caught out lying if the details are too strong. But then it came over her again. The 'Fuck it' feeling. And with it, she hit send. 'Steph!?' a voice bellowed over the contact centre, 'What the hell?' It was Charlene. 'Sorry mate, this was the only seat free earlier!' She lied. Charlene pulled a sad face to Steph, made a love heart with her hands and found a seat a few rows away. Steph, looking around carefully to see if the team leader was around, slid her phone from the pocket on the back of her chair and typed to her mum. 'I've done it mum, I've asked them to put my wages in your account.' Sliding the phone back down, Steph was filled with a sense of achievement. She'd made a new step, one she hadn't done before, to getting better and becoming free of her addiction.

Chapter 9

As Steph took the coat from the back of her chair and waved bye to Charlene across the rows of people, all on the phone, she felt disappointment that she'd not had a reply yet from HR. She'd really wanted to go home and prove to her mum that she'd made the step and confirm the money would now be paid into her account every month. But she still felt proud of what she'd done. As she walked out of the automatic door at the front of the building, she could see Adrian in the car park of the building opposite. She made her way toward the old Focus, climbed inside and lent over to give him a kiss. 'Good day?' asked Adrian. 'Yeah not too bad, you?'. She didn't tell Adrian about what she'd done that day, or the night before. She felt lucky to have come out of the experience as well as she did. She didn't feel unwell in anyway and knew it could have ended so differently. 'You hungry?' asked Adrian 'Well I hope so because I've booked us in at Flounders.' He said again, not giving Steph a chance to answer. Flounders was a restaurant they'd been to a few times. It was hugely over priced but the food was nice. Remembering the limited funds she had in her account, she nervously smiled and thanked Adrian. He started the car and they made their way to the restaurant.

As they reached Flounders and walked in, they found a table next to the window that they'd sat at before. It gave a beautiful view of the fields over the road and she saw the sheep in there which always reminded Steph of her grandad. The waiter came over and took the order for two large glasses of red wine from Adrian. Steph gave him the look to which Adrian replied 'I'm only having the one!'

The pair opened the oversized menu's that were laid on the table in front of them. 'I don't even need to look' said Adrian, knowing he would order the same thing as he had every time they'd been here. Steph laughed at his comment as she scanned the price column of the menu. It was so expensive! She had a month to make £50.00 last, she really couldn't afford anything from this menu. 'I'll just have a salad, I'm not that hungry' she told Adrian, knowing this was the cheapest thing available. The waiter returned with their drinks and took their orders for food.

'I was worried about you last night' said Adrian. 'It was just a migraine honestly, I get them sometimes.' Replied Steph. The pair chatted about the normal day to day things, how his family was, how her family was and what they'd got planned for the week. As the food arrived, Steph looked at her pathetic salad, stomach rumbling and wishing she had something more substantial. 'I can't believe you've ordered that' said Adrian, stuffing his mouth with the side order of chips accompanying the huge burger on his plate. Steph looked at Adrian and told herself 'This is worth getting better for. So that I can come back here and order what I want, and sit with Adrian and actually enjoy it, and not be worried about the waiter coming with the card machine at the end of the meal.' She liked Adrian. He was kind and he seemed to really like Steph. Of course, he only knew the parts about Steph he let her know. Would he still like her if he knew the truth? Of course he wouldn't, nobody would like an addict, destined for bankruptcy!

'Oh my god I'm stuffed!' exclaimed Adrian, sliding down his chair, holding his stomach. 'You greedy bastard! I can't believe you've eaten all of that. Where the hell do you put it?' asked Steph.

The pair sat for a while longer whilst Steph finished her glass of wine. Once she had, it was time for the bill. Adrian waved down the waiter and politely asked if they could have the bill and the card machine. 'This one's on me' said Adrian as he winked at Steph. She was so relieved! 'Awhh, thank you Adrian. You're so nice.' So, she'd still got £50. She could scrimp through the month on that she but she felt so guilty that Adrian had paid again. He often paid for the meals they went out for and she knew soon enough she would need to return the gestures. 'You stopping at mine tonight?' asked Adrian, putting away his wallet. Steph didn't really want to. Adrian lived with his mum, dad, big sister and little brother. She liked his family but she always felt a little uncomfortable around them for some reason. But, filled with guilt for the salad he'd just bought her, she agreed and the pair headed back to Adrian's house.

Guilt and gambling go hand in hand. Steph would feel guilty about the most ridiculous things. She'd feel guilty if she ever said no to anyone, which often meant she ended up doing things she didn't really want to do. She'd feel guilty if someone else was having a hard time, even if it had nothing to do with her. She'd feel like everything bad in the world was her fault and so, would do anything and everything for others, never putting herself first. Apart from on payday – On payday, nobody else mattered. When she was on that website, or sat at that machine, the only things that existed in the world were her and that screen.

Steph and Adrian walked through the front door and they were met by the border terriers the family owned. Steph loved dogs. She'd always wanted one but her mum never let her. She enjoyed so much being sat with a dog and feeling the innocence of the animal and nothing but love. They walked through the hallway into the kitchen where all of the family were sat around the table. Steph did enjoy being there sometimes. They were quite a traditional family. They all sat at the table at mealtimes. There were no phones and the family would talk and laugh together. Steph had never had that growing up. She didn't even have a dining table and her sisters moved out at such a young age that she couldn't ever remember a time where they all sat as a family like Adrian's family did. Adrian and Steph joined the family around the table.

Adrian's mum had an obvious drinking problem. Every night, she'd repeatedly fill her glass from the box of wine she'd buy. Very often, she'd just fall asleep on the sofa watching TV but sometimes, she got really angry and would start shouting or crying and looking for an argument that someone in the family would usually facilitate for her. This is what made Steph uncomfortable but at the same time, Steph could relate to Adrian's mum. She knew that she had her own conjoined twin. Steph knew first hand how hard it was to ignore the screams and so felt sorry for Deidre. Nobody ever addressed the obvious drinking problem she had, something Steph knew Deidre would be grateful of.

Steph always thought that the family were strangely over protective of Adrian. He was an adult now but they would still want to know where he was, they'd still shout at him if he didn't clean the house or if he'd spent too much money. One night, when they first started seeing each other, Adrian stopped at Steph's flat. In the early hours, his family came banging on the flat door and barged their way through when Steph answered it.

His mum was screaming at him saying how worried she'd been about him and started hitting him. Steph couldn't believe it. How did they even know where she lived? It made her feel sorry for Adrian more than anything else, and so, they continued their relationship.

'Have you eaten?' Asked Adrian's dad.

'I'm surprised he can walk!' replied Steph jokingly, tapping Adrian's belly. The pair spent an hour or so with the family before making their way to the bedroom. They climbed into the single bed together and Adrian, feeling very tired from his full belly and long day at work, quickly began snoring. Steph lay next to him as still as she could, being sure not to disturb him. As she did, she heard the shouting begin from downstairs. She couldn't make out what they were saying but she could tell it was Diedre and her Daughter Amanda. She listened for the next half an hour as the shouting got louder and she heard Amanda storm her way upstairs into the bedroom next door. Adrian was still sound asleep, snoring on every in breath. Steph thought he must just be used to it by now, or he's eaten so much he's fallen into a food coma. She could hear crying through the thin wall, coming from the next room. Steph and Amanda had grown quite close recently since she'd being seeing Adrian. She was a lovely girl but Steph knew, trying to talk to her or Deidre once they'd had a drink was pointless. Instead, she rolled over, tried to pull the duvet from under Adrian who wouldn't move, and went to sleep.

When she woke up, Adrian had already gone to work. He always started at around 6am so Steph knew that when she stopped there, he wouldn't be there when she woke up. She always felt a little awkward though, going down to the family without Adrian being there. She got ready for work, hoping she would have a return email from HR. She moved around the room as quietly as she possibly could, hoping Amanda and Deidre would still be sleeping off the wine from the night before. She crept downstairs and took her coat off the coat peg.

'Steph?' a weary voice shouted from the kitchen. Shit. Deidre was awake. 'Yeah it's only me D' she replied. She walked into the kitchen where D was sat in her pink fluffy dressing gown, hands wrapped around the black coffee Steph knew she was drinking to try and get rid of the headache she'd got. 'you ok?' asked Steph.

'Me? Yeah I'm fine darling. You got everything you need for work? Have you got some lunch?' D asked. D was lovely when she was sober. Steph actually really liked her and a part of her wished they could be open with each other about their addictions, it might make it easier for both of them. But, knowing this could never happen, she told D she had everything she needed, thanked her and wished her a nice day. She walked out of the door and made the short walk to work. Adrian only lived around the corner from work so it was easier when she stopped there.

On the way to work she got a message from Adrian 'Have a good day beautiful, I love waking up next to you. Even if you do snore like a pig and dribble on my duvet! xxx' Three kisses. She knew he really liked her. 'Me too mister ☺ xxx' was Steph's reply. She crossed off the message and went to call her mum. 'Hi mum, are you ok?' she asked, quite relieved her mum had answered the phone. They continued the conversation they had every day and Steph told her mum again about the email she'd sent to HR. Her mum told her she was proud and to let her know what they say. The phone call ended and Steph, who for the first time in a long time felt good and optimistic, walked into work.

Chapter 10

From: HR   RE: Pay

Hi Steph,

I'm really sorry to hear about that! How awful! Not a problem, if you let me have the details you need your wages paying into we can arrange it for you. It's not something we should do on a long term basis so if you can let us know as soon as possible your new account details, we can arrange to get it paid into your account again.

Kind regards,

HR team

'Yes!' Steph whispered to herself, surrounded by other employee's on the phone. This was it, the first day of the rest of Steph's life. She snuck out her phone once more and took a photo, immediately sending it to her mum. What a brilliant day! Steph could feel her phone vibrating in her pocket. She was desperate to look at but there were so many team leaders around now and she knew she'd get in trouble. It kept vibrating and she could tell it was someone trying to call her, not the short vibration that she knew was a message. Who was trying to get hold of her so desperately? Things like this always filled her with anxiety. Had something bad happened? Was it one of her sisters? She couldn't wait anymore so she rushed her way through the call she was now on. She knew if one of her team leaders listened to this conversation they wouldn't be happy with it but she needed to know who was trying to ring her. She put herself on 'not ready' on the phone system and made her way to the toilet. As she locked the cubicle door and sat on the toilet, she read the notifications displayed on the screen of her phone. 3 missed calls and 2 new emails. She opened and the numbers were an 03 number. She knew this was a debt collector. She had a huge amount of debt now and was used to debt collectors trying to contact her. She regularly changed her number so they couldn't contact her anymore and didn't even open letters anymore. She deleted the emails without reading them and swiped away the missed calls from her phone. She would often worry about her level of debt which usually pushed her online to try and win the money to pay them off, leaving her with even less money and then having to take out another loan, increasing her overall debt yet again. A vicious cycle. So she'd decided to just ignore all of her debts and hope they'd go away. The worst advice she'd ever given herself.

She flushed the toilet, even though she'd not actually been, and walked out of the toilets back to her seat in the call centre. She began to think about her debts. If she wanted to ever truly get better, and make a life with Adrian, she needed to get them sorted. She didn't want letters coming through and keep changing her number. She'd made a good step this week already to get better and so this was the perfect time to sort some of her debts out too. She remembered when her mum was really struggling and she left her with that council tax bill. Her mum had been able to get a debt relief order which cleared the council tax bill altogether. 'I wonder if I could get that?' she thought.

When she got to her mums flat later that day, she asked her mum how she had managed to get a debt relief order. Her mum explained that she'd called a debt charity who went through her income and all of her debts and they arranged everything for her. They searched online for the charity that her mum and used and Steph called the number. As she was on hold, she turned to her mum and said 'I told you I'd do it mum. I'm really trying this time.'

'I know you are sweetheart, I'm so proud.' Said her mum.

After being on hold for a while, Steph started speaking to a woman at the other end of the phone. She was so lovely, she listened to everything Steph said. Steph actually told her about her gambling and how hard she was finding things and not once did the woman at the end of the phone judge her. She listened and genuinely tried to help her. She asked Steph to go through the debts she had. Steph reeled off debt after debt after debt. She felt hugely embarrassed but she figured there must be millions like her if there is an actual charity for this kind of thing. After over an hour on the phone, the woman advised Steph that she didn't qualify for the same as her mum but that a debt management plan was the best option for her. 'What's that?' asked Steph. The friendly woman went on to explain that they would put all of Steph's debt into one direct debit payment a month, a payment she could afford, and they would distribute it to her creditors. They talked through it some more and it was decided, out of Steph's wage, she could afford a payment of £527 a month. Steph thought to herself, how bloody embarrassing. I have all that disposable income a month and here I am, not being able to afford food. Steph and the woman agreed everything. Steph explain very proudly that the money would need to come out of her mums account as that's where her money would be paid into now. The woman took the details and they agreed a day after payday would be when the money would leave the account. Steph couldn't thank the stranger at the end of the month for everything she'd done for her. A huge wait had been lifted from her shoulders and for the first time in years, Steph felt like the screaming was getting quieter.

She hung up the phone and gave her mum the biggest hug she ever had. Her mum actually had to pull her off because she squeezed her so tight! 'It's happening mum, I'm getting better.'

Chapter 11

5 months had passed and Steph had never been happier in her life. The money was going into her mums account which she didn't have access to. Her relationship with Adrian was going amazingly and she's had no more sick days from work. She couldn't believe it. All these years she'd been trapped and she was finally feeling free. She'd also proved to her mum that she could do it. She'd stopped having to send those payday messages and instead, they grew closer and laughed and were best of friends. Steph had also become really close again to Leanne. Recently, Leanne had been having some of her own financial difficulties. She'd been telling Steph that she wasn't sure how she was going to carry on without any additional income. She'd got her own debts, the rent to pay on her own and she simply didn't earn enough to do it all. That's when Steph offered to move in with Leanne. She was in a much better place now, happy with her life, in control of her own mind. She had an opportunity to help out her best friend and get out of that bed she shared with her mum. Leanne was over the moon at the thought of splitting the bills and living with her childhood friend. They'd agreed to wait until the following payday to make it happen, given they'd already paid their bills for this month, and that's when Steph would move in.

Steph told her mum about the plan, knowing secretly she'd be pleased that she would be getting her own space back. Her mum was pleased for Steph but was concerned about the money. 'How will we manage it?' asked her mum anxiously.

'Mum it's been 5 months now. I really feel so much better and I don't feel like it will happen again honestly. I really feel ready to have my card back.' Steph genuinely meant it. She didn't hear the screams of the conjoined twin so loudly anymore and believed that she was in control now. Still anxious, but understanding, Steph's mum handed her the bank card.

The next person to tell about the news was Adrian. She rang him and told him what they girls had agreed and how excited she was to be living with her best friend. Things recently had been hard for Adrian. His mum's drinking had got worse and there were more arguments than ever before. 'Can I come with you? I want to wake up with you every day and I really need to get out of here.' Steph was silent as she tried to take in what Adrian was asking. She knew at this point, she loved Adrian. They'd said it to each other not so long ago and she really felt as though she would spend her life with him but she didn't imagine it would be so soon they'd start living together. 'I'd love it too Adrian. Let me check with Leanne.' She responded. They talked a little more about how excited they were at the thought of living with each other and ended the call with the understanding that Steph would speak to Leanne about Adrian making the move too.

'Leanne. What if Adrian came too? We'd share the room I'm moving into obviously but it would mean we could split the bills three ways.' – That was the message she sent to Leanne. She had that feeling in her stomach again. The one she'd not had for 5 months now. The swirling in her stomach as she waited for a response. 'OMG YES YES YES' Steph's body filled with a feeling of happiness and excitement as she read the message. She couldn't believe it. She'd be moving into a house with her amazing boyfriend and her absolute best friend. And best of all, she'd be gamble free and happy! She rang Adrian back and told him the news. The giddy, love struck youngsters could not be happier and looked forward to the 28th. A date that had previously brought Steph so much misery, would be the best day of her life so far.

The 28th came and Steph and Adrian moved into the 2 bed house. Setting up the tiny space into their own. The room was too small to get a bedframe in so they slept on a mattress on the floor. They didn't mind though. They would be together, away from the drinking, away from the gambling. They went and got their first food shop as a couple. Only ready meals and frozen veg but they were proud. For the first time, they felt like adults, completely in love. Adrian still didn't know about the addiction Steph had hidden all of her adult life, but it didn't matter now. It was gone and there was no need for him to know.

Another thing that had changed for Steph was her love for her job. She did love work in the call centre however, she'd found herself bored and looking for a new challenge, especially since gambling wasn't consuming all of her thoughts anymore! She knew she could never afford to just quit, but she'd started the search for a new job. There was one that caught her eye. It was in another call centre but it was dealing with complaints. She loved problem solving, ironically as for so many years she hadn't resolved any of her own. But the thought of dealing with angry customers and turning it around, finding out what had gone wrong intrigued and excited her. And so a few weeks ago, she'd sent off her CV and waited for a response.

That night, her and Adrian laid on the mattress on the floor, thinking about how happy they were. How this tiny space was theirs together. They talked to each other about their plans for the next day. Adrian was at work so he'd be out of the house by 6am. Leanne worked in the same contact centre as Steph and she knew she was on an early shift so she'd be out of the house for 7.30am. But it was Steph's day off tomorrow. She'd planned on cleaning her new home top to bottom, and going into town to look for some pictures to hang on the walls of their tiny bedroom. Completely smitten, they kissed each other good night and fell to sleep.

It was 9:30am the next day Steph woke up. The house was empty. She opened her eyes and looked around the little room and smiled. She went down the stairs into the kitchen and made herself a coffee, lit a cigarette and called her mum. Her mum answered and asked how she'd got on with the move. Did she like it? Was the room ok? Did she go food shopping? And once again, was she ok? It was at that moment in clicked in Steph's head as to what her mum was actually asking. The 29th of the month and with Steph in control of her own money again, her mum was asking if she'd gambled. The thought had genuinely never even entered Steph's mind. 'Honestly mum I haven't. I haven't even thought about it. I'm so happy mum I wont screw it up by gambling.' Her mum, still anxious told Steph how proud she was. They'd agreed that Steph would go for tea at her mum's flat one day next and ended the call.

Steph then got on with the cleaning. She scrubbed every inch of that house, other than Leanne's room, and was so proud. By this time, it was 2.30pm. She'd decided against going into town given it was chucking it down outside. Sat on the sofa, with no one to talk to and nothing on TV, she began to aimlessly scroll through Facebook on her phone. She didn't even read any of the posts on there, she just scrolled though to make sure there was nothing from her sisters. As she scrolled, an advert filled the screen. '50 FREE SPINS' it read, with a picture of the game Steph had once loved so much. She stopped scrolling and stared at the advert. 'No!' she told herself and continued scrolling. Her thumb seemed to drag the page up much slower than it previously had. Her thumb now scrolling in the opposite direction, slowly pulled the advert back into view. *£20 deposit required. As she sat in that living room, alone, she thought 'If I just do £20.00, I'll get the free spins and I'll not deposit anymore. I'll definitely just do £20.00. 50 free spins is too good to miss!'

She clicked on the advert. As it asked her to register her details to create her account, she could feel the scream of the conjoined twin getting ever so slightly louder. 'I'm only doing £20.00!' she told herself. 'I'll be fine, I've not done it for ages. I can control it now.' She registered her details and just like that, her account had been created. It was now ready to accept the £20.00 she needed to claim those spins. She stood up and went to the pocket of her coat where she knew she'd had her mothers bank card the day before. She pulled it out and entered the details into the website. CVV code was the last thing to be entered. She hesitated as she read the three digits on the back of her mums card.

'I shouldn't do this.' Was the last thought she had before she hit deposit.

She rolled away the £20.00 on a £2 stake. The feeling as she did it this time wasn't dread or guilt It was excitement. The thrill those spinning wheels gave her. The 'near misses' when 2 of the 3 bonus symbols would drop. There really is no feeling quite like it. The £20.00 lasted around 3 minutes before she'd got no credit left. She went on to play the 50 free spins. '20p!' She shouted out loud. The free spins that had led her down this path were a 20p stake. Steph knew she wouldn't make anything from a 20p stake and felt robbed by the advert. She rolled away the free spins, completely disgusted. She didn't even watch all of the spins because she was so annoyed at the stake. £1.13 was the total won from those spins.

Steph now felt completely cheated. She was a very sore loser. She knew and it often believed this was an attribute to her gambling. The fact she couldn't walk away feeling like it had beaten her, even though it always did. It was that feeling, that feeling of anger that led Steph to deposit £100.00. She didn't realise it at the time, but even with a 5 month break, it had taken 1 advert, a CVV code and an empty house to lead her straight back into the black hole she'd managed to climb out of. Back into that state of numbness. Not feeling, not thinking. It was just her and the slot.

48 minutes in total. It took 48 minutes to clear Steph's bank account completely. She was now having a panic attack. A full blown panic attack. 'What the fuck have I done? Why? WHY?' she screamed to herself over and over again, now pacing the carpet of a new house. Fighting for breath now as the panic took over her whole body, she sat and tried to calm herself down. 'You've already paid the rent, got shopping, and the debt management direct debit has already left. You've only spent the shopping money and bus fare money. You're going to be ok.' Was what she told herself to try and gain back control the amount of oxygen she was inhaling. 'You've paid mum back so you can think of a reason to ask for money. It's just this month.'

Those famous words again leaving her mouth. The 'It's just this month' which previously had lasted years. What was about to follow was a string of lies and deceit that, for the past 5 months, Steph had enjoyed not doing.

She looked at the clock and saw it was now 4.30pm. Both Leanne and Adrian would be home soon. Neither, even though they were the closest people to Steph, knew of her problem and she couldn't tell them now. She pulled a frozen lasagne from the freezer and put it in the oven, ready for her housemates return. It was time once again, to paint on that fake smile she'd mastered and hide her true self from the world.

Steph decided to wait a week, until she next needed a food shop, to ask her mum for money. The bank account her mum had let her use for wages was one she never used. She didn't have online banking or anything for the account so she knew she would never find out what she'd done.

Steph faked her way through the rest of the week, pretending everything was ok to Leanne and Adrian whilst hiding her absolute disappointment in herself and anger behind her smile. It was the next Saturday her and Adrian had planned to do the food shop. All Friday morning at work, she'd been thinking about what she could possibly tell her mum had happened so that she could ask for money.

One thing gambling had also made Steph very good at was living on very little money. She knew she didn't need hundreds of pounds to get through the month on. All she would need is money for tobacco and food. She could manipulate her way through the supermarket shop to spend as little as possible. Swapping big brands for own brands, convincing Adrian they had enough of certain products and that they needed to stop buying certain things because it was a waste of money. Steph could live on £25 a week easy and so, she knew she didn't need to get hundreds of pounds out of her mum. It was 3 weeks until payday now so she just needed £75.00 to get through.

'Hey mum, could I borrow £75.00 until payday please? You don't need to worry, I haven't gambled or anything, I just need to ...'

She couldn't think of an end to the message. She couldn't think of a reason she needed the money for. A reason that wouldn't lead her mum to suspect anything. She needed something original that she'd never used before. Her trail of thought was interrupted by a call that came through her headset. 'Good morning you're through to Steph, how can I help?' she answered, as she did every call at work. The conversation continued and she helped the old man on the other end of the phone with his query. A pretty good call all in all, she wouldn't mind if her team leader listened to that one! The guy told her at the end of the call 'thank you for you're help Steph, I can enjoy my birthday now knowing it's all sorted!'

'Hey mum, could I borrow £75.00 until payday please? You don't need to worry, I haven't gambled or anything, I just didn't realise it was Amanda's birthday and we've all been invited to Leeds for a meal and a night out. You know with me paying this debt management plan I don't have a lot left but I don't want them to know that! xxx'

It was perfect. Once more, she was filled with guilt, but, it was believable and it may mean she can get through to payday with no-one knowing the slip up she'd made. She was determined though she wouldn't slip again. It was one slip and that's it.

'Yeah of course you can. I'll send it you now.xxx'

She'd done it. She'd got the money she needed to get through the month. Feeling relieved, she continued with her shift and went food shopping the next day with Adrian.

Chapter 12

27th. Thank god. She'd made it. She'd got through the month with no one finding out about her slip up last payday. Tomorrow she could fix the mess she'd made and get back on the straight and narrow. Her and Adrian were as smitten as ever and she was enjoying time with Leanne. They'd spend time together chatting, watching TV, doing their hair. All the girly stuff she felt she'd missed out with her own sisters. She had work today so she knew the day would go by quickly and she wouldn't have to spend too much time thinking about money before she'd be home, going to bed and waking up tomorrow fixing it all. She also knew she was at work tomorrow so there wouldn't be any risk of her being left at home alone and having the chance to gamble. All would be good again tomorrow.

She went to work in a pretty good mood. The first half of the day flew by because it was so busy with calls. The most they'd had in a morning for a while.

It was Steph's dinner time. She rolled herself a cigarette at her desk and made the walk out to the smoking shelter. As she did, she checked her phone.

RE: Job application

Hi Steph,

We've been passed you're CV with interest in the complaints handler position and we would like to arrange an interview with you. Would you be available at any time next week? Please let me know by return and we can get it booked in for you. We are holding interviews Monday – Wednesday so if you could make it early next week that would be brilliant.

Kind regards

No way! She'd been offered an interview. She knew she was off on Tuesday so it was perfect! She replied excitedly, making sure no one around her could see what she was putting. She triple checked her email for spelling mistakes before sending it back and letting them know she could make any time on Tuesday. Filled once more with excitement, she messaged Adrian to tell him what had happened.

'Well done babe! You'll smash it I know you will. You'll be the bread winner if you get this job haha!' replied Adrian. He was right. This job was really well paid. It would mean she had more spare income each month that she would get her mum to save for her. Things were looking up.

Steph finished her shift and made her way home. She put another ready meal in the oven, ready for Adrian coming home and started to research the company she was going for an interview with. She wanted the job so much now and would make sure she was fully prepped for it. As Leanne came home too, the three watched TV, drank wine and headed off to bed. A good day all in all. As Steph lay on the mattress on the floor, wrapped in the arms of Adrian, she should have felt happier than she had all month. But she didn't. Instead, the only thought that run through her mind was gambling. Her mind becoming a calculator, she went over and over what she could gamble and still afford to pay her bills. All month she'd spent thinking about how she would make things better. All month worrying. All month being determined she would get back on track tomorrow, replaced with 'I can gamble £100 and still afford to pay my bills.' Reassuring herself that she wouldn't be alone tomorrow and so couldn't gamble replaced with 'I could do it on my lunch, just hide in the toilet.' Steph couldn't sleep at all. The conjoined twin screaming so loud in her ear now that she was actually excited to get on the website and shut her up. She knew her wages went in at 00:00 and so she was periodically checking the time on her phone, being sure to keep the bright light from waking Adrian. 11:58pm. Was the time on the 5th check. She slid her phone off of it's charger, carefully moved Adrian's arm from around her and tip toed on the end of the mattress, down the stairs into the bathroom. Once again, on a toilet seat late at night with her phone in hand, she loaded up the website. It was more difficult than it was when she had her own card because she didn't have online banking to check the money had gone in with her mums card. She attempted to deposit. Declined. She couldn't understand. It should be in by now! The time just turning 00:01. She gave it another minute and tried again. £200 the amount in the deposit box. Deposit successful. 'Thank god!' he said to herself. The thought of not being able gamble petrified Steph, almost more than actually losing her money. This was it! This time, Steph didn't feel nervous or scared or have any thought about what she would do if she would lose. She was excited because she knew, she knew undoubtedly it was her turn to win.

'Fuck it' she whispered to herself as she set the stake to £5. And there, in that downstairs toilet, she began to press the little red button once more.

The girl gambler, sat once again alone, unable to control herself, now having no conscious mind. All that mattered now was she had money and she was gambling. She'd rolled away £170 before she hit the bonus. But she did hit it and that was all that mattered. She loved the sound it made on the bonus rounds so she increased the volume from silent to just one bar of sound. It was very faint but she could hear it. Her body was shaking uncontrollably. She was so hot though. There was sweat dripping from forehead now. All she was doing was sat on a toilet but this was the affect gambling had on her. Not only mentally, but physically it changed her.

£4,000! This was the most she had ever won! £4000 from a £5 spin. She stood up and jumped around the bathroom as quietly as she could, silently squealing to herself. There was nobody. Nobody in the world she could share her good news with but she didn't care. She knew it was her turn to win. She didn't know how, she just knew. The bonus round ended and £4030 was the credit on the screen. She looked at those four numbers and it gave her a feeling she'd never had before. A feeling of appreciation, of success. Steph had finally done it. As she stared at the number, so did her twin.

'I'll just play the £30 and I'll withdraw the rest' This is something she always did. She'd set a number in her head and she would just roll her money away to this figure. She'd stop at this number and walk away. She would! 7 spins later, she'd not hit what she needed. She stared again, as she always did before she made a bad decision, at the credit now showing £4000. 'I'll just play it to £3500, that's still more than I've ever had before! And I'll do it on a £10.00 spin so I'm even more likely to hit the bonus!' That was how she justified to herself that she wouldn't withdraw any winnings at this point. Steph knew.

Once she'd set herself a limit on her losses, and she continued to spin past it even once, the chances of her stopping at all became lower and lower. Like the odds on a horse. As she spent the £30 she'd promised herself she's stop at, the odds of her stopping at all were now 100/1.

10 minutes later, she was at £3150. She'd gone well past the £500 she'd promised. 'Right, £150 more and that is it. I am not coming away with less than £3000.' was the next thing she told herself. Her odds of being successful now going 150/1.

She did stop at £3000. She took herself back onto the home screen and went through the menu to withdraw. Please enter the amount you would like to withdraw filled the box so she rarely got to fill in. Steph entered £2000. 'Look, £2000 is more than I have ever won still and it will still help me out. But I might hit the bonus again with this £1000.' She went back to the game she loved so much and began to spin. Steph levels of anger getting higher and higher with every spin that didn't give her the thousands of pounds she was looking for. Every 2 seconds, her credit dropping another £10.00. Not once, not once did she hit the bonus again. How? How can you spend £1000 at not hit it?

Steph locked her phone and went back up to bed. She was angry, angry that the game had beaten her. £2000 she'd spent. £2030 actually since her last bonus round. She tried to counteract the thoughts with the £2000 that was sitting patiently, waiting to be paid into her account. She started to imagine what she would do with the money. The truth being that she couldn't think of anything she wanted to do with it. She didn't particularly like buying clothes, there wasn't anything she wanted for herself. But still, she was so thrilled. Even to just have a bank balance of £2000 and not buy anything was enough for her. Her anger replaced in part with excitement now. She lay on that mattress, too overcome with excitement and anger at the same time, to ever fall asleep. She kept replaying that bonus round over and over and over again in her head. It was so beautiful. The colours, the sound everything about it Steph just loved. It made her happier than anything else in the world. The bonus round is what she chased every month. It was like a drug to her. She started the think about the lines that were on there, and how big each win was on them. 'Imagine how much I'd win on a £20 stake.' She played, in her head, what the bonus round would look like on a £20 stake. She could change her life if she hit it on that.

Once more, she slid her phone off of her charger, and made her way to the toilet. She knew in the back of her brain what was about to happen but she pushed it as far back as she could. Perched once again on the toilet seat, she typed in the website. She went into the menu and clicked 'reverse withdrawal'. She hated that she could do this. She'd done it every time she managed to withdraw anything. The money would sit in there and scream at her until she went in and withdrew it. He wished so much that the websites would not give her the option. She couldn't reverse her deposits so why could she reverse her withdrawal?

Immediately, the credit changed from £0 to £2000. She went straight back into the withdraw section of the page and withdrew £1000. 'I'll still be happy with £1000 even if I lose but I'll use this £1000 to hit the bonus.' Whispered the twin in her ear.

Within seconds, she was back on that game. That beautiful game that had, not an hour earlier, given her more money than she'd ever had in her life. Increasing her stake to £20.00, she began to spin. 5 spins = £100 down. 10 spins = £200 down. She couldn't believe how quickly her credit was going down. And in no time at all, it was all gone. 'NO!' she quietly screamed through her teeth. She impatiently navigated her way back to the part of the menu where she was able to reverse the last £1000 she'd, not 10 minutes before, requested to withdraw. Back to the game, back to the £20 spin. The odds now of Steph walking away with anything that payday morning, 1,000,000/1

Steph was furious. She'd been cheated. How could she have rolled through £4000 without hitting the bonus again? An absolute con and she'd been cheated. She began to punch herself in the head out of upset and anger. 'No, I wont be beaten!'

She typed £400 into the deposit box.

3 minutes later, she typed again £400 into the deposit box.

12 minutes after that, she typed £400 into the deposit box. This time, a message displayed 'Transaction declined: Insufficient funds'

In less than 3 hours, Steph had spent £5000. She'd spent almost all of her own wage on top of the £4000 she'd won. She wasn't better. She was worse than she'd ever been before. There was no hope for her. What the hell was she going to do?

There was no getting back to sleep this time. No way she'd be able to nod off and wake up in a few hours with a plan. £5000. How? How the hell had she rolled her way through £5000? She began again to panic. Trying silently to take back control of her breath as she paced around the cold, tiled floor of the bathroom. She went to the back door and chained smoked 3 cigarettes. On the last drag, she took the cigarette, glowing red on the end from the heat and stubbed it out on her arm. 'It's what you deserve' she told herself as the tip burned through the layers of her skin. It didn't even hurt that much. She couldn't feel anything. The loss of £5000 had acted as her anaesthetic. Even the sadness and despair had left her now. Back once more, to that complete emptiness and numbness she always felt when her head was finally free of the screaming she listened to everyday, telling her to gamble.

She sat on the sofa, the light slowly beginning to fill the room from sunrise. Adrian would be awake soon and going to work. She didn't know where she was going to find the energy from this time to paint the smile on her face that hid all of her secrets. She didn't know what she was going to tell Leanne, her best friend who'd she'd moved in to try and help out of her own issues. She'd just created her more.

The usual money making thoughts ran through her head. Could she get a loan? No, especially not now she was in a debt management plan. Could she borrow from family? No. Her mum had already said she wouldn't lend her any more money. It was looking more and more likely that telling Adrian and Leanne was the only option. The thought made her feel sick.

She heard Adrian stomping around upstairs. Shit. Shit! She couldn't do it. She couldn't face him. She couldn't tell him. He'd hate her. She heard the footsteps coming down the stairs, she had about 5 seconds before he would see her puffy eyes from crying and would know something was wrong. She quickly laid down and closed her eyes. She'd decided pretending to be asleep and avoiding any interaction was the only thing she could do. As she laid, eyes closed, trying to force herself to look as naturally asleep as possible, she heard him head to the kitchen and click the kettle. He walked towards her. She knew he was stood over her. She'd got that feeling you get when you know someone is looking at you and seemed to be stood there for ages. Did he know? Was he staring at her in disgust? Her heart was pounding out of her chest. She heard him take a step and reach for the blanket on the other sofa. She felt the air flow across her body as he was wafting the blanket and then put it over her body. Steph, still keeping her eyes closed and trying to look as natural as possible, turned away from him as the blanket covered her. She heard Adrian go back to kitchen and make himself a cup of tea. 'Just fuck off to work' she thought as she lay there as still as possible, pretending to be asleep. Finally, she heard Adrian get up and put his empty cup in the sink. She could hear him putting on his steel toe capped boots, walk back over and kiss Steph on the forehead and leave for work.

Even though Adrian had gone, she lay in the same position, eyes closed for a while. All she could see in her mind was that bonus round. Going over and over and over it in her mind, exactly how it had played out. She needed, as a minimum, to find the rent money for Leanne. She couldn't fail on her 2nd payment, she couldn't let her down like that. Her mind went into mission mode. She'd do whatever it took to find the money she needed to pay Leanne. She looked over at the big clock on the living room wall. It was 7.30am. She had a few hours before Leanne would ask her to transfer the money for the rent. Her share of the rent and bills was £220. She went over in her head how much she'd spent earlier that morning. Not having online banking made it harder than normal.

'I deposited £200 first. Then £400, then another £400. The last £400 I tried got declined.' She told herself as she tried to remember exactly how it had played out. She decided to ring the number on the bank card. She knew it would tell her the available balance on there and her actual balance. She made her way to the bathroom and, for the third time this morning, sat on the toilet as she dialled the number. As she lied her way through the automated security questions, answering as her mum as it was her account, she reached the part she needed.

'You're balance is One. Thousand. Two. Hundred. And twelve. Pounds.' Read the robotic voice over the phone. 'Your available balance is. Two. Hundred. And twelve. Pounds'. Quickly hanging up the phone, Steph felt sick. All that money she'd got paid this morning and that was all she was left with not even 12 hours later. She did however, also feel slightly relieved. She was only £8 off what she needed to pay Leanne. Mission one, pay rent completed, near enough. She would draw out the cash and tell Leanne she'd used some for dinner at work and would give her the missing £8 tomorrow.

Chapter 13

Steph's anxiety was through the roof. As she tried to force herself to get ready for work, her heart would start randomly beating so fast that it felt like it was going to come straight out of chest. She did have a heart condition so it always worried her even more when it started beating fast. She had to take a heart tablet everyday to slow it down but then she'd do things to speed it up again!

She really didn't feel up to work. She wanted to stay at home and work out a plan. That's all she would be thinking about all the time she was working anyway. Even though Leanne was sorted, she still needed to pay her debt management plan, her mum and live for the month. Every time she thought about it her heart raced again. She'd decided she would go to work. She didn't want to start the sickness pattern again and have eyes staring at her. As she put on her work shirt, she winced as the sleeve went over her arm. It was the burn. It looked a real mess and it was really sore. It was just above her wrist so she would need to wear a long sleeved shirt for a few days to make sure nobody saw. She slid her handbag over her shoulder and made her way to work.

Steph had to sit down a few times as she walked to work. She'd go into panic again and her chest would hurt and she'd feel dizzy. She didn't know how she was going to make it through the day today. But she continued to march to work, too scared to call in sick. As she reached work, she was completely out of breath and still in panic mode. She sat down on the big green chair in reception, bent over trying to catch her breath. She could see the receptionist staring at her. 'Are you ok Steph?' she shouted over the tall reception desk. Steph couldn't reply. She couldn't even breath properly. A minute later her boss walked into reception. He put his arm over her and asked her if she was ok. 'Yeah I'm ok' she panted. 'Look Steph, go home. You don't look well and there's no way you can work in this state. Do you need a lift?' She couldn't think of anything worse than being stuck in a car with Jamie in an awkward silence. 'No it's ok. I'll ring Adrian.' She said. Jamie turned to the receptionist and told her to ring him if there were any problems. There was no way she was ringing Adrian. Her mind wasn't working well enough today to come up with the lies she needed to as to why she needed picking up from work. She pulled her phone from her pocket and pretended to call him. 'Adrian I don't feel well. Will you pick me up please?' She said down the phone. She waited a few seconds before saying 'Ok, yeah at the bottom of the road is fine. I'll start walking now.' She pretended to hang up the phone and put it in her pocket. 'He's only around the corner so he will pick me up from the bottom of the road' she lied to the receptionist. 'Ok Steph, well be careful and I hope you feel better soon.' Steph made her way back towards the main road and walked to the closest bus stop. She kept her hood up the whole time to be sure no one from the contact centre recognised it was her. She really didn't feel well at all but she needed to get to a cash machine and withdraw Leanne's rent.

As she boarded the bus, a heater wasn't what she looked for this time. She needed a seat near the window because she felt like she was going to pass out. Hood still up, she opened the window closest to her and rested her head against it as the bus made it's way into town. She couldn't shift this sick feeling. She just couldn't believe what she'd done. More money than she'd ever seen and she'd lost it all. Why couldn't she stop herself? Why, even though it would sort all of her problems and more, why could she not just take the money? The questions ran through her head all the way into town. She stepped off of the bus and couldn't even bring herself to say thank you today. She hurried off, hood up and never turned to face the driver. She felt guilty after. It didn't cost anything to be polite and it wasn't his fault she'd spent all of her wages.

She arrived at the cash machine that so often had spit out her wages, ready for her to feed them into another machine. She fed in her card, wincing as her coat brushed past the burn on her arm. The screen presented her with the option to view her available balance. She did not need to see it. She felt ill enough already without another reminder of what she'd done! She withdrew the £210 she was able to. She waited as it made that familiar churning noise and snatched the notes from the slot.

She hurried back onto the bus, trying to be faster than her thoughts about gambling. She knew there was a very real risk of the betting shop calling her so loudly that she couldn't help but go in so she marched to the bus stop as fast as she could to make sure she couldn't be beckoned it by it's screams. Steph felt so ill, so hopeless and so tired. She needed to get home and just go to bed. Not necessarily to sleep but just to be still and silent. As she arrived at back door of her house, she somehow found the strength to find the key and open the door. She didn't however, have the strength to make it up the stairs. She collapsed onto the sofa. Steph wasn't sure when she came around if she'd actually lost consciousness or just fallen asleep. Quickly, she stuffed her hand into the pocket of the coat that she'd slept in. Phew, the £200 was there. She carefully placed it under the mug on top of the microwave so that she could tell Leanne, when she got home, it was there for her.

She sat back on the sofa and started the monthly cycle about she could get the money for the rest of the month. What lies she could tell, what rules she could break and how she could manipulate people into giving her what she needed. She hated it. She absolutely hated it. It was so contradictory to her thoughts that weren't taken over by her addiction. When she wasn't thinking about gambling, she was thinking about how she could help people. She often thought about how sorry she felt for the homeless. How she wished she could give them a place to stay because she would hate being in the cold like that. She'd think about her family and how she'd do anything for any single one of them. How she'd give them her last pound if it meant they could get what they needed. Her addiction truly had changed her as a person.

She did manage to get through the month as she always did. She did go to her interview and to her huge surprise, was successful. But with the bigger wage came the bigger gambles. She told her mum in the end. She'd spent so many pay checks on the sites now that she had no other option.

She'd run out of things she could do month of month to get money and hide her secret. Her mum did break her promise about giving her anymore money. How could she not when Steph was sat crying and begging her to help her? Steph knew too, she knew her mum would give her money. She knew what to say to extract it from her. She'd cancelled the direct debits for her debt management plan too. She didn't pay any bills in fact, ever. If she could pay her rent, she'd be ok.

And this cycle continued for another year. The trauma of what she'd done on her payday's now faded pretty quickly and somehow, she would still believe her payday gamble would go well. Every payday, gambling more than she could afford. Her bets got bigger and bigger. She rarely played on less than a £20 stake now. And sometimes, she would win. Sometimes, she even managed to get some money in her account from her withdrawals, managing to avoid the 'reverse withdrawal' screams. However, it was never in there for more than 24 hours before she'd deposit again, to the same site, to the same game. And with this cycle she also had the depression, the hurt, the illness and the wishing she wasn't here anymore. Every month. Everyday. Steph wished to be free. Free from the screaming, free from the thoughts and free from addiction. On the outside, people saw a bright, happy smile. On the inside was a prisoner. A girl gambler who had lost all control.

Chapter 14

'We need to move.' Said Leanne. Steph's heart sank. Was she kicking her out? She loved Leanne so much. Her best friend, her sister. Did she know what Steph was doing month on month? Could she see how unhappy she was? 'There isn't enough room here and the tenancy is coming to an end and I really don't want to renew it' explained Leanne. Steph felt some relief that her friend wasn't asking her to move out. 'I've found this beautiful cottage. Detached, 2 bedrooms where you and Adrian can have an actual bed frame!' Steph looked at the photo's of the cute cottage on Leanne's phone. Of course, all she was looking at really was the price for the rent and the deposit needed. £750 a month, £750 deposit plus one months rent up front. Her mind running the calculations through as quickly as she could. £1500 divided by 3 was £500.

'Yeah it looks nice.' Steph replied.

'I'm arranging a viewing' said Leanne. She walked to the back door where you could get a better signal and spoke to a husky sounding man who told Leanne the three could go later that day to view the house. 'Brilliant, thank you we'll see you later.' Leanne ended the call. 'We can go and see it later! Tell Adrian to go straight there from work and we'll meet him there.'

Steph messaged Adrian the details and arranged to meet him after work at the cottage. Steph wasn't sure how she felt about it given the higher rent and the deposit needed but, as she always did, agreed and went along with the plan.

As Leanne went upstairs to get ready, Steph quickly grabbed her phone and opened the calendar. 8 more days until payday. She could tell Leanne that she wouldn't have the money until payday and hopefully that would be ok and the new landlord would wait. The final option was Steph's gran.

Her gran was a little old lady who Steph had so much respect for. She was the most generous, loving person in the world and she'd often help Steph when she needed it. It was very rare though that she would ask her nan for money as she knew that it upset her. Steph's Nan had lost her husband and best friend. She'd experienced so much heart break over the past few years. Steph felt guilty all the time and avoided upsetting her whenever she possibly could. She really didn't want to ask her nan.. She'd already cancelled her debt management plan months ago and so had creditors chasing every day and still owed her mum hundreds.

'Come on then!' Leanne shouted. 'Lets go see our new house!' The girls climbed into Leanne's car and made the short journey to the new house. It was literally around the corner. They actually could have walked there. Steph was secretly hoping that they wouldn't get it so that she wouldn't have to find the £500 deposit needed. They pulled onto the drive and looked up to the beautiful detached cottage. It was made of old stone. Not like the new builds. You could tell this was an old house and it was gorgeous. Adrian pulled onto the drive a few seconds later. As they all stepped out of the cars Adrian shouted 'This is well nice!'

'I know!' replied Leanne. 'I actually love it!'

As they knocked on the front door they were greeted by a fat ginger guy and a slimmer, dark haired middle aged woman. 'Adrian!' the guy shouted. 'Well I had no idea it was you!'

Leanne and Steph looked at Adrian. 'Bloody hell mate! I didn't know this was yours!' It turned out that Adrian knew the guy. He used to work for him in his old warehouse. The landlord and Adrian chatted for 5 minutes before he invited them into the house to look around. The front door opened up into the dining room. It was pretty big and had red tiles on the floor. Some of them were cracked but you could tell this was original flooring. It was vintage! 'Oh my god!' cried Leanne, 'it's beautiful!' The three made their way around the house. There was a living room that was a little smaller than the dining room but it had a big, modern fireplace and wood floors. The kitchen was tiny. It was barely big enough to hold the three of them at the same time! In the kitchen was a door which they opened to reveal a steep staircase. 'Ohhh, that's weird.' Said Steph. She'd never seen a layout like this before.

The three made their way up the extremely steep staircase as Adrian made a joke about climbing them when he was drunk. Immediately to the left of the top step was the bathroom. 'Why the hell is the bathroom carpeted?' asked Leanne. It had a cream carpet all the way through and an oddly shaped bath. It was a big bath though and Steph was partial to locking herself in a bathroom for some me time, some gambling time. 'I like it' replied Steph.

They went on into the first bedroom that was absolutely huge. It had windows bigger than they'd ever seen. 'I call this one!' called Leanne as they walked into the second bedroom. Again, a really good size. As much as Steph was worried about the money, she did actually like this house and did like the idea of having a proper bedroom with Adrian. They made their way back downstairs and met the landlord and his wife. 'It's really nice Gary' said Adrian to the bloke he knew.

'Look' said Gary 'Because it you Adrian, I'll offer it to you now. I wouldn't usually do this but I know you and I know you'll look after it for us.' The three looked at each other excitedly 'Yes! We'll take it.' Said Leanne. Steph, heart sinking, used that fake smile once more to hide her nervousness about the money she needed to find. 'Gary, we get paid at the end of the month, can we move in then and give you the money?'

'Thank you!' shouted Steph in her head, so grateful that Adrian was on the same wave length as her. If they could wait until payday, she could just transfer Adrian the deposit before she went on, as she knew full well she would, to lose the rest.

'Yeah no problem mate, the 1st ok?' Asked Gary.

The three agreed on a move in date of the 1st, that being the day they would pay Gary the deposit needed and the rent date going forward. They were so lucky. Within a few hours they'd seen a house and it was now theirs to rent! More importantly, they didn't need to pay anything until payday.

'Well done you!' said Steph to Adrian and she climbed in his car for the short journey home. 'We only got it because of you!' Adrian gave Steph a kiss and said 'The first bloody thing we are doing is buying a bed!'

Chapter 15

'Yes!' whispered Steph. £1900 read the credit bar. She was in her usual 3am payday position, on the toilet as her best friend and boyfriend lay sleeping. 'I'll just roll it to £1500' 5000/1 she would actually stop then. Suddenly, the door opened. She quickly locked her phone and shoved it between her legs. It was Adrian 'What the hell are you doing?' he asked, eyes still squinting as he tried to adjust them to the light in the bathroom.

Heart absolutely pounding, to the point it was painful. Steph replied 'I think I've come on my period. I've got really bad pains.' She usually had time to think about her lies but she didn't this time. This had never happened before. Why was he awake? What was he doing? Had he seen what was on her phone?

'Oh, I need a wee.' Was Adrian's only response.

'Ok, one sec' She pretended to wipe and flushed the toilet. Thankfully, she actually had done a wee when she came down, and had just sat with her pyjama bottoms and pants at her ankles for the last hour. She made her way back to bed. Her heart was absolutely racing, palms sweating and she felt like her eyes we're about the fall out of her head. What was more worrying for her was the fact she was mid spin! What if it had landed on the bonus? What if locking her phone made her lose connection and lose her winnings? She heard Adrian climbing back up the stairs. She laid, facing the opposite direction to him and he fell into the bed next to her. He put his arm around her and squeezed her. It was only a minute or two before he was snoring again but she knew he wasn't in a deep enough sleep for her to attempt to move. He'd definitely wake up. She couldn't light up her phone because she knew as soon as she unlocked it, it would open the slot she was on and he would see. So, she had no choice but to lay there and wait. She was furious, calling Adrian every name under the sun in her head. With no chance of getting to sleep, because of the anticipation of what was going to display on her phone when she opened it, she kept her eyes closed and wished the time to go by faster so she could get back to her gambling as quickly as she could. This was the loudest she'd ever heard the screaming in her head. It was absolutely unbearable.

Finally, she heard Adrian's alarm go off. She must have been laid there, still as a the dead, for 2 hours. She heard Adrian reach under his pillow for the phone, telling him it was time to wake up. He clicked the snooze button and didn't move. 'No!' Steph thought. 'Fucking wake up!' It was another 10 minutes before it sounded again. Again, he pressed the dreaded snooze button. 'It's waking me up Adrian, fucking get up or turn it off' said Steph, hoping he get up. Adrian fidgeted for a few minutes before lifting his body upright, stretching his arms as he yawned and started to get dressed. 'Thank fuck' Steph thought to herself. She knew within the next few minutes, he'd be making his way downstairs for his morning brew and she could finally get back to her game. She listened to every move Adrian made trying to make out what he was doing. Putting his socks on, putting his shirt on, putting his jumper on. She narrated it all in her head, constantly wishing he would hurry up. Finally, he stepped out of the door and went downstairs. Steph waited to hear him click the kettle before she grabbed her phone and returned to the page she'd left it on.

'Connection lost' read the screen. She quickly refreshed and was taken back to the game. She began to spin and was reunited with that state of mind. Where she heard, saw and thought of nothing other than what was on the screen in front of her. It was actually really peaceful. The dread, angst, hate and upset only ever came at the end of the spins. As she was doing it, it was always pretty tranquil. She'd now got £600 left in her bank account and £500 credit on her game. She stared at it for a while. And then, she exited the game and withdrew the £500. They made the move in a couple of days and she could not be the reason this went wrong. She couldn't let this be the time they found out about her secret. The embarrassment and shame this time, was stronger than the urge to gamble. She actually did wait for the money to hit her bank this time too. When she got her new job, she needed to have an account in her own name and so, she'd got a very basic account. The only one they'd let her have with the credit score she did, but it did come with online banking so moving money and checking how much she'd got was so much easier. Steph was proud. Proud that she was going to pay. Proud that she'd walked away.

Moving day came and the three loaded the van that Adrian had rented. Steph could drive but she never had enough money to actually buy a car and keep it on the road and her credit score gave her 0% chance of getting accepted for finance. So, Adrian drove and shifted furniture from one house to the next. It was a hugely stressful day. Getting everything in and finding a place for it. Building the furniture that they'd spent hours taking down to move. But no matter the stress, Steph felt good. She felt good that she wasn't letting the little team down with money and she wasn't the reason they didn't get this house. She did transfer the money to Adrian and she did put money towards the bed they'd bought. Adrian and Steph laid in their new bed, finally not laying on a mattress on the floor and quickly fell to sleep, exhausted from lugging around the furniture all day.

Steph slept really well that night. She didn't wake up once, even though she'd got unspent money in her account. Usually, having money in there would trigger the screaming in her head that she would just give in to. But that night, she slept soundly. When she woke up, she was excited to get the clothes out of her wardrobe in her new bedroom and get ready for work.

Steph was enjoying her new job. When she first started, she was really unsure and felt really uncomfortable. It was an office filled with women of a similar age to her and, in her personal life, she often avoided these types of groups. She knew they tended to be bitchy and she couldn't afford to get involved in any of that. She relied on her wages far too much. The girls had all been nice to her to be fair, along with her boss, but she couldn't stop the thoughts that ran through her mind that they hated her, that they were all bitching about her and that she needed to leave. She never took her coat off and she'd heard some people make comments about it. When Steph had anorexia, she'd learnt if she wore an oversized coat, and kept it on, no one would see how thin or fat she was. It was more than a parker. It was a coat of armour it protected her.

Today, she got ready and made the walk into town for the bus to work. It always took forever as it was quite far away but it was her own fault. If she hadn't made such a mess of her life, she'd have been able to afford a car. She got on the bus and found the seat she looked for every day. As she rested her head against the window, she watched the people walking through town. It was generally the same faces every day. The same people, with the same breakfast they'd got from Greggs or Mcdonalds, catching the same bus to do the same job as everyday. 'There must be more to life than this' Steph thought to herself. Directly opposite from the bus stop was a bookies. She knew one of the girls that worked in there from her time working in the bookies. They'd been on few nights out together with Naomi. Waiting, outside of the bookies was a man. They didn't even open for 45 minutes. No matter how bad Steph's addiction was, she'd never be caught waiting for it to open.

Her addiction had moved much more to online now. It was so easy. They were available 24/7, it was fast, you could deposit immediately and there were more games than what you could play on a physical machine. The jackpots were much higher too. Steph, of course, had excluded herself from a few websites. Generally after she gambled and lost everything and promised herself she would never do it again she'd fill out the form that would men she couldn't use that particular site anymore. But the beauty of online gambling was, there was always another site. Every month a new site would be doing the rounds where you could register in seconds and before you knew it, you were playing all of your wages away. So self-excluding, really, didn't mean anything at all. You could always do it again.

The bus began to move and Steph stared at the man, waiting outside the bookies as the bus drove past him. She felt sympathy, which turned to empathy, which turned to understanding, which turned to exactly the same frame of mind that the guy had. She needed to gamble. And, as Steph travelled on a bus to work, she was able to deposit the last of her wages. Every. Last. Penny. Once more, she was in that place. Although her head free from voices screaming, although perfectly silent, she was in a place where she didn't want to be anymore. It was strange now. Because she'd been through this so many times, the despair and the panic weren't as strong when she gambled. Truth be told, it was because she felt this even when she didn't gamble. There wasn't a day that went by for Steph anymore that she didn't wish she was dead. She didn't wish she was free from addiction. Steph couldn't remember the last time she felt happy. She knew it was gambling that did this to her. She knew, if she just didn't gamble, she wouldn't feel like this. But it was too hard. Steph sat on that bus, now without a penny in her account and felt tired. Exhausted, actually. But it wasn't the kind of exhaustion that any amount of sleep could fix. Steph was tired of fighting. She'd been fighting all her life. She fought what her dad and her Auntie did, the negative thoughts in put in her head. She fought what her mum's ex had done to her, when he touched her bum and made her feel uncomfortable. She fought anorexia and the screams that put in her head about her needing to be thin. She fought anxiety everyday and she'd tried, for too long, to fight the voices. Fight the screams and the need to gamble. Steph was too tired now, to fight anymore.

Steph went through the day at work as she always did. Not speaking to anyone, not interacting, just doing the job she needed to do. She got on the bus home completely numb, without any kind of thought or feeling running through her body or mind. She got home and made her way upstairs. She stood, naked, on the carpeted bathroom floor as she watched the bath fill higher and higher with water. She locked the door and got into the oddly shaped tub. Eyes closed, she felt the slightly too hot water embrace her body. She couldn't move too quickly or it would burn her too much. And so, she lay there completely still whilst the temperature, very slowly, began to fall. All that was running through Steph's mind was that she couldn't do this anymore. How gambling had completely changed her. How she wanted to be free and be the person she actually was, not the twin that so often took over her. 'You win.' She whispered to herself. Slowly, she slid her body down bath. She felt her chin touch the water. Then her lips. Next her nose. Within a few seconds, her whole head was underneath the water. She opened her eyes as she was completely submerged under the water. She could feel the temperature of the water on her eyeballs that was quite uncomfortable. As more and more seconds passed, she began to feel herself struggling with the lack of oxygen. The struggle got harder and her hands began to shake. She squeezed her fists as tight as she could and closed her eyes. As another few seconds went by, she began to feel as though her head was about to explode, but she refused to give in. She knew what happened when people drown. She knew that your body takes one huge breath, and it was that breath that killed you. You couldn't stop the breath though, no matter how hard you tried. It was your bodies natural instinct. She knew it was coming. As her hands shook uncontrollably and she squeezed her eyes as tightly shut as possible, there was a huge bang on the door. With the bang, Steph lifted her head out of the water with a huge gasp for air. 'I need the fucking toilet!' Shouted Leanne's voice through the little wooden door. 'Hurry up!'.

Steph was gutted. Absolutely gutted. Why did she lift her head? She knew she was so close this time to freeing herself. She pulled the plug from the bath and wrapped herself in a towel. She unlocked the door and Leanne barged through. 'Who has a fucking bath at this time!' she shouted as she slammed the door, leaving Steph dripping wet on the other side. Leanne had no idea what she had just done. No idea she had just saved Steph's life. Steph sat on the end of her new bed, wrapped in her towel and sobbed.

She sobbed uncontrollably. The type where it's silent until you take a huge inhale. She didn't want anyone to hear her but she couldn't stop it. She could hear footsteps on the stairs, getting closer and closer. She'd usually be able to paint on her smile and make out it was nothing but not this time. This time there was no hiding her hurt. Adrian walked through the door. He saw Steph, curled in a ball on the bed sobbing in nothing but a towel. Like a baby who just couldn't stop. He dropped his bag and ran to her, asking over and over again what was wrong. Steph was completely unable to answer. She simply could not stop crying. 'Steph please, please tell me what's happened. Is it your mum? Please Steph talk to me.' Adrian pleaded. Still unable to talk, Steph just grabbed Adrian's hand and cried into it.

After 10 minutes or so, Steph managed to get some control of her body back. Adrian, who had resorted to simply rubbing her back until she was able to speak again, asked her again what was wrong. Steph wiped her eyes on the wet towel she was wrapped in and looked Adrian in the face. She stared at him. The man she shared her life with who, actually, didn't know her at all. She knew this was it. It was time to share her secret. Tears still rolling down her face, heart absolutely pounding, worse than ever before now at what she was about to do said to Adrian, 'I'm an addict. I'm a gambling addict.'

Chapter 16

'What?' replied Adrian. Steph once more began to sob. 'I'm an addict Adrian. I don't even want to live anymore. I can't get it out of my head and I can't fight it anymore. Every payday, every day.' She said between sobs. Adrian, somewhat taken back, began to rub the back of Steph again. It was clear he was trying to process the information he'd just received.

'So you gamble?' asked Adrian. Steph, unable once more to speak, nodded her head in agreement. 'How long for?' again asked Adrian. Steph stood up from the bed and began to pace the bedroom. This was it. She was going to be completely honest with Adrian. Her heart was beating faster and faster. She took a deep breath and tried to compose herself.

'7 1/2 years Adrian now. For 71/2 years, I've thought about nothing but gambling. Every payday, I find a way to spend all my wages. I've tried to stop, I really have. I honestly don't want to be like this Adrian. I hate it so much and so many times, I've tried to end it all but I can't even do that properly.'

Adrian sat, staring at Steph but not saying a word. 'I'm sorry.' Said Steph, hoping it would prompt some sort of response from him.

'Why didn't you tell me? We've been together for over a year now. Why didn't you say anything?'

'Because I was scared of this, Adrian. I was scared you'd look at me different. I was scared it would ruin everything and you wouldn't want me anymore.'

A few more seconds of awkward silence passed. 'I'm sorry' cried Steph once more. Adrian stood up, stood in front of Steph and wrapped her in his arms, tighter than the towel she had was holding her. He kissed her forehead and whispered 'It's ok.' Steph let out the biggest cry she ever had and her legs gave way. Adrian held her up. She was so relieved. Her biggest secret, her darkest demon she'd let out. And it didn't scare him. He was still there, holding Steph up. Together they stood. Steph had no idea how long they'd been stood there for but it was so nice. It felt good to share her secret.

'Shit, Leanne!' said Steph to Adrian.

'She's not here, she passed me on the stairs as I was coming up and she went out. Steph felt relieved that Leanne had not heard the sobs.

The couple made their way downstairs and both had a cigarette at the back door. Adrian began to ask Steph questions about how long, when it started, how much she'd gambled and so much more. She knew she owed it to Adrian to answer the questions but she was so tired, so sick and tired of talking and thinking about gambling that she just wanted it to end.

'Do you have any money left?' asked Adrian. With that question Steph's heart sunk. Instinctively, she wanted to lie and tell Adrian she had enough money left and that everything would be ok but she knew she couldn't this time. 'No' said Steph, looking at him holding her tears back. 'What? Nothing at all?' He probed again. 'No I told you Adrian, I did every penny. I have no idea how I will get through this month.'

Adrian didn't have much money either and he wasn't too good with money himself. Every payday he would buy something ridiculous and he never had much money left the following week.

'Don't worry. We'll sort it.' He said to Steph, once more taking her into his arms.

Adrian took out his phone and started typing something in. 'What do you want to eat?' he asked, 'We're having a takeaway and we will talk through all of this.' Steph chose the same pizza as she always did and went upstairs where Adrian took out a pen and piece of paper and asked Steph to talk him through what she still needed to pay.

She talked Adrian through everything she owed and what she needed money for this month. She explained everything to him. For the first time in their relationship, Steph told Adrian who she really was. Adrian was trying to be really supportive although Steph could tell the disappointment in his face as he went on writing down what she needed. She really did love him. She wanted to get better not only for her, not only to stop the constant screaming in her head but for him, her mum and Leanne. She wanted to stop hurting people.

As Steph looked at the piece of paper that revealed just how much trouble she had gotten herself into, tears began once more to roll down her face. Adrian got out his phone and logged into his banking app. She could see he didn't have much money in it and he wouldn't be able to lend her the money she needed to get her out of this mess. She did wonder why so soon after payday he had so little money too but she didn't question it. He was being so good with her, she had no right to ask anyone questions about money management! He clicked on the overdraft section of his account. He applied for a £500 overdraft. He pressed the apply button and immediately, Steph saw the word approved. She again began to cry. She clung on to Adrian and repeatedly thanked him.

'You promise me now Steph, no more. You cannot go through this anymore. We can't continue as we are, working full time and scraping through every month.'

Steph promised him faithfully that would be it. That she wouldn't gamble again.

'I'll transfer my wages to you, you can have my bank card. Thank you so much honestly Adrian. I love you.' Filled with love and a glimmer of hope, Steph hugged Adrian as tight as she could.

Adrian went on to ask her questions about the addiction that had trapped her. How it felt, why she did it, what made her start. Steph answered more honestly than she ever had before. 'You know you're mum with drink Adrian, well I'm exactly the same with gambling. No matter how much she might not want to drink, or hates the arguments, it's too hard to fight the urge, the need to do the thing you're addicted to. It's like you can't rest. You can't think, you can't feel about anything other than gambling. It's like a monster has taken over your body and the only way to get rid of it is to gamble.'

She knew Adrian could never completely understand. The same as the woman at gamblers anonymous couldn't, or her mum couldn't because they'd never suffered addiction and Steph knew, unless you'd felt it, you could never know truly just what it was like.

They talked for hours and hours, about everything Steph had done, what it felt like and how hard it was. They enjoyed their pizza, although Steph didn't have much of an appetite, and went to sleep.

The next morning when Steph woke up, Adrian had already gone to work as usual. She looked at her phone and there was a message from Adrian. 'I love you. I wish you had shared it with me sooner. I'll help you get through this and we will be ok xxx' It filled Steph with hope and relief. He knew about her now and he was still there. Filled with a new sense of determination, Steph once again set out her plan for recovery.

Steph for the next two months, didn't gamble a penny. She sent everything to Adrian for the bills and managed to pay everything she needed to. Things were going well for her now, now that she had someone to share her secret with.

One day, Adrian sent Steph a picture message. On it was a puppy Bullmastiff. 'Oh my god that's beautiful!' replied Steph. 'I hope you like it because I'm picking her up tomorrow.'

Steph had always wanted a dog. Adrian loved dogs too. He often did some dog training on the side of his regular job and he was never happier than when he was surrounded by dogs in the open air. Steph was never allowed a dog as she grew up. Her mum told her she was allergic but she was pretty sure her mum just didn't like dogs and so that was her excuse.

'Are you joking???? Oh my god Adrian!!!!! Thank you SO much. Thank you so so much!!!'

Steph couldn't believe it. She was getting her very own puppy. She knew this would help her recovery. She would save money and make sure she had everything she needed to take care of it. She would save for vet bills, she'd walk it everyday. She would love this puppy like it was her own child.

That night, Adrian met Steph at her mums shop. She was selling clothes now and was renting a tiny shop to do it from just outside of town. He walked up to the big window at the front, puppy in arms. Steph had never been so happy or excited in her entire life. This meant even more to her than the bonus round did. She took the puppy from Adrian and didn't put it down for over an hour. She showered it with love and promised the pup that she would give it a good life. She knew this dog was going to play a key role in getting her better. Steph must have said thank you to Adrian a million times that night.

Over the next few months, Steph did really well. She did have a few relapses but she told Adrian when she did and they'd fix them together. They'd taken, between them, a number of payday loans and had racked up a fair bit of debt, however, Steph did always pay what she owed now. Even if she'd had a slip, Leanne and Adrian got their money first. It was important to her that they got paid and they wouldn't have to worry about rent.

A few weeks ago, Steph had managed to finance a car! When she applied, she really didn't think there was any chance at all. She'd got so much debt, so many payday loans and so when she got the email, and saw 'approved' in the title, she screamed with excitement. How had they let her have a car? She just filled out the application whilst she was on the bus, fed up of having to get so early to get to work. The payments were ridiculously high but, because she'd managed to get to a place where she was paying what she needed to before she would gamble, so she was confident she could keep up the payments. Adrian remained pretty bad with money still. He would pay what he needed too but they would often find themselves short at the end of the month or struggling for food. Steph never asked why he struggled so much as she didn't feel she could, given what she did with her money. But, now she had Bo to think about too. The most beautiful, kindest dog she'd ever known with the loveliest temperament in the world. This dog was Steph's absolute best friend and she would do anything in the world for it.

Chapter 17

As Steph sat at her work desk, she could feel her phone vibrating over and over again. She wondered who could need her so desperately at this time? She thought it would probably be the debt collectors again. It buzzed once more and Steph gave in. She grabbed her phone from her coat pocket and stepped out of the office into the corridor. 3 missed calls and a message from Leanne. 'I've taken tablets, I'm sorry.'

Leanne had been struggling with her mental health lately. She'd been drinking a lot more and she'd often hurt herself. Steph knew how a bad mental state could affect a person and so she always made sure she was there for Leanne. She'd often gone to the hospital with her after she'd taken tablets, or scratched her way through layers of skin until it was infected. Every time it happened, she swore to be there, and she was.

She ran back into the office and shouted to her manager 'I have to go, it's Leanne.' Her boss replied, 'It's fine, go. Go!' She jumped in her car and made her way to the cottage they shared. On the way, she called Leanne's mum. Steph and Leanne's mum were the only ones who knew how to take care of Leanne when she was in this state. She didn't need fuss or someone being overly nice to her. She needed someone to clean up the mess, put her in bed and just keep an eye to make sure she was ok. Leanne and Steph were pretty similar like that. They would be able to sit in each others company yet be completely silent. It wasn't ever an awkward silence, they were happy just to be near each other but understood that, you don't need to be constantly talking. They both loved silence and time for themselves. It worked perfectly and Steph often thought this was the reason they'd become so close and we're friends for so long.

'Mads' Steph shouted at the car through her hands free speaker ' You need to go to ours now, Leanne's taken tablets again.'

'Right, on my way.' Replied Leanne's mum.

Steph didn't remember the drive from work to her house. She knew she'd broken the speed limit a few times but all that mattered in that moment, was getting to her best friend. As she reached the driveway, Leanne's mum was already there. Adrian's car wasn't there so he must have still been at work. Steph ran through the front door and up the steep staircase to Leanne's room. As she burst through the door, Mad's said 'She's ok, she's ok don't worry.' She was nursing the cuts to Leanne's wrists, applying some antiseptic cream and covering the cuts with a bandage. Steph grabbed Leanne and hugged her as tightly as she could. 'I'm so sorry Leanne, I'm here. I promise I'm here.'

Leanne didn't respond. Steph didn't know if it was the drink or the overdose on anti-depressants but Leanne seemed completely out of it. 'I'll ring an ambulance' said Steph to Mads.

'No!' cried Leanne suddenly, 'I'm not going there again.'

Steph and Leanne had been in the hospital a few weeks earlier after she'd done the same thing. Leanne luckily, didn't need any treatment but the ambulance crew were shocked at the level of alcohol in her blood. They admitted her for the night and Steph stayed with her every minute. She even climbed into the hospital bed Leanne was in and cuddled her until she fell to sleep. She remembered how scared she was she would lose her true sister, her only friend.

Mad's made Leanne drink some water and laid her to sleep. Leanne was asleep almost before she hit the pillow, but Steph was worried. As her and Mad's made their way out of the bedroom Steph whispered ' We need to get her checked!' Mad's told her she'd only taken a few of the anti depressants. She'd seen this so many times now, she knew what required a hospital visit and what didn't and Steph really did trust her completely.

'I'll have a coffee with you now to make sure she doesn't start being sick or anything. If she's fine, I'll get off. Just keep an ear out for her during the night.' Instructed Mads to Steph.

Together they had a coffee, being sure to whisper in case they heard any noise from Leanne's room. They didn't. Steph talked with Mads for a while about how long this had gone on for. 'They just don't help her' explained Steph. Leanne had been to the doctors before about her mental health. They always seemed to just fob her off and give her anti depressants which just didn't help her. It was frustrating for Steph and Mads too because all they wanted was for Leanne to be ok and happy.

Mads went up before she left, to check Leanne was ok. She came down and saw how nervous Steph was. 'Are you sure we don't need to ring a doctor?' asked Steph.

'No, I promise she will be fine. Just ring me if you have any trouble.' Mad's told Steph. Steph, feeling somewhat comforted by the confidence in Mad's tone, said bye and listened intently for any noise from Leanne's room.

Adrian came home from work and Steph told him to be quiet as soon as he walked through. Bo wanted to make a fuss and she was trying to keep her calm too, so that nothing would wake Leanne. Steph told Adrian what had happened. He wasn't too supportive of these episodes with Leanne but Steph didn't care. She was her best friend and she would be there for her no matter what.

The next day, Leanne walked downstairs at around lunch time. Adrian had gone off to his mums. He seemed to always be there lately. Steph always knew they were a close family but he was a huge mummies boy. Steph had enjoyed the morning with Bo. She took her for a walk and they cuddled on the sofa. Leanne came downstairs and without saying a word, put on the TV and started to watch her favourite programme. Steph knew it was one of the times they Leanne needed space and not to be talked to and Steph honoured that for her.

As Leanne reached out for her drink that was on the coffee table, Steph noticed the bloodied bandage still wrapped around her wrist. She thought how sore it must have been. Steph started to think about how hard it must be for Leanne. She had her own demons to fight, just like Steph did. The more Steph thought about it, the more upset she started to feel. Leanne always reached out to Steph when she was struggling or she needed someone to talk to. Why couldn't she do the same? Why had she allowed, for all these years, Leanne to feel like she was suffering alone? She began to feel more upset and overwhelmed. She stood up and made her way into the dining room. She sat at the large dining room table and Bo followed her. Steph began to cry. She was usually so good at hiding her emotions but she was completely overwhelmed in this moment. She'd realised that, whilst she thought she was protecting herself and others from her addiction, she'd left her very best friend feeling as though she was the only one who had mental health problems. As she sat there, she made a decision. She wanted to do anything she could to help Leanne and so, she would once again, share her biggest secret.

Once again, her heart was going at a pace that she knew wasn't healthy. She was there for a few minutes before she heard Leanne get up off of the sofa. This was it. As Leanne walked through the door into the dining room, she saw Steph with her head in her hands crying. 'What the matter?' said Leanne, completely shocked at what she was witnessing. Leanne had very rarely seen Steph cry. She'd always done such a good job of hiding it, it was a shock for Leanne to see. She pulled the other dining chair up next to Steph and began to rub her back, exactly the same as Adrian had done when he found out about the real Steph.

'I need to tell you something. You tell me about your issues and how you struggle and I don't want you to feel on your own.' Wept Steph. 'Ok, you're scaring me Steph. What is it?' replied Leanne. 'I have issues too Leanne. I'm a gambling addict.'

Steph wanted the world to implode in that moment. It would be easier for her to die than explain what she needed to.

'What?' asked Leanne.

'I've been an addict for years and I really don't want to do it anymore. But I wanted you to know, you're not alone.'

It felt, in those few moments, like a wheel was spinning. The two options were 'She will be nice' or 'She will hate you.' She waited to see which it landed on and how Leanne would respond. As he wheel began to slow, Leanne squeezed Steph as tightly as she possibly could. 'Oh Steph.' She cried as she squeezed. Both girls crying once more, Steph felt closer to Leanne than ever before.

'I genuinely had no idea Steph. How the hell have you kept this hidden for all this time?' Asked Leanne. 'I hate it Leanne. It's honestly killing me. I haven't done it for a few month' she lied, 'So I really feel like I'm getting better. But you're not on your own Leanne. You're not. I can't tell you how many times I've wanted to end it all and I've come so close.' Leanne began to cry and thanked Steph for telling her.

That day, the girls talked about their issues. They shared each others demons. This was it. The most important people now in Steph's life, knew who she really was.

Steph laid in bed that night feeling like the weight of the world had fallen off of her shoulders now. She had a fantastic boyfriend, her best friend and her family who all knew who she was. Who she truly was. They all knew her secret and none of them hated her. None of them left her, none of them had kicked off and kicked her out. Maybe this time, maybe, she really would be ok?

Chapter 18

Steph was out on her usual walk with Bo. She'd found that walking Bo did help her clear her mind and sometimes, helped relieved the urge to gamble. Steph was proud of herself. Although she was still gambling, she was paying what she needed to. She was happy where she was, she had a dog that she absolutely adored and even had a car. She never thought that she would get to this point. As she walked back from the park with Bo, her thoughts wandered to her and Adrian. He'd not been around too much lately. He was spending a lot of time with his family and she just didn't feel that closeness they once had. She loved him infinitely. She'd changed her life around for him and their future. She'd really tried hard for Adrian, harder than ever before. And she would keep trying because he was worth it. Their life together was worth getting better for.

As she walked through the door and put Bo, who had mud up to her knees from the muddy run, into her crate to dry off, she could feel her phone vibrating in her pocket. It was Belle. Belle usually called Steph when she needed something. Even more so since she had a car. She didn't mind though, she'd do whatever she could to help.

'Steph, can you take me shopping later?' asked Belle who at this point, was 8 months pregnant. 'Yeah sure, what time?' replied Steph.

'Whenever really, I don't mind'

The sisters agreed that Steph would go and take Belle shopping now. She picked up the car seat that was Amelie's and got into the drivers side of her car. Her car wasn't brand new but it was hers and she loved it. She started the car and drove the 3 minute drive to Belle's house.

As Amelie opened the front door and ran towards Steph, with her arms wide open for a cuddle, Steph bent to her knees and greeted Amelie with the cuddle she'd wanted. 'Are you ok princess?' Asked Steph. Amelie reassured Steph that she was and began to tell her how excited she was about her little sister that would soon be born. Steph put Amelie in the car seat and waited for Belle. She watched her squeeze her 8 month pregnant belly through her front door and waddle towards the car. 'Bloody hell Belle, you're massive!' Said Steph to her sister as she lowered herself into the passenger seat. 'Thanks!' replied Belle.

Belle asked how Steph had been with the gambling and the usual chat they had. Steph told her how happy she was and how, even though she was still gambling disposable income, she was on top of her bills. Steph waited in the car with Amelie whilst Belle went shopping. She played Amelie's favourite songs through the car's Bluetooth and they both sang along.

As Belle struggled to walk with the trolley because of her huge stomach, Steph got out of the car and helped her unload the shopping into the boot. She told Belle to get into the car as she took the trolley back to the trolley park. As she did, she saw a scratch card on the floor. She always loved checking them, without touching them, to see if someone by mistake had discarded it with money on! They never did. She lingered around the trolley park, trying to casually read the symbols underneath the half scratched paint. There was nothing on it. She made her way back to the car and fastened her seatbelt.

'Steph' said Belle in a way that let Steph know she was about the ask her a serious question. 'Have you and Adrian been ok?'

Steph, confused and a little frightened replied 'Yeah, why?'

Steph's heart sank immediately. She'd gone to her go to of lying and pretending everything was ok. Steph had always felt second best to Belle. This was fuelled by the fact that, on more than one occasion, Steph's boyfriends had ended up liking and seeing Belle. It happened with her first boyfriend. The first guy she ever slept with. He ended up being in a year long relationship with Belle. Then her first serious boyfriend. Belle once told Steph, when they were arguing, that she'd kissed him. Belle had denied it ever since and said she only said it to hurt her but Steph remained sceptical. Amelie's Dad was actually Lillie's ex boyfriend. Belle had kept their relationship a secret from all of the family but when the truth came out, Belle and Lilly didn't speak for a long time. Steph was scared that history was about to repeat itself. Adrian wasn't a particularly good looking guy and she was sure he loved her far too much to ever cheat.

'I've been getting weird snapchats from Adrian. He's always fully clothed and stuff but he'll just send me a snapchat of his groin and ask me what I'm doing but he's doing it more and more.'

No. Please lord no, don't let it be true. She'd changed her whole life for Adrian. She did everything to make sure they had a good life. She'd shared her darkest secret with him. Was he really going to do this to her, after he knew about her insecurities with Belle?

'He's never said anymore than that but it's just weird' Belle added.

'Do me a favour. Snapchat him back and start flirting. Just gentle flirting. I need to know Belle, I need to know if he wants to cheat.'

Belle took some convincing but eventually agreed. The sisters agreed that later that evening, Belle would reply to his snapchat. Steph had the same feeling she did as when she gambled. It was all she could think about and she just needed to get the end result.

Adrian still wasn't home when Steph got there. She had no idea where he was. She spent the day cuddling Bo and praying that he wasn't the same as the others. That he wouldn't be lured in by her sisters flirtatious personality. She convinced herself he wouldn't and that their relationship meant more to him than that but still, at the back of her mind was that thought that he would. And of course, with any stress that ever entered Steph's head, followed thoughts of gambling. She picked up her phone and entered the website but, at that moment, she heard Adrian's car pull onto the drive. She pressed the home screen button on her phone and stood at the window with Bo, who was stood on two legs at the window excited to see Adrian. He jumped out of his car and waved to them both as he walked towards the front door. As he walked through, he gave Steph a kiss on the forehead and gave Bo a fuss as he always did.

'Where have you been?' asked Steph.

'At my mums babe. My dad needed help with the computer.' Replied Adrian. Why was Steph now questioning what he had told her? She never did before.

'What's for tea?' asked Adrian.

Steph told him that she was planning on making a pasta dish to which he agreed. Steph went into the kitchen and began cooking tea. She knew it wouldn't be long now before Adrian got the snapchat on his phone. As she was cooking, Adrian grabbed hold of Steph from behind and hugged her. 'I love you I do' he said in Steph's ear as he kissed her on the cheek.

Surely he couldn't be thinking about cheating? The man who Steph had turned her life around for. Granted not completely, but she really did try. He loved Steph far too much to ever do that to her.

The couple sat down to the dining room table and ate. Steph 'accidentally' dropped a slice of garlic bread and some pieces of pasta on the floor for Bo. The couple talked about their day and what they had planned for the evening. Adrian had suggested he might go out with one of his mates. Steph's stomach hit the floor. For one, Adrian didn't have any mates and two, he never went out. Steph played along though. He explained to her that an old school friend had said that he wanted a night out and had invited Adrian. Steph went along with what she was sure were lies. 'Go and enjoy yourself' said Steph to Adrian.

Had Belle already messaged him? Was he telling the truth? She didn't know anymore and she hated the fact that these questions ran through her mind. 'Shall we go and play on the PlayStation for a while before I go?' asked Adrian. The PlayStation was the one thing Steph was hugely proud of. She'd ordered it for Adrian one payday. She'd decided that, to thank him for being so good to her, she would buy it him and prove that she was able to avoid gambling. She remembered how proud she was of herself and how happy it made Adrian. She loved to see him happy. He deserved to be happy.

As Adrian stood at the PlayStation, putting the disk into the slot, he looked at his phone. 'Oh.' He said. 'I'm not going now babe, he's cancelled'

He must have been telling the truth. Belle would have messaged Steph by now if she'd messaged him. Maybe he really was supposed to be going with his mates? Steph felt relieved but still anxious as she waited for the snap chat from Belle to arrive.

Steph was playing on the PlayStation and Adrian was laid on the bed next to her on his phone. Steph heard it. Adrian thought she didn't but she did. That vibration on his hand. She also knew, this was a snap chat. This was it. It was time. She could see form the corner of her eye, Adrian tilting the phone away from Steph so that she couldn't see what was on the screen.

Adrian got up and walked to the bathroom, phone in hand. 'I need the toilet' he said. Steph felt sick. He'd gone to snap chat her sister. She quickly checked her phone and there was a message from Belle. 'I've just put. Nothing much. Lonely on my own ☹ you? X' This confirmed where Adrian was and what he was doing. He was in the bathroom for about 20 minutes, completely oblivious to the fact that Steph was getting updates from her sister as to what he was putting.

It was pretty tame at this point though but obviously flirtatious. 'I'm sure you can find some strapping young lad to come round and keep you entertained' and 'don't be so daft, you're stunning!' were the types of comments Adrian had made.

Adrian flushed the toilet and came back into the bedroom. 'Babe, he's changed his bloody mind! We are going!' Adrian lied to Steph. 'Oh right, what, now?' asked Steph playing along. 'Yeah! Chuffing idiot honestly. I'm going to get ready now and drive round to his. I'll leave my car there and you can take me to pick it up in the morning yeah?' Asked Adrian as he put on a new shirt and seemed to try and drowned himself in aftershave. 'Yeah alright' replied Steph.

Not even 10 minutes later, he was ready to leave the house. Steph gave him a huge cuddle. She held on for longer than normal because she was scared. She was scared this would be the last cuddle she would ever give him. And with that, he walked out of the door and into his car. Steph had a cigarette at the back door and let Bo outside. She tried to drag it out as much as she could and prayed that he really was meeting his friend and that Belle wouldn't send her anymore messages. She shouted Bo inside and made her way up the stairs, praying with every step.

As her and Bo bounced on the bed, she grabbed her phone from the bedside table. 3 new messages – Belle

Text 1 - 'Steph he's put – Well I'll come and keep you entertained if you want!'

Text 2 – 'OMG Steph he's asked me to prove I'm serious. I said how and he said TITS'

Text 3 – 'You better ring him now, he's sat outside in the car! He is not coming in Steph. You need to tell him you know!'

Time stopped as she read those messages. It was like her gambling state. She couldn't see anything other than her screen. She couldn't hear anything at all. Once again, her man had fallen for Belle. An 8 month pregnant Belle. All the secrets she shared with him, all the memories she'd made with him, all the love she felt for him he'd discarded like one of her cigarette ends.

She messaged Adrian and told him she knew. That he'd not to come home that night and that he should go to his mothers.

Steph, cuddling Bo as tightly as she could, laid in that same spot all night. How, how could he do this to her? She'd changed for him, she tried for him but still, it was second best to one night with Belle. She checked all night for any response from Adrian. There was nothing. Steph once more, found herself alone on the bed, sobbing like a child.

Chapter 19

It was Bo that woke Steph up the next morning, rubbing her nose against her face to let her know she needed to go out. Steph lifted her head from the bed. She was still in the same position she'd fallen to sleep sobbing in. She got up and let Bo out. She looked around and couldn't bear to be in the house. She still couldn't believe what he'd done. How badly he'd hurt her. Steph grabbed Bo's lead and they went for a walk to the field.

Had Adrian done this with anyone else? Had he cheated on her before? A thousand questions ran through Steph's head. It was ironic really. She'd finally opened up to Adrian, letting him know who she was and it turned out, she didn't know him at all. Steph watched Bo run up and down the field. She loved to watch her run. She was a big bullmastiff so she wasn't exactly graceful but watching her run so freely, enjoying herself so much gave Steph so much joy.

They made their way home and Bo went into her crate to dry off. Leanne was upstairs. She was out last night and must not have got home until the early hours of the morning. Steph knew that meant she wouldn't be awake until this afternoon. She sat on the sofa and looked at her phone. There were missed calls from her mum and Belle. Messages from them both asking if she was ok. But nothing from Adrian. Not a message, not a missed call, nothing. Did he not even care what he'd done? He really had no interest in saving their relationship at all.

Gambling was at the very front of her mind now. She was fighting as hard as she possibly could but it was hard. It was the perfect time for her to do it. She was on her own, she was sad and she did have some money in her account. But she didn't want to. She had no idea how she would cope without Adrian and so instead, she called her mum.

Steph told her mum everything. How she was feeling, what he'd done, how they'd found out. Her mum listened but genuinely didn't know what to say. Nothing she could say would make it better. Steph could hear her mum was worried. 'Don't worry mum, I'll be ok' Steph said. 'I'll give you a ring later.' Her mum agreed and they ended the call. Steph let Bo out of the crate and once more, cried into her. Bo just Let Steph cry on her. She never moved, just occasionally looked up and licked her face as if to tell Steph it was ok and she was there for her.

She sat with Bo for a while and decided she would go to Belle's. She drove around the corner and opened the front door of her little sister's house. Amelie came running towards her and gave her a huge hug, followed by Belle. 'I'm so sorry' said Belle. Come here.

Steph spent a few hours at her sister's. She just didn't know what to say and would randomly begin to cry. Nothing could make her feel better and still, she had no contact at all from Adrian. Steph, feeling no better at all, made her way back home to Bo and Leanne. Bo was excited to see her, like she was every time she went home. Leanne was still in bed. Steph beckoned Bo up stairs and once more, they laid in bed together and fell to sleep. By the time they woke up, it was dark again. Steph stretched and half expected to feel Adrian on the other side of the bed. When she realised he wasn't, she felt sick. She checked her phone and still nothing. She felt so hurt. So lost. It was 7.30pm now. She left Bo sound asleep on the bed and walked into Leanne's room. She crawled into the double bed where Leanne was laid. Leanne was awake watching TV. Leanne put her arm around Steph and Steph whispered 'He' gone Leanne. Adrian's gone.' Leanne, confused at the statement replied 'What ? Where has he gone?' Steph once more, began to cry. Leanne, panicking now sat up. 'Steph. Where is Adrian? What's happened?'

Steph told her best friend what had happened. She told her that she'd told him recently about her gambling. She told her about the messages and the fact it was pregnant Belle he had gone to try and see. To try and sleep with. Leanne was angry. 'You fucking what!?' she shouted. 'Right! Give me his number! Now!' Steph refused and asked her best friend just to lay with her. It was a familiar scene. The two girls, two best friends laid in bed upset only this time, it was Leanne holding Steph as she cried herself back to sleep.

The girls slept right through to the following morning. Steph got up and let Bo out and checked her phone as she did. Her heart sunk as she saw Adrian's name.

'I'll be round at 11 to get my stuff.' That was all the text read. No apology. No excuses. No explanation. Just that he would be there for his stuff. Steph ran back up the stairs and told Leanne about the text. Steph had gone into panic mode. 'It's ok, it's ok!' Shouted Leanne. 'I'll be here'

Steph couldn't calm down. She was in full blown panic mode. She was pacing, watching the clock the whole time. 11am came around faster than she'd hoped. Leanne and Steph sat in Leanne's room, waiting to hear the car pull up on the drive. It was about 5 past 11 when the car pulled on the drive. Leanne grabbed Steph's hand. 'We will be fine. I'm here' she told Steph, staring straight into her eyes. Steph was so thankful Leanne was there with her. She could not do this on her own. As she had been all her life, Leanne was there for her.

All of a sudden, the front door burst open. There were voices talking and shouting. His mum and Dad had come with him! Leanne barged her way downstairs and there were Adrian and his mum and dad. 'You fucking scum!' screamed Leanne. 'How fucking dare you!'

Immediately, Adrian's argumentative mother began to scream. 'Him the scumbag!? She's the fucking addict!' Steph felt in that second, as though she had been stabbed straight in the heart. She heard Adrian shout 'I just can't do it anymore that's why I'm leaving. I cannot deal with the constant gambling.' Steph sat on the floor, absolutely crushed. He'd told his family it was her gambling that was the reason they'd split up. He'd clearly not told them what he'd done with her sister. Even though she'd paid him every penny for the bills that they needed to pay, even though she'd done her absolute best to turn things around, even though he knew how much she hated her addiction and how hard she'd fought, he'd thrown it all in her face. He'd used her darkest secret against her. She couldn't listen to anymore. She walked into the kitchen and made eye contact with him for a second. She didn't know who she was looking at though. It wasn't her Adrian. It wasn't the loving, caring man she knew. She walked straight through the dining room, avoiding contact with his mum or dad. Put Bo on the lead and jumped into her car. As soon as she did, she burst into tears. She couldn't even see the road now for tears but somehow, managed to safely pull up and Belle's house. She walked in, absolutely sobbing and unable to hide her tears from Amelie.

An hour or so passed and she'd managed to gain some composure. 'Has he gone? I'm so sorry Leanne, I just couldn't listen to it anymore.' She texted Leanne.

'Don't you dare apologise! Yeah he's gone now. Come home xxx' was Leanne's reply. Steph thanked Belle for letting her and Bo go there, gave her a hug, and made her way back home. Despite their arguments, Belle was a good sister.

As she walked through the door, she saw the TV was gone in the living room. He'd really left them without a TV even though he had one in every room at his mums house. Leanne marched up to her and gave her a hug. 'I'm so sorry, I tried to stop them.' Steph squeezed her back and told her not to worry and apologised for leaving her with them.

Steph went upstairs as Adrian didn't really own anything downstairs, other than the TV. When she walked in, she was faced with a wardrobe with a broken door and a huge empty space in the middle of the room. He'd taken their bed. He'd actually taken the bed they'd bought. 'Selfish bastard!' she shouted. He didn't even have anywhere he'd have been able to put it. He'd taken a chest of drawers and the TV from their room too. Steph, after years of relationship, was left with nothing other than an empty space. Leanne followed Steph into the room 'You can sleep with me don't worry. Selfish prick.' Steph just couldn't believe what he'd done. Her hurt now, had turned to anger.

Steph called her mum and told her frantically what had happened. 'You're joking!' her mum screamed down the phone. 'No! even my bed mum.' Replied Steph. She was on the phone to her mum for a while, telling her what Adrian had done. Steph's mum had told Steph she would buy her a new bed and she'd get it delivered as soon as she could. She was so amazing. She promised to help Steph in whatever way she could.

Steph ended the call with her mum and sat on the sofa's with Bo and Leanne. This was her family now.

Steph made herself comfortable on the sofa as she got ready to go to sleep. Leanne kissed her on the forehead and reassured her again that she was welcome to share her bed with her but Steph refused.

She tried for while to get to sleep. Bo was on the sofa with her. The big old lump who took up more of the sofa than she did. Her thoughts would keep going to Adrian. How could he just stop caring like that? How could he have told his family it was all her gambling after all she'd tried for him? Steph began to cry again. She'd cried more recently than she had in her entire life. As sleep continued to evade her, she pulled out her phone and began to look at the photo's of her and Adrian. From the time they went to Ireland, the time they went to London. The nights out they'd had and the house parties. Steph scrolled the top bar of her phone down to check the time. It was 20 past midnight now and she had work in the morning. She knew though, she wasn't going to get any sleep tonight.

Suddenly, the thoughts came flooding back into her mind. Her conjoined twin was laid on that sofa with Steph and Bo. And she was starting to scream. Steph desperately needed some quiet time. A break from the thoughts in her head and nothing did that for her quite like gambling.

Within seconds, she'd landed on the gambling site. There were the homely lights, the adverts, the games. It was a feeling of familiarity and security. Even though she knew, she absolutely knew how this would end, she'd well and truly reached fuck it mode. She enjoyed the spinning this time. The difference was that she wasn't even doing it to win. The thought of a bonus didn't get her excited. It was simply the silence she craved and the feeling of numbness she needed. She didn't even know how much she'd deposited. She just kept going until it declined anymore transactions. She knew it couldn't have been much because it was only 4 days until payday and so she didn't have much in her account. Money spent, twin silenced and hurt temporarily frozen by the magical effects gambling now had on her body, she fell to sleep.

Chapter 20

The next few days went by and Steph went to work as normal. She didn't tell anyone about her break up other than the two friends she'd made there. Amy and Betty. She'd been out with the pair a few times and really did enjoy their company. They were both mad about dogs too so they often went together on dog walks and would always have something to talk about. The three became really close. Steph and Amy had become closer lately too. Amy was going through a similar situation having just split up with her girlfriend. There was no big fight, no cheating or anything. They'd just grown apart and decided it was best to move on from each other. Steph remembered when she first got the job. It was near Christmas and she'd picked Amy out of the hat for secret santa. 'The only thing I know that she likes is girls!' Steph really struggled to know what to buy for her. The three often laughed at what Steph knew about Amy at this point.

Steph felt lucky to have two good friends like she did. When Amy found out about what had happened, she tried her best to help Steph. She would message her most evenings to make sure she was ok and she even gave her a TV, as she knew Adrian had taken theirs. The three were stood in the cigarette shelter one day when Steph felt her phone vibrate. She could feel the colour drain from her face as she read Adrian on the screen. She stubbed out her cigarette and told the girls she needed to toilet. Off she went and locked herself in so she could be alone to read the message from her ex.

'I'm sorry Steph. I really am. I miss you and Bo and I should never have done that. I want our little family back'

Steph could feel herself welling up at the message. It really hurt but she knew she'd never be able to trust him again after this. Especially not because it was Belle he had chosen to try and sleep with. She decided in that moment, it wasn't the right time to reply. She couldn't get her head around it and she needed time to properly think of a response. She did though message Amy, and told her what Adrian had sent. Amy and Betty had no idea about Steph's gambling. She'd learned from Adrian that it would only get thrown in her face if she told people.

'What you gunna do?' replied Amy.

'I have no idea. I'm not replying yet' said Steph.

As Steph made her way home that evening, she ran over and over in her mind what she could reply to Adrian. She didn't even have any money in her account until the day after tomorrow so she couldn't even gamble away the thoughts.

She reached home and took Bo on her usual walk, thinking all the way around about Adrian's message and her response. As Bo was drying off from the muddy puddles, she sat, coffee in hand and began to type.

'I know I made it hard for us Adrian, but I tried my best for you. I paid you everything and made sure my gambling didn't affect you as much as possible. I know I've left us in a mess and riddled with debt but why? Why did you tell your mum and dad it was me? You knew how hard it was for me to tell you about my addiction. And why Belle, Adrian. Anyone but Belle I could cope with, but not her' She re-read the message 6 times before sending it.

A few minutes later, her phone buzzed again.

'I know. It was hard for us but I know you tried. I've ruined it now. I know that and I need to live with that. I need to come and pick my sky box up. Is it ok if I come and get it tomorrow?'

The pair messaged for most of the night. It felt like, although Steph was unbelievably angry and hurt by Adrian, they were finding grounds to be friends on. They talked about memories they had with each other and Steph even laughed at one message about the time he'd slipped when walking Bo.

'Would it be ok if I just spent an hour with Bo tomorrow? Just to take her on a walk? You can come with us if you want?' asked Adrian.

Steph agreed that he could take Bo for a walk but she wouldn't go with them. It would be too painful for her. And with that, the messages stopped and Steph lay on the sofa to go to sleep with Bo.

The next day came and Adrian knocked on the door. Steph opened it and her heart sank a little and she'd wanted to cry. He didn't look angry like the last time she'd saw him. He looked like the Adrian she had always known. He smiled at Steph and walked into the living room and disconnected the sky box. 'You ok?' he asked as he looked as Steph with big sad eyes. 'Yeah I'm alright' said Steph, holding back her tears. Adrian began to fuss Bo and put on her lead. 'I'm going to go to the reservoir with her if that's ok?' He had often taken Bo to the reservoir before and Steph knew that Bo loved the water so she agreed. 'no more than 2 hours though please Adrian.' He agreed and popped Bo in the boot of his car.

Steph went upstairs and climbed into bed with Leanne. 'You ok?' asked Leanne, knowing that Steph was dreading seeing Adrian. Steph didn't answer. She just cuddled closer into her best friend and watched the film that was on the TV.

2 hours 20 minutes passed when Steph messaged Adrian. 'Adrian where are you? You said no more than 2 hours' She gave him the benefit of the doubt. They could have hit traffic or anything.

It was another hour when she messaged him again 'Adrian you promised. Please, please bring her back.'

45 minutes later, Steph received a message.

'Bo is staying with me. You aren't fit to look after her. I hope you're happy at everything you've done and you will never see her again.'

No. He hadn't done this to her. He hadn't. She felt like she was falling. Like she was falling down a black hole.

Steph screamed. 'No!' she was hysterical. 'Bo!' She cried. She collapsed at the top of the stairs. The dog that had helped her so much, that gave her a sense of responsibility, that helped her with her gambling and taught her unconditional love, had gone.

Steph was absolutely heart broken. Leanne tried to console her and said the pair would go to the house he lived at now with his parents and get Bo back. Steph refused. She knew his family and they weren't scared to have a huge fight in the street. Bo was in Adrian's name. He bought her, even if she was a gift to Steph. She didn't believe she had any chance of winning back the dog that had helped her so much and so, resigned to the fact that she'd lost her now. She couldn't believe who Adrian actually was. She genuinely believed he'd loved her, and he would never have done anything like this to her. She text Adrian 7 times, begging him to bring Bo back but received no response. She didn't know how she would get through any of this. No Adrian, no Bo. She couldn't do this on her own.

It was now 3am on payday and with no Bo, Steph was at the lowest she'd ever felt. Lower than the when she swallowed those pink pills. Lower than when she lowered her head underneath the water. At least when she did those things, she had Adrian and even though she didn't have Bo then, at least she'd never known her. At least she didn't have this huge hole in her life. When she'd previously tried to end her life, she thought she had a good man. So what did she have now to stop her? She had Leanne but she had her own demons to fight. She had her mum and her sisters but she didn't see them everyday. They weren't by her side to fight her conjoined twin when she was left alone with it. And Steph knew all too well by now that, she wasn't strong enough to fight it on her own. Steph had nothing to lose.

She wiped the tears from her cheek and grabbed her phone. She was already completely numb so she didn't actually know what she wanted to achieve from the gamble she was about have. She had zero interest in winning any money but still, she felt that somehow going onto the website and depositing every penny she had in her account was what she needed to do. Was she trying to punish herself? Steph had no idea why her mind worked this way and at this point, she didn't care either.

She put that faithful website into phone and deposited £1000. This was more than she'd ever deposited before in one go but she really didn't care. She wanted to hurt herself. She wanted to punish herself with another loss. She wanted to get the inevitable out of the way as quickly as she could. She wasn't looking for the thrill of it now. She wasn't looking for the numbness it made her feel. She simply wanted to get to the point, that she knew she would eventually be in anyway, as quickly as possible. She went straight for a £20.00 spin to get through the credit bar as quickly as she could. Within 20 minutes, she'd hit £0.00. She couldn't even remember the spins. She couldn't even tell you if she'd hit a bonus or not. She actually felt some relief as she put down her phone, bank account £1000 lighter and laid her head back on the sofa to fall asleep.

Chapter 21

For the next few days, Steph walked around like a zombie. She couldn't remember going to work. She couldn't remember getting home. She couldn't remember conversations she'd had on the phone. She didn't eat for a while but this was nothing new. Her two coping mechanisms in life were starvation and gambling. After she'd gambled, she transferred Leanne her increased share of the rent. She was shocked she'd got enough money left in her account to pay it to be honest. But she transferred it and really didn't care at all that she didn't have a spare penny. She had enough for a pouch of tobacco and that was all that mattered.

Steph made her way home one day from work. Not remembering the day at all. She walked through the front door to find the table laid, the candles lit and plates of all of her favourite foods across the table. Stood at the kitchen door was Leanne. 'I'm worried about you Steph, I know you feel alone but you're not. I'm here. I want to help you and I love you.'

For the first time in a while, Steph felt something. She felt love. A tear came into her eye as her body filled with a warm feeling that she had for her best friend. She was right. She wasn't alone. She had Leanne.

'You are so amazing Leanne, I love you so much.'

The friends sat down and ate. Steph was full after just a few bites. Her stomach must have shrunk due to the lack of food consumed recently but she did enjoy what she ate. The girls talked as they used to, avoiding the subject of Adrian and Bo. Steph felt a tiny glimmer of hope. A glimmer of Steph shining back through. After tea, the girls pushed together the sofa's, brought down the duvet from Leanne's room and sat together watching pretty little liars. Steph felt happy. She'd been reminded of the bond her and her best friend had and that, after so many years, it was truly unbreakable. This night was exactly what Steph needed.

Steph did decide to stay in Leanne's bed tonight. Her new bed her mum had bought her should be here tomorrow. The delivery took a while because of the mattress her mum had ordered with it but Steph was excited. She'd have a bed that Adrian had never slept in. That was just hers.

Steph woke up feeling a bit better. She had a streak of optimism today. She was going to put up her new bed and go and see her mum to thank her. She put on some clean clothes and brushed her hair. She still didn't quite feel up to put putting make up on yet but her mum wouldn't mind her not wearing any. She went downstairs and looked for her car key. It was at that moment Steph thought 'Shit. My car insurance.'

She'd gambled every penny she had outside of paying Leanne. Her insurance was due now, along with her car finance. She quickly stopped looking for her car key and grabbed her phone. Another feeling came back to Steph. Worry. She was petrified. She surely couldn't lose her car too!

She hadn't bothered for the last few days to check her emails at all. She didn't want to see the failed direct debit notifications and the debt collectors telling her she'd missed payments. She opened up the Gmail app and waited for the emails to flood though.

'Final notice of cancellation' read the email.

She didn't even read the email. She knew what it meant. She scrolled to the bottom of the email and pressed the number displayed on there. She put the phone to her ear and began to pace. 'Hello?' she asked frantically as she got through. The woman on the other end ran through the script she needed, confirming data protection for Steph.

'You're about to cancel my policy but please don't, please. My partner has just left me unexpectedly and I've had to pay more rent than usual and all of my bills. Please, please don't cancel my insurance. I'll pay it all next month I promise' Steph pleaded with the woman at the other end of the phone. The woman put Steph on hold to see what she could do. Steph was again praying. Steph didn't even believe in god yet all she seemed to do was pray.

The woman came back and agreed that Steph would make 2 payments on her next payday. 'Thank you so much. Thank you.'

Steph put down the phone and went back to her emails. That was strange, nothing from her finance company yet. Steph, along with her other bad habits, had a terrible habit of leaving things until the last minute. She only actioned debts on the last day she had to pay. She'd only call who she needed to at the final letter of demand and would procrastinate on almost any task until the last possible moment she could. Not seeing any notification from her finance company, she proceeded to her car and made the journey to her mums house, feeling relieved that she wasn't driving uninsured.

She got to her mums flat and gave her one of those long meaningful hugs that let her know she really loved her. She stayed there for hours. Telling her mum everything that had happened and how upset she was and how much she missed Bo. Her mum agreed with her about what an awful man Adrian was but also that, she'd never expected it of him. They had some lunch together and on occasion, Steph's mum made her laugh. It was nice. Steph's mum had a magical power. A power of making Steph feel safe, no matter how much trouble she'd gotten herself in. 'Has your bed come yet? Asked Steph's mum.

'Shit!' she replied. She checked the time and the expected delivery time text she'd noticed received earlier. 'It's due in an hour, I'd best go mum. I want to put it up and sleep in it tonight!'

'Ok, well listen Steph. You will be ok. I've transferred you £100 for your food for the rest of this month. Please Steph, buy food with it and tobacco.'

Steph's thoughts, as soon as her mum said it, was to gamble it. 'Oh mum you don't need to do that! I'll be ok, I always am.' Replied Steph, thinking all the time that she couldn't wait to get home now and gamble the money.

'I want you to have it, but promise me Steph, promise you'll buy food with it'

'I will mum, I promise' lied Steph once more.

Steph gave her mum a hug and hopped into her car. She drove 5 minutes down the road before the screaming for her to gamble this money was too much. She found a side street where she was sure no-one would see her and pulled up on the side of the road.

'You absolute bitch. You've just promised your mum you wouldn't do it, knowing full well you would. Do you think she can afford to keep giving you money? It's not like she earns loads.' All of these thoughts were going through her mind as she was typing in the website that she loved so much. The insults she was hurling at herself still weren't enough to stop her from what she was about to do.

Sat on the side of the road, Steph began to spin. She told herself she'd do a £5 stake for now but then drop to a £2 stake if she hadn't hit a bonus by £50. She stared at the screen, praying again for someone, somewhere in the universe to let her win. She reached £70. She stopped for a moment as she saw a couple walking on the pavement towards her car. She didn't want them to know she was such a pathetic loser that'd pulled up to gamble. She lowered the phone to below her steering wheel so that no one could see what she was doing. She thought about whether she should go to a £2 spin but convinced herself that, to win the money she needed, she really needed to be on a £5 stake when she hit it. She continued to spin. £40. £35. £30. £25. £20. £15. £10. £5. £0.

She'd not even been able to make it home before she gambled this time but she did feel the excitement, the want for a bonus and the disappointment and self-hatred when she lost it. She started her car again, absolutely fuming with herself. All the way home she repeated 'You are absolutely disgusting. Is there any wonder you've lost everything good you had? You don't deserve anything you're a manipulative, evil bitch.'

She got home and pulled onto the driveway. As she walked through the door, she half expected Bo to jump up at her, but of course she didn't. She sat on the chair at the dining room table, head in hands again, and thought about what a mess she was in. How could she wake up in such a good mood and ruin everything? She thought about the things she hadn't paid, and the things she still needed to pay this month. Paying any of her debts was out of the question. There was no way her mum would give her anymore and she didn't have Adrian to rely on this time to help. Her trail of though was interrupted by a knock on the door. It was her bed. She took the boxes inside and the double mattress that was incredibly heavy. She didn't have the strength tonight to put it up.

Feeding herself was never a concern for Steph. She could quite happily go without food. She didn't mind starving herself and gambling her own food money. It was only when it was someone else that might be affected that she panicked. Truth be told, Steph didn't care what happened to her as long as the people she loved were ok. She truly believed, she deserved to suffer.

Leanne was a vegetarian and so, she did her own shopping and cooked for herself the majority of the time. It was perfect because it meant Steph wouldn't need to be with her when she went food shopping and wouldn't have to contribute to bill. Steph could easily live off of coco pops for a month. All she needed was tobacco and petrol for her car. Right now, she wasn't sure how she would get the money for it but with a full pouch of tobacco and half a tank of fuel, she didn't need to worry about this right now.

Her phone buzzed on the table. It was Amy. 'Hey you. How you doing? I've not heard from you for a few days and you've been really quiet at work. Is everything ok? X'

Steph smiled. It was nice of Amy to reach out to her. She obviously wasn't going to tell Amy about the gambling or anything but she really appreciated her reaching out to her.

'Yeah, I'm alright mate. I'm missing Bo like mad but I'll be ok. What you up to tomorrow? I've got a bed here I need to put up and I can't even move this mattress, never mind carry it up the stairs. Fancy helping me? X' Steph replied.

'Yeah ok ☺ I'll come round tomorrow morning if that's ok ? x'

Steph was looking forward to having Amy round. It would be a new face and she could finally sleep in a proper bed again.

The next day, Steph opened the door to Amy, who was presented with the mattress and the boxes of flat pack pieces that would build Steph's new bed.

'As if you didn't build it last night you lazy cow' said Amy

'How on earth could I possibly do this on my own?' Asked Steph.

Amy and Steph dragged the mattress up the steep stairs, which seemed even steeper when dragging a mattress up them and built the bed. It took them ages as both were useless at flat pack. Once it was done, Steph jumped onto the mattress. 'Oh my god! It's so comfortable!' shouted Steph. Amy laughed as she watched Steph star fish on the bed. 'Better than the sofa!' said Amy.

'Thank you so much Amy honestly. I really appreciate it.'

'No problem, just ring me if you ever need anything! Was the TV ok? ' asked Amy.

'Amazing!' said Steph. 'I'll get another and give it you back I promise' said Steph, knowing full well she'd never have enough money to buy a TV.

As Amy and Steph made their way downstairs, Amy asked Steph if she fancied a drink somewhere. Steph's heart sank. She knew she couldn't even afford a pint. 'Ahh, I'm sorry I've promised Belle I'd watch Amelie' lied Steph.

'No problem' replied Amy. 'Well just give me a ring if you need anything.'

Steph thanked Amy and saw her out.

Steph found herself once again, sat alone in the house. The only thought in her mind about how she could get money to gamble. She ran through every possible way in her head. How could she do it? Who could she get to transfer her money so that she could deposit? The need to gamble wasn't leaving her, even though there was no money she had to gamble. She searched in her phone 'No deposit free spins.' There were loads of sites offering them! She knew the websites tricks. That you could only win a maximum amount of about £50 and you needed to wager that 50X before you could actually withdraw any money. Basically, making it completely impossible to win but she didn't care. She needed in this moment, to spin a wheel. Steph signed up to 8 different sites that day. All offering between 10 – 20 free spins at a 20p stake.

Her addiction was now so bad, that she needed to just play the game. Without any realistic chance of her winning, she needed to spin the slots.

Chapter 22

5 days until payday now. She'd learnt that as long as she had a pound on her card, she could buy fuel. The machine would pre authorise £1 and not take the money for a couple of days and when it did, it would just leave her bank overdrawn and not return the payment so she didn't have to worry about the police or anything. She'd also managed get her mum to pick her up a packet of tobacco when she needed it. She told her she would bring her the cash which of course, she didn't. But her mum was kind enough to tell her to just give it her on payday. She'd managed to stay out of the house when Leanne was at home at tea time and tell her she'd eaten out so didn't need anything making. Steph had run out of coco pops 2 days ago. She hadn't eaten in 2 days and she was starting to suffer now. She often went a day here or there without eating a thing, usually after gambling. But she was really feeling it this time. Leanne had very little food left in the house at this point too as they got paid at similar times and she always held off buying food until payday.

Steph was driving home, planning on raiding the sofa's to see if there was any change that had fallen down that she could use for some food. She got a call as she was driving. It was her mum.

'Steph! Belles had the baby!'

Belle had had a difficult pregnancy. Steph had taken her to hospital at the drop of a hat a number of times when the baby wasn't moving, when Belle was ill, when anything wasn't right. They'd told her a few weeks ago that there wasn't enough water around the baby and that they may have to induce early. Steph was a little hurt that, after it had been her there all the way through the pregnancy, it was Lillie that got to be there for the birth. But this was some good news, finally something good to celebrate.

'Ahhh yay! Are they both ok?' Asked Steph to her mum.

'Yeah they're fine. She's named her Hettie'

Steph screwed her nose up at the name but it did grow on her eventually.

'Can you come and pick me up and we will go to the hospital and bring them home?' asked Steph's mum.

'Yeah no problem, I'll come over now.'

Perfect! She could pick her mum up and tell her she'd not eaten and she'd forgotten her card. That way, her mum would get her something to eat from the hospital.

Steph made her way to her mums house, picked her up and drove them both to the hospital. Steph casually mentioning on the way how hungry she was. Her mum didn't pick up on her hints, she was too excited to see her newest grandchild.

Steph had always felt like she'd let her mum down when it came to grandkids. She was the only one of her sisters not to have a child but realistically, she couldn't afford to feed herself, never mind a baby. She also had been told that she would struggle to conceive naturally, given issues with her ovaries and her womb. Steph didn't mind though. She really was in no way fit to be a mother at the moment and there were always other options if the time came where she was ready.

They parked up at the hospital and got a ticket from the machine. 'I don't have any money on me mum, can you pay for the parking?' her mum agreed and they made their way to the ward Belle and Hettie were on.

She was beautiful. A perfect little girl. Steph had gone into that head space again staring at Hettie. Where nothing else mattered. She didn't hear or see anything around her, other than that beautiful little girl that lay asleep in her arms. Little Hettie had cuddles with Steph and her mum before a nurse came and told them they were allowed to leave. Steph had never driven so carefully in all her life, driving them home. Steph's mum had agreed to stay with the girls for a few days until Belle had recovered from giving birth as Hettie's dad wasn't around. Steph dropped them all off at Belle's house and kissed her mum, sister, Amelie and Hettie goodbye.

As she got back into her car, her stomach growled. She'd not managed to get any food that whole time. She made the short drive home and raided the cupboard. She made sure she didn't eat any of Leanne's food. It wasn't fair for her to eat anything Leanne had paid for. She found a packet of noodles hidden right at the back. She'd never been so happy to see noodles in her life. She cooked them too quickly, meaning they were still a bit hard but she didn't care. It was enough to fill the hole in her tummy.

Steph remembered when she lived alone in the flat above the sandwich flat and couldn't afford to eat. She'd finished work one day and really needed some food now but didn't have a penny. She'd been given a Marks and Spencer's voucher for Christmas from work. She'd spent the voucher on Christmas present for her family but that evening, she went into the store and picked up a tin of soup. She was that desperate to eat, after losing all of her money to gambling. She attempted to pay for the tin of soup on the voucher. There wasn't even enough money on it for that. She went hungry once more.

Steph told her best friend all about the day and little Hettie as they watched their favourite programme again. She still missed Bo but she was starting to feel like she was getting back on track.

As the pair sat there, Steph's phone vibrated. It was Amy, asking Steph again how she was and telling her about her dog that had slipped the lead today. Steph spoke to Amy right up until she climbed into her new bed. She snuggled into the duvet with a full belly, her best and longest standing friend in the world downstairs, a really good friend she'd spoken to all night and a new niece in the world. Today was a good day.

Steph had managed, for the last few days, to go to Belle's for tea to help her mum and Belle look after Amelie and Hettie. It was payday tomorrow so she'd make sure she had enough money to do a food shop. By now Steph had completely lost any desire to get better. Although she had good days, all in all Steph was a very lonely, sad person. She didn't enjoy anything in life anymore. Nothing interested her. She simply existed, day by day, painting the best smile she could on her face to make people think she was doing alright. Steph was ill. And she was trapped in her illness. And as her addiction got worse, and grew in age, it got harder. The determination Steph used to feel not to gamble anymore had gone. She had completely resigned herself to the knowledge that, whether she truly wanted to or not, she would gamble the biggest portion of her wage away.

This month though, Steph really needed to pay her finance on her car and her insurance. She needed to make two payments on both. She needed to get the gas and electricity sorted. Since Adrian had left, she had a bigger portion of the bills to pay. Her own debts, her payday loans, had no chance of getting paid, once again. She really needed to try tomorrow to keep some money safe to pay some bills.

She'd arranged to go on a dog walk with Amy today after work. She missed walking, and the joy she felt watching Bo run. Amy picked her up from her house and they went to a local walk nearby. There were never any other people on the walk so it was perfect to let the dogs off and have a run. Steph watched Amy's two dogs running through the field. It made her smile but it didn't give her the same feeling it did when she watched Bo run.

'I proper miss Bo' said Steph to Amy.

'I know, I bet you do. You can watch these idiot's whenever you want though if that'll make you feel better' Amy joked.

Steph found it easy to talk to Amy. She was really laid back and seemed to listen to what Steph had to say. Steph was glad she'd made a new friend. They managed to get the dogs back onto the leads and they drove back to Amy's house.

'I'll drop the dogs off first then take you home if that's ok?' Asked Amy to Steph.

'Yeah that's fine, no problem' replied Steph.

They pulled into Amy's drive and Steph looked at the house. It was a brand new build. 'She must be loaded' thought Steph to herself as Amy unloaded the dogs into the house. 'I'll not be a minute' shouted Amy.

Steph stayed in the car looking at the house. 'Nice car, nice house.' She thought to herself. Amy was the same age as Steph so she'd done really well for herself! Not like Steph, the addict who'd been living off of coco pops for the past 3 weeks.

Amy got back in the car and drove Steph home. 'Are you like, rich?' asked Steph to Amy. Amy laughed 'No! I wish!'

'You're house looks dead nice and your car is lovely' Said Steph. 'Thanks' replied Amy 'But I'm definitely not rich.'

Amy dropped Steph off at her house and the girls waved goodbye to each other. Steph went inside and made herself a cup of coffee and rolled a cigarette at the back door. Her thoughts turning to gambling. Steph was scared. She was scared that she'd gamble more than she could afford again tomorrow. She knew it was coming. She knew that soon enough, she'd have money in her account and she'd be able to do nothing other than gamble it. What could she do to make sure she didn't gamble her rent and car money? Steph wrote down on a piece of paper what she needed to pay tomorrow.

'£830'

That was the figure written on the paper. That was just for her insurance, finance and rent though. That didn't include any of her other bills or her food. But again Steph told herself, she didn't need to eat. She didn't need shopping and she didn't deserve it anyway. It was strange the way the her thoughts changed the closer it go to payday.

Here it was. 2.17am on payday. Her bodies natural alarm clock had once again reminded her it was payday. Had told her that it was time now. It was time to wake up and satisfy the greedy twin that couldn't even give let her have a full night's sleep. As she sat up in her bed making her way onto one of the dozens of website's she's registered to, her stomach churned. She was scared. She knew how important it was that she had the money for her car and insurance.

She decided to go for a game she hadn't played before. If she could win enough money to pay everything off, including her debts, she could have a fresh start. Telling herself she would be sensible this time, she deposited £100. After spinning just £20 of it, she decided against the new game. She decided that she needed to be on her original game, her favourite game, that was the only one that was going to give her that bonus that had previously allowed her to win so much. £80.00 in credit, she left the game and searched for her favourite. For a second, she was worried this new site didn't have it but then, as she pressed the little magnifying glass, there is was. She clicked the icon that took her back to that place where she found herself every morning of payday. Sat within those reels. On a £5 stake, she spun. She'd won £400 on her first spin! She could have withdrawn this and been ok. £400 would mean she could pay the arrears on her insurance and her finance. Both payments were huge as it was her first insurance and her finance was exploiting the fact she had terrible credit and so was charging her over £300 a month for a car that wasn't worth half what she would end up paying for it. To Steph though, it wasn't enough. She'd written that number down on the piece of paper and this, she'd convinced herself, was how much she needed to win. Increasing her stake now to £10, which in Steph's mind was a completely sensible and rational thing to do, she spun the reels.

It wasn't long before she reached £0. She'd only deposited £100 at this point so the panic and fear hadn't set in because she knew, she had money in her account to continue to deposit to win it back. She was though, a little disappointed that she'd spent all that and not hit a bonus round yet. Steph so many times had told herself it was a con. It was chasing those three bonus symbols that always led her to gamble every penny. She'd always cry with frustration and ask how she could roll away so much money and not hit it once. It was clearly fixed. The thought never was strong enough to deter her from doing it again though.

Fuelled slightly with disappointment at this point, she deposited £200. Still convincing herself that she was being sensible.

'£600 and not hit one fucking bonus. What an absolute joke.'

Fuelled now by absolute determination that she would win, that she would hit the bonus and it was due to pay out, Steph deposited a further £500. She was in that state of mind now where she didn't actually know or care how much she had in her bank. All that mattered was hitting this bonus. 'The more I put on, the more chance I have of hitting it' She continued to tell herself.

She was completely fixated on the reels. They spun and spun and spun, taking her credit down another £10 every time she did. But at £210, she'd done it. She'd got those three little golden symbols that had become the symbol of her life. She was so excited. She couldn't sit still in her bed. Her hands were sweating and her heart pounding out of her chest. This was going to make everything better. She'd never got the bonus on a £10 spin before. On a £5 one she won £4000 so imagine how much this was going to get her. Steph couldn't even remember how to breath at this point.

The bonus round gave Steph 12 free spins but the winnings were multiplied on every spin so the potential for winning was huge. She knew it was her turn to win.

The first spin began. No win.

That was ok. She knew that they'd often leave it until a few spins in before the winning spins came.

Second spin. No win.

Third spin. No win

Fourth spin. No win.

What the hell? 4 spins in on the bonus and no win yet. Steph was getting nervous. She'd always won when she got a bonus. Surely you couldn't get a bonus and not win anything?

Fifth spin. £40 win.

Phew. Here it was, it started the winnings late but they were coming.

Sixth spin. No win.

Seventh spin. No win

Eighth spin. No win.

Steph's whole body was now completely tense. She hurt she was tensing that much. She was screaming in her head. How could this be happening? How could the bonus she loved so much be letting her down? How could she have spent so much money, hit the bonus and it not pay out?

Ninth spin. No win

Tenth spin. £100 win.

'That's not enough!' screamed Steph in her head, hands wrapped so tightly around the phone she thought it may break. These last 2 spins needed to be huge wins.

Eleventh spin. No win.

Twelfth Spin. £60 win.

Steph dropped her phone on the bed, clenched her fists and her whole body and screamed silently. She was so angry. How could this happen. How on a £10 stake could she hit the bonus and come out with £200? She cried and began to punch her pillow in anger. She buried her head in the pillow and screamed again.

Now ,feeling completely cheated by the game and the bonus she loved so much, she went into a state of rage. She picked up her phone and told herself 'It will not fucking beat me!'. Increasing her stake to £20, she spun viciously. 'You fucking owe me' she repeated to the phone and the game. 'You cannot do that. You owe me.'

Steph rolled away all of the credit left on the screen, followed by every last pence in her account. She even made a small last deposit of £26.00 as that was all she had left. None of it brought her the bonus again. None of it got her the £830 she'd needed. All it had done is what it did every month. Left her broke, unable to pay any of her bills and this month, had stolen her car too.

Steph felt like her heart had been ripped straight out of her chest. She felt like the bonus that she loved so much, that she yearned for every month for the past 10 years had cheated on her. How? How had she hit it and it not won more than £200? Steph had never felt so angry in her entire life. She wasn't even thinking about her bills right now. She was thinking that she needed to deposit more to get the bonus that was owed to her. Her mind was racing back to previous times she'd needed money and how she'd got it.

She remembered a time she had cleared her bank account at a bookies. She stood outside the shop and applied for a payday loan. She'd been accepted at that point and they would only take 10 minutes to transfer the money. She remembered keep putting her card in the machine, time after time checking if it had gone in yet. It was easy when her credit rating wasn't as bad as it was now, to get money. The money finally went in and Steph proceeded to go back into the shop to roll away the loan money too.

Even though she knew she would never be accepted for another loan, she searched for any loan providers she'd not already taken from. She found a weird looking site. She didn't care though. She filled out the application. The whole world knew her bank details at this point. And there it was, unfortunately. 'Unfortunately, we can not offer you the amount you are looking for however, we are able to offer you £300'

Steph couldn't believe it. She was already behind on payments. As if they would let her have anything! She reduced the amount from £1000 to £300. An email came through with a contract agreement and she signed. She of course didn't actually read the contract, she just signed it.

Congratulations! The next email read. Your money will be with you in within the next 5 minutes.

The repayments for a £300 loan were over £80 a month. It was so easy to get into debt. How could someone as desperate as Steph, with a credit score and payment history as bad as hers, get a loan with repayments this high within 30 minutes and have the cash in her account? It was madness. But she didn't care. She opened the bedroom window and had a cigarette, refreshing her banking app every few seconds to see if the money had gone in. Not once did a thought enter her head about how she would pay it back, or any of the other things she needed to pay this month. That money was going straight back onto her game for her to get the bonus it owed her.

It was there. £300. Steph, still amazed that any company would actually lend her money, immediately deposited it onto the site. Straight onto a £10 spin, she gambled her way through all of that £300. Not hitting the bonus once. She went straight from the gambling website to 'payday loan searcher' website. A website that searched a number of payday loans and showed her anyone that was willing to lend to her. She had yet another cigarette, pacing her bedroom floor and there it was. 'We're sorry. We've been unable to match you with a lender.'

It was then. That second when she read that sentence, that Steph came out of her gambling state and back to earth. It was like a scene in a film, when something bad happens and the camera zooms down onto a person. Dropping her phone to the floor, her body completely still, paralysed through shock and fear she said to herself 'What have I done?'

The panic attack followed. Walking around her bed over and over and over again. Unable to breathe and heart going faster than it ever had before. She was shaking uncontrollably. She couldn't even roll a cigarette she was shaking so much. Steph was going at 90 miles per hour. Pulling her hair, crying and pacing with just 6 words repeating themselves over and over 'What am I going to do?'

Her breathing got even faster and so did her heart. She'd got actual pains in her chest at this point and they were getting stronger. She sat on the bed and tried to take deep breaths but her panic ridden body wouldn't allow it. As another stabbing pain ran through her chest, Steph began to feel dizzy. Her heart couldn't take this and she hadn't taken her tablets all month. She was panicking even more now about the pains and the dizziness. Unable again to take any control back over her body, and the dizziness getting worse, Steph felt her eyes roll into the back of her head as she fell backward onto the bed.

Chapter 23

It was banging of doors that bought Steph back round. She had no idea how long she'd been unconscious for but she knew she had a pounding headache. She lifted herself from the position she'd passed out in and held her head as the blood seemed to pound to her brain. It was Leanne getting ready for work that she could hear. She looked at the time and she was running late for work too, but she couldn't do it. There was no way she could work today. Aside from the fact she'd got a huge problem to deal with, she was in so much pain with her head that she wasn't even capable of driving.

She messaged Amy and told her how ill she was and how much her head hurt and that she wouldn't be in.

'Oh no! I hope you're ok mate. Let me know if you need anything x' replied Amy.

Steph then messaged her boss, apologising but explaining she simply wasn't well enough to come in. She didn't feel as nervous as she usually did when she called in sick because she wasn't actually lying this time. She really was in too much pain to work.

She made her way into the drawer where her and Leanne kept the painkillers. It was one of those drawers that every household has. Where you put all of the stuff you think you might need even though you never will. It was full of letters, documents, phone chargers and nappy bags she used to use with Bo. She rummaged around, finding a pack of ibuprofen. 2 wouldn't cut it. It wouldn't get rid of this headache. She popped 4 of the bright pink pills. Not to overdose but to try and shift this pain she was in. She was in so much pain that she couldn't even think about what she'd done earlier that morning. All that she could think about was relieving the huge amount of pain she was in. She couldn't even manage a cigarette. She made her way back to her bedroom, passing Leanne on the stairs.

'Fucking hell you look like shit! Are you ok?' asked Leanne.

'Migraine' replied Steph as she continued towards her bedroom.

Steph didn't even hear if Leanne had replied or not. She just climbed into bed and rested her head on the pillow, praying that the pain would go away. She wasn't sure how long it was before she'd managed to nod off.

Steph awoke 6 hours later. She couldn't believe how long she'd slept for. She moved her head slowly, trying to work out if the pain had gone or not. It had. 'Thank god' she said to herself. She felt almost like she had a hangover. That fuzzy head, dry mouth feeling you get after a hard night out.

As she drank a glass of water, she got that churning stomach in her feeling. For a moment or two, she'd forgotten what she'd done but it was back in her mind now and again, the same question running through her brain. 'What am I going to do?'

Steph spent the rest of that afternoon searching for solutions on her phone. She applied for every single loan that she hadn't previously applied for and was rejected on all. There had been a few times though, that it had said guarantor loan company would help her. She'd seen them loads of times before but she didn't know anyone that was willing to be a guarantor for her. Her mum's credit wasn't good enough, her sister's didn't have good credit either and her dad didn't work. She needed a solution. She had literally nothing and more debt than before. She needed to pay her rent and somehow, find a way to keep her car on the road. How the hell would she wriggle her way out of it this time?

Her thought process was interrupted as Leanne walked through the door. She popped her head around the living room door and asked Steph if she was ok and if she was feeling better. Steph told her she was feeling loads better now. Leanne asked Steph if she wanted a takeaway. 'My treat' Leanne insisted. Steph once again was reminded of how kind and beautiful, inside and out, her best friend was.

The girls pulled the sofas together again and got the duvets. Their pizza's arrived after half an hour or so. Steph really struggled to eat. She told Leanne it was due to her feeling so ill earlier that day but Steph had gone some time now without eating properly, and she struggled with large meals.

The girls sat together as they often did and watched TV. Steph couldn't concentrate on what was on the TV because she was so worried about what she was going to do. Within the next few days, Leanne would be asking for her rent money, ready for it leaving her account.

Steph started to think about the times Leanne had needed her. Steph was always there, no matter what. At her hospital bedside, in Leanne's bed when she was sad, leaving work to be with her to make sure she was ok. Leanne's other friends didn't know how to deal with some of Leanne's episodes but Steph did. She knew what she needed and when to just leave her alone to give her time to heal. Leanne's friends would even message Steph sometimes and ask her what they should do, because they knew too, Steph was the one who looked after Leanne.

And right now, Steph needed help. Leanne always told her, she would do anything for her. And Steph knew she meant it. But the guilt she felt asking anyone for anything, always stopped Steph from going to her. But she had no option this time.

Heart pounding once more, she sat and psyched herself up for what she was about to ask.

'Leanne, I need your help...'

'Leanne looked at her and could see Steph welling up. She knew it was serious.'

'What is it?' asked Leanne.

'I need to ask you Leanne, if you would guarantor a loan for me. I'm behind on the payments for my car and I have debts I need to pay off. I'm in a such a mess Leanne and I just don't know what to do.' At this point, tears were once again rolling down her face.

She'd prepared herself for what was about to come. For the shouting, for the 'Do you really expect me to do that for a gambling addict?' She'd pictured in her head that it would be like one of the arguments she'd had with Belle. Where Belle called her vicious names and threw the fact she was an addict, and all of the horrible things she'd done, in her face.

Leanne looked at Steph and pulled a face as though she was about to cry. 'Of course I will' she said, as she gave Steph a hug. Steph absolutely burst in tears. How had she thought her best friend of all this time would react so badly? Why had she convinced herself she'd say horrible things. Leanne had never done this to her. She was her absolute best friend and always would be.

Leanne and Steph went for a cigarette as Steph told her about the loan company who would lend her money if she had guarantor. Although Leanne didn't have a lot of money, she did have a good credit score. She'd always paid her bills on time and was sensible when it came to paying things off. 'How much do you need?' asked Leanne.

Steph knew to pay her insurance and finance so they were up to date, to pay off the payday loan she'd taken out earlier that day and to get up to date on the payments she's missed on the others, she needed around £3000'

'£4000' replied Steph to Leanne. She would use the other £1000 as an emergency fund she told herself.

'Bloody hell! I didn't know it was that much!' said Leanne.

Steph filled in the application form. She put in her income and expenditure, obviously leaving out gambling. Once she'd done her part, an email was sent to Leanne as her guarantor, for her to fill her section in. She went through the same only, she filled it in honestly. The repayment on this loan was just over £200 a month. If Steph didn't gamble, she could easily afford that.

'You do realise Steph that if you don't pay this I will have to, and I really can't afford to. You must not let me down.'

Steph reassured Leanne that she did understand and that she would never let her down. Leanne submitted her application. It wasn't one of them though that said congratulations or unfortunately straight away. It told her she would have a decision within 48 hours. Steph gave Leanne a hug and thanked her again. She promised she would get things sorted.

The girls went to bed but once again, Steph couldn't sleep. She ran though all the scenario's in her head of the outcome of this loan decision. What if got rejected? What the hell would she do then? If it was accepted, she was going to pay everything off. She really was this time.

The next morning came and she went to work. She couldn't focus at all. Constantly checking her emails to see the outcome of the loan the friends had requested. She made it through to lunch time and still nothing. She was so anxious. Amy had tried all day to talk to her but she just wasn't able to hold a conversation. She was giving her really short, blunt answers. She didn't mean to. She liked Amy but she couldn't fit anything more than the decision of this loan in her brain right now.

She was on the phone to a customer when she felt her phone buzz. This was it. She knew it. The customer on the phone had a complaint she wanted dealing with there and then. The office Steph worked in was a small one and so everyone could hear her on the phone so she knew she couldn't try and hurry her way through the call. She listened to the customer and talked through her issues, the whole time wishing she would get off of the phone so that she could go and read the email. 20 minutes that call lasted. Steph was so relieved when the customer hung up on her. She quickly grabbed her coat and ran to the toilet. She pulled out her phone as she sat in the locked cubicle and slowly pulled down the notification bar on the top. It was them! She'd feared she'd been anticipating it so much that it would just be an email from Facebook or something stupid.

The title of the email – Your loan agreement.

She couldn't tell just from the title if they'd been accepted or not. She clicked the email. Her body full of anticipation. 'Approved'

Steph literally jumped from the toilet she was sat on, overcome with joy. Leanne had done it. She'd sorted things out for her. Steph was going to be ok! Steph was jumping up and down in the cubicle she was in. She was so happy. This was going to turn her whole life around!

Steph went back into work and messaged Amy on the skype chat they had. 'Heyyy, just had some dead good news. Sorry if I seemed off today mate, I've just got a lot going on at the moment but it should be ok now. Fancy a dog walk soon? Xx'

Steph had a really bad habit of making plans when she was on a high. Immediately after she'd won, she would often tell her mum or one of her sisters that they should go away somewhere, or book something together or do something. Of course it never happened because Steph would lose all of the money she'd planned to do it with and have to come up with some ridiculous lie as to why she couldn't.

Amy said she was glad that Steph was ok and they arranged to go on a dog walk together at the weekend.

As Steph drove home that evening, she concentrated on getting the money into her account. That was the next thing. They might have been approved but she needed to get it into her bank account, nothing was final until that happened. She got home and opened the door. She was absolutely gutted that Leanne wasn't home yet. She didn't want to pester her about the loan or the money but her brain wasn't going to let her forget about it until the money actually hit her account. She tried to keep herself busy until Leanne got home. She'd try and do the pots, or sweep the floor but there was no point. Nothing was going to distract her mind from telling her over and over again she needed this money in her account.

She was stood at the back door chain smoking when she heard the car pull up on the drive. This was it! She needed to act casual, like she wasn't as desperate as she was.

Steph had hidden her true self and her true feelings for so long that, she felt it wasn't ok to be herself. Leanne knew she was desperate so why had she convinced herself he needed to hide it? She thought that showing any sign of upset or distress was a sign of weakness. She had to constantly pretend to everyone that she was ok. The reasons she wasn't ok were all her own doing so it would be selfish of her to let anyone know what she was actually feeling.

Leanne walked through the door and ran through the kitchen up the stairs. 'I need the toilet!' she shouted to Steph. Steph laughed, hiding how gutted she was at the fact that she hadn't immediately struck up a conversation with Steph about the money that was now in Leanne's account. Leanne was on the toilet for ages. It was killing Steph! She wished she would just hurry up so her brain could begin to rest. She listened as closely as she could for any sign that Leanne was leaving the bathroom. She heard the taps starting to run. Leanne was having a bath! Steph, full of anger and desperation paced around the living room, doing that silent scream again with her whole body tensed and her face screwed up. Was Leanne doing it on purpose?

The reality was that Leanne simply needed a bath. She had a headache and she'd arranged to meet a friend later that evening. She is no way was trying to put Steph through anymore angst. She was just getting ready for her night out. But Steph simply wasn't able to think of it this way. How could it not have been at the front of Leanne's mind when it was literally all Steph could think about? She had another cigarette to try and calm herself down. Leanne was in the bath for half an hour! It was absolute torture. But as she heard the water drain from the bath, she was filled again with anxiety. She heard footsteps coming down the stairs. She repositioned herself on the sofa cushion she was sat in to look as natural as possible. Why? Why did she feel the need to hide what she was feeling? She heard the back door open as Leanne had a cigarette now. Steph was stuck. Crippled with anxiousness and anticipation. She pretended to look at her phone. She was scrolling through Facebook but wasn't reading a single post, she was just scrolling. She heard the door close and her heart racing even faster now. She waited for the steps towards the living room but instead, she heard footsteps going back up the stairs. Was this a joke? What the hell? How had Leanne still not come to speak to her?

She couldn't bare it anymore. She went up to the room that her best friend was in. She could see her, sat on the bedroom floor, doing her hair in the mirror. 'Hey, you ok?' asked Steph.

'Yeah I'm in a bloody right rush. Why did I even agree to go out Steph when all I want to do is get in bed and eat shit?' Leanne asked jokingly. Leanne's joke made Steph feel more comfortable. Like Leanne wasn't mad at her.

Steph had a terrible complex about people being mad at her. She always thought, all the time, someone was mad at her for something. Even when she'd done nothing at all wrong, she feared that people we're mad at her. She thought it was linked to the guilt she carried around all day, every day because of her gambling.

'You might enjoy it when you're out' replied Steph, psyching herself up to ask about the loan.

'Oh, I've transferred you that money by the way.' Said Leanne, so casually. Like it was nothing. Like Steph hadn't been driving herself crazy over it for the last few hours.

'Oh have you?' replied Steph, feeling a huge sense of relief. How had she missed that? How had she not checked her bank all the time she was waiting for Leanne?

'Yeah but I've kept the rent money for this month so I've just transferred you the rest if that's alright?' asked Leanne.

'Of course! Leanne I can't thank you enough I really can't. I promise, I'll never ever let you down with a payment. Thank you so much.'

'You better not! But you're more than welcome. Now piss off because I need to get changed.'

Steph gave Leanne a hug and left her bedroom. Those feelings of frustration, anger, defeat and anticipation now replaced with pure happiness and absolute exhaustion. What a rollercoaster of emotions the last 24 hours had been.

As she made her way downstairs, she heard a knock at the door. It must have been one of Leanne's friends. She opened the door and Amy was stood on the other side. 'I don't care what you say, you're eating this.' She held up the white plastic bag filled with Chinese food. 'I noticed you didn't eat anything at dinner time today and I know full well you wont bother to cook for yourself so you're having this.'

Steph remembered feeling so bad. The guilt again. She'd not really responded much to Amy today and she'd completely forgotten that Amy was going through a break up. She was probably lonely and wanted a friend and Steph had just ignored her.

'Oh my god! As if! That's so nice, come in.'

Steph got a couple of plates out of the cupboard and plated her and Amy some food up. She shouted Leanne and ask if she wanted any but she didn't. 'This is so nice of you Amy, thank you.'

'It's ok' replied Amy, smiling.

The pair sat in the living room, put the TV on and tucked into their Chinese. Leanne came down and asked the pair how she looked. 'Your tits look massive!' shouted Steph.

'Thanks' replied Leanne as she pushed up her boobs and walked out of the door.

With a full belly now, and feeling completely exhausted, Steph tried her best to stay awake. Her friend had come round to make sure she was ok. She couldn't fall asleep! Amy was talking to Steph about her and her partners break up. How it was really lonely at home now but she was glad she had the dogs for company. Steph again, became overcome with guilt. Her friend was lonely and she'd been too wrapped up in her own issues to even notice. She made a promise to herself that she would be there for Amy.

Amy said she'd better get back to the dogs now. Steph thanked her again for the food and saw her out. She was relieved when Amy left because she was so tired, she just wanted to go to bed. As she had her last cigarette of the day, she grabbed her phone and went straight onto the website of her insurance company. She paid the outstanding balance and did exactly the same for her finance company. She climbed the stairs and crawled into bed. She felt happy. She hadn't gambled today, even with money in her account. She did what she promised she would. That night, her twin let her sleep the whole night through. With more money in her account than she'd ever had, she managed to get a full nights sleep.

Chapter 24

Steph felt great the next day. She'd had a full nights sleep, her car was safe and her insurance up to date. Her rent was paid and she had enough money to clear her bills. The smile she would wear today would not be a fake one, it would be real. So many years of depression, so many years of sadness, all relieved with £4000. She wouldn't fail this time she was sure of it. She would do everything she needed to in order to get herself out of the trap she had been stuck in for so long. Sure, it couldn't pay all of her debts off, she'd racked up so much by now, but it could definitely get her back on track.

She went to work in the good mood she had woken up in. Her customers were very lucky if they got to speak to her today, they'd get the best service ever! She thanked Amy again on Skype for the meal last night. Amy knew she was having a rough time and went out of her way to make her feel better whilst Steph had been completely ignorant to the hurt Amy was feeling.

'Dinner is on me today.' Steph messaged Amy. It was the least she could do after last night. Amy often went home to her dogs at dinner as she didn't have anyone else at home now who could let them out. Sometimes, she'd take Steph with her so she could see the dogs. Steph enjoyed seeing them even though it always made her miss Bo.

'Ok' replied Amy.

They got in Amy's car at lunch time and made their way to Amy's house, stopping at the sandwich shop around the corner from her house on the way. Steph placed the orders for them both and paid on her card. She was filled with pride at the fact she could afford a sandwich. It sounded silly but being able to buy not only herself, but her friend a sandwich was something she was very rarely able to do so the fact she could now, made her feel good. They fussed the dogs and ate their sandwiches. Steph sneaked the dogs some of her sandwich when Amy wasn't looking. Once they'd finished, they made their way back to work. Amy looked really happy. Steph remembered thinking she'd hoped it had cheered her up a bit.

Steph got in her own car after work and drove to Belle's to see Hettie and Amelie. Hettie was so peaceful and lazy. She loved children and secretly, the thought of never having one of her own bothered her a bit. But she had plenty of nieces and nephews she could love and watch grow. Belle was really struggling now too, financially. Neither of Steph's niece's fathers had anything to do with the girls or paid anything towards them. Belle was a young woman with two children to feed and only had her benefits to survive on. Steph remembered wishing she could help her but she never had enough money to. Whenever she won she would try and help but that was a rarity. Steph's mum and nan helped Belle a lot though. They bought all the kids clothes, food for the little family and everything the kids needed. Steph and all of her sister's were lucky to have such a good mum.

Steph got home and she was glad it was Friday night. She'd got herself a couple of bottles of fruity cider, even though she didn't drink, some snacks and planned on watching Mean Girls on TV. She was going to enjoy just chilling on her own tonight as she knew Leanne was going out.

She was snuggled up on the sofa, snacks in hand about to put on one of her favourite films when her phone rang. It was mum. 'You ok mum?' she asked as she didn't usually ring her at this time. 'Yeah I'm fine Steph, I just wanted to make sure you're ok. We haven't spoken much for a few days and I miss you.'

There it was again. The guilt. It filled her body as she listened to the statement from her mum. 'Oh mum I'm so sorry. I've just been busy at work honestly. I'm absolutely fine mum I promise.' Within the call, Steph must have apologised 15 times. Her mum wasn't trying to make her feel bad but that's what Steph's mind told her was happening. It also told her she was a bitch. She was happy to take money from her mum when she needed it and go there when she was sad but she didn't bother when she was happy. What a selfish cow she was.

The feelings of happiness had gone now. She was filled with guilt and sadness once more, feeling sorry for mum and what she'd done to her. She went back to the sofa where she had planned to have a nice evening, enjoying the film which she didn't feel like doing now. She couldn't do anything but feel. Feel how she'd let her mum down. Feel the guilt take over her body. Feel the self-hatred. And hear. Hear the thoughts in her head telling her what a disgusting piece of shit she was. Hear them asking how she could do what she had done and how could she be so selfish. Hearing them tell her how her mum was sat alone in that flat, after Steph had taken all of her money and how sad her mum was. She just wanted the thoughts and the feelings to stop.

'Steph. No!' She actually said out loud. 'Do not do it Steph. Leanne did this for you to help you. She wont do it again. You promised her.' She continued to talk to herself out loud. 'Do not ruin this chance you have, please!'

She was arguing with her twin. Steph knew what these thoughts and feelings were leading up to. It was her twin. The ugly monster pushing and pushing her to do something she didn't want to do. She begged herself. She begged that the urge to gamble would leave her. 'Please, please, leave me alone.' The battle happening in Steph's body was a huge one. Her addiction was like a dark cloud in her head, slowly making its way across her brain as the real Steph, the kind Steph was the sunshine trying to keep the cloud at bay. The battle went on and on, inside Steph's brain. The dark cloud pushing as hard as it could as the rays of sunshine tried to intercept it in its path. She didn't know when, but her brain now was covered completely in a dark cloud. The sunshine had lost. It had been forced out of Steph's head completely and the dark cloud began to rain, flooding Steph's brain with thoughts of gambling.

Chapter 25

There was a knocking at the door that woke Steph up the next morning. She ran downstairs and opened the door. It was Amy and her two dogs. 'Shit!' said Steph as she opened the door. 'I'm so sorry, I completely forgot!' She'd forgotten completely about the dog walk she'd arranged with her. Another move she'd made when she was on a high. 'Come in, I'll be 5 minutes I'll just chuck some clothes on.' Steph left Amy and the dogs in the dining room, the dogs licking the red tiled floor as she ran up the stairs. She really didn't want to go. She was tired and just wanted to get some more sleep but she'd made a promise that she would be there for Amy, as she had been for her. She found some old jogging bottoms and a hoodie and threw them on, not even changing her underwear in an effort to be as quick as she could. She felt guilty that she'd forgotten about the walk. She chucked her hair into a bun and went back downstairs. 'I look an absolute mess but we're only walking aren't we.' She said to Amy.

'Yeah. I've only got my scruffs on, don't worry.' Amy replied.

The girls walked for miles and miles. The sun was blazing by the time they got back to Steph's house. Steph filled up one of Bo's old water bowls and let the panting pups have a drink. They both seemed to drink loads.

'Jesus! They we're thirsty!' said Amy. 'Do you fancy going for something to eat or a pint?' asked Amy. Steph really didn't want to. She wanted to be on her own but once more, the guilt of not going won. 'Yeah alright' replied Steph. 'I'm only going like this though, I'm not getting changed.'

The pair put the dogs in Amy's car and travelled to the pub down the road. They wanted to get the dogs out as quickly as they could as it was really hot. The pub they went to had a big beer garden with huge umbrellas and water bowls. The chose a table with the most shade and the dogs laid underneath the umbrella. They were both shattered after the walk so they were really well behaved and just fell straight to sleep. Amy brought over two pints. One of lager and one of Guinness for Steph. She didn't like larger and never drank anymore but Guinness she could stomach.

They talked for a while and drank their pints. They'd decided in the end just to order a bowl of chips. It was too hot to eat anything more than that. The pair talked about their recent heart breaks. Amy's partner hadn't cheated on her like Adrian had so it was a little different but still, the feeling of having someone there beside you for years and then suddenly being on your own is hard. Steph knew it was this loneliness pushing Amy into spending more time with her.

Amy dropped Steph back off home and thanked her for today. Steph waked through the door and ran, as quickly as she could straight upstairs. She peered around the door of Leanne's bedroom to make sure she wasn't home. She wasn't. She ran into her room, got herself sat up in the bed and went to the gambling site.

The credit bar read £1025.

Last night, when the cloud took over her brain, she deposited £500 onto a site she'd not used before. She'd turned this into £1525 after hitting a bonus. She withdrew £500 so her bank would be back at the position it was before she gambled, leaving her with £1025 to play with. She liked this new site. It had given her the bonus straight away.

She turned the volume up on her phone. It was rare she got to listen to the music with the games because she'd be playing in silence, listening for anyone around her so she could make sure he wasn't caught. But right now she was completely alone with £1025 to play with as she wished. A head full of dark, rainy cloud, there was nothing but gambling and winning on her mind.

As she was spinning, her mum started calling her. She hated it when this happened because it interrupted her play. She couldn't see the reels and couldn't get to the button to spin. She wouldn't answer though. She'd just watch it, telling it to hurry up and get off of her phone so she could carry on playing. All the feelings of guilt she'd had the night before didn't matter now. They didn't exist.

That's what the dark cloud did to her. It completely put the parts of her brain that were kind, loving and cared about her family and friends into complete shade. Imagine your brain is in sections. One for family. One for friends. One for work. One for concentration. And they are all plugged in to a plug socket. Usually, they're full of light, sparks flying everywhere lighting up your face. What happened when Steph gambled was the dark cloud would cover her brain and begin to rain. It would completely flood those sections so that the electricity didn't work anymore. They were dark, lifeless and no longer working.

She continued to spin. She didn't bother telling herself this time that she'd stop at £750 or £500. There was no point. She knew she wouldn't.

She stared at the screen. She must have been staring at it for at least a minute as she thought about what she would do next. It was like a tombola drum spinning around and around in her head. What thought would come out first? Would it be a thought to stop or continue. The drum turned and turned and turned. It started to slow and a piece of paper fell out. It unfolded itself and the thought that Steph had was...

'I can still afford to pay most of my stuff if I do another grand. Really, it's like I haven't even deposited anything anyway because I've withdrawn that £500 back.'

Another grand was deposited. She often thought, how the hell do they let me gamble this much?

She had, on more than one occasion, challenged some of the sites she had played on as to why they let her gamble so much. She thought she had a very good argument but she never won. They never gave her any of her money back.

And yet again, she lost her money. 'I can afford another £500 and I'll still be alright' she kidded herself.

She deposited the next £500. Her heart started racing again but it was ok. She'd got £500 due to go in account from the website so she was going to be ok. Steph had lost, once again, all concept of the value of money. When she had £4000 in her account, £500 was nothing. When she was gambling, she wouldn't even ever bother depositing less than £100 because £100 was absolutely nothing in the gambling world. She'd think £4.00 for a jar of coffee was ridiculously priced but £500 for a few spins of a gambling game was peanuts.

Steph went on to lose that £500 too. She could feel the rage taking over her body but she tried to calm it down 'It's ok, I still have money.'

She ran through the calculations in her head.

'I had £4000. Minus the £500 I deposited last night, minus the £1500 today. But then I have £500 coming back from that website. So I have £2500 left when that £500 goes in so I'll be fine even if I do one last £500. No more than that though. One more £500 is all I can afford.'

It took seconds for her to convince herself it was fine to deposit yet another £500. She played away that £500 exactly the same as the previous £1500, without a win. Although she was angry and upset, she wasn't in a state like she was the other night because she knew she had money in her account. She knew she could afford to eat, and live and didn't have to worry all month about how she was going to get through things.

She really did exit the website after that last £500. She walked downstairs to the back door to have her cigarette and as she did, she opened her banking app. She knew there would be £1500 in there, she'd run through the calculations a million times in her head and it would soon be back up to £2000 when that £500 hit her account. As the banking app showed her the available balance, she felt sick. 'No!' she said aloud, 'That's not right!'

Her available balance was £670. How!? She'd run through so many times. She looked at the transactions. And there it was. The £830. She'd completely forgotten that she had paid her insurance, finance and rent. She still had other stuff to pay! She's not brought any of her other loans up to date. 'It'll be ok, I'll get that £500 then I'll have £1170. It'll be ok.' Were the thoughts she pushed around her brain. There was one thought that dominated her brain though. The thought that one last £500 would probably do it. That one last £500 deposit would definitely trigger the bonus. She was sure it would.

She walked about frantically. She was hurting. She was trying her absolute hardest to stop this thought. To stop herself from reacting. She was in pain. And that's the other thing that people didn't understand. The actual agony a person felt when they were in the middle of an urge. The complete struggle they were going through. No-one ever saw the fact that she did try. She tried her hardest. She fought every single day of her life. She really did try not to let the gabling thoughts win.

She couldn't be alone right now. She needed to get out of the house. She knew how much danger she was in at this moment. She didn't want to lose everything. She'd lost enough already and she didn't want it to happen again. She didn't want to be left on her own with the twin.

She grabbed her car key and made her way to her mums shop. All the time she was driving, the twin screaming at her like something from a horror movie. She kept her eyes fixed on the road and just concentrated on getting to her mums. She didn't need to tell her mum what she was going through, what was happening at this moment but she could at least be with her. She couldn't gamble if she was with her mum.

As she pulled up outside of her mum's shop, she pulled down the sun visa on the car and made sure she looked ok. She had the unhappiest face ever. She really was struggling in this moment but she couldn't let anyone see that. She took a deep breath, slapped a smile on her face and walked into the shop. 'You ok mum?' asked Steph.

'Ahhh Steph!' Her mum walked over and gave her a hug. 'Are you ok? You don't look very well!'

'I'm fine mum I'm just tired.' Was Steph's generic response, as it was to everyone who'd ever told her she didn't look well.

Steph sat with her mum for the next couple of hours. She apologised for missing her call and made up a lie about leaving her phone upstairs whilst she was cleaning. The lies rolled off her tongue now but better that than the truth. Better that than letting her down again. She was safe when someone else was in the room. It meant she couldn't gamble.

An advert came on the TV her mum had in the back of the shop, about a gambling website. She hated it when that happened. It always felt really awkward, like an elephant in the room. They only ever advertise gambling as people having a great time with their friends. She'd never seen an advert where there was a young girl crying her eyes out because she couldn't afford to eat or Matt stood outside the bookies at ridiculous clock in a morning.

Steph felt calmer now. Her mum had worked her magic and made Steph feel safe once more. She gave her a cuddle, a kiss and promised she would come again soon. Steph sat in her car and took another deep breath. She took off her handbrake and set off home.

She'd been driving for 7 minutes before she found a side street where she parked up and put £300 on the website. Although she felt calm, the moment she left her mum and was on her own, her twin spawned itself again and continued to scream in her ear as it had done all the way there. Steph was actually crying before she gambled this time. There was no excitement, no hope of a win. The only reason she was doing this was because the urge was so strong, the thoughts in her head so loud and painful. It felt like someone had a gun to her head, making her do it, even though it was the last thing she wanted. She begged for herself to stop, to not do what she was about to do.

She didn't only do that £300, she went on to do another £300. She checked her bank, ready to see the next to nothing balance. But it wasn't! The £500 had actually gone in! This was the shortest time it had ever taken! But she wished it hadn't because she knew, she knew she was mid gambling session and she couldn't stop. She deposited that £500 too. Steph was absolutely distraught. She was hopeless. She was an absolute lost cause. Why should anybody try and help her? All she'd do is lie to them and gamble anyway. Her distraught now replaced with anger. Not at the game though. At herself. She could convince herself all she wanted she had an evil twin, that deep down she was a nice person but the truth was, she wasn't. She told herself now, she was a piece of work from the devil himself. She was a leech. She was vermin. The sooner she was dead, the better for everyone.

She drove her car home, all the way looking for a wall she could she smash into that would be fatal. She drove straight past her house. She pulled up outside of the shop at the end of her street. It was a really run down, old shop. The shelves were never stacked and the few bits they did have in there were always out of date. Steph only ever went into this shop for three things. Coco pops, Tobacco and scratch cards. She walked through the door and the little bell attached the hinge of the door rang. The counter was near the front of the shop which she immediately stood in front of. She said to the dark haired stranger on the other side '3 number 3's please and a bottle of vodka.' The kind man stood on the other side turned around and picked a small bottle of vodka up from the shelf. Steph could see the dust on the top so she knew it must have been sat on that shelf for god knows how many months but she didn't care. He pulled the long reel of cards from the plastic casing and tore off after the third had been pulled out. '£32.99 please' the man asked as he pushed the card machine towards her. Steph, card already in hand realised she'd have to actually put her pin in as it was over the £30 limit. 'Fucks sake' she whispered under her breath. She waited for the card machine to show approved on the screen. She knew she'd got £70.00 at this point. It took forever. Eventually, it showed the message approved and asked her to remove her card. She heard the machine begin to print a receipt but she wasn't waiting anymore. She took her scratch cards and vodka and walked back out of the door.

She climbed into her car and searched for something to scratch the paint on the cards with. She found a one pence piece stuck in gap between the seat and backrest of the passengers seat and scratched away. She laughed out loud after scratching. She started laughing hysterically. All three cards had lost. Three £5 scratch cards in a row and they were all losers. She opened her bottle of vodka and took a gulp. She screwed her face up at the disgusting, bitter taste now filling her mouth. She put the lid back on and moved her car down the road, onto her drive. Leanne's car wasn't here. Thank god.

Steph went upstairs and sat in her bed. She forced the bottle of vodka down her throat. She never drank anymore. It always made her so sick she just never did it but right now, she felt it was what she needed. She was more concerned about the germs that were entering her body from the dirty glass she was drinking directly from than the effects of the vodka but still continued to pour the disgusting substance into her mouth from the bottle.

'It's not even fucking doing anything' she thought, as she'd almost finished the bottle now. She picked up her phone and began to search for things in google. Her first search was 'how to kill yourself without any pain.' The number for Samaritans came up immediately. She scrolled past and read an article that had all of these ideas about how to do it. She closed it off because it scared her how intently she was thinking about actually going through with it. Killing herself wasn't an option now. Leanne was a guarantor on her loan. She couldn't leave her with his debt and ruin her life too.

She stood up for a cigarette and felt the effects of the vodka. The room started to spin. She began to laugh to herself again. Was she going crazy? Drunk now, and with a feeling of happiness running through her, she attempted to roll a cigarette. There was more tobacco on her bedroom floor than there was in the cigarette she'd managed to roll herself. She picked up her phone and tried to make out the time on the screen. Immediately, she was distracted by a message that had come through. She squinted as she wobbled on the bedroom windowsill trying to read the message. 'Amy – The dogs are absolutely shattered still!'

Steph smiled at the message and attempted to reply. 'Awwhhhhh, ad ther? I enguyed it tooo. I'n so deunk hahshsha' was the message she managed to type out and reply. She threw her phone across the room. 'Fuck off' she shouted to it. Slurring her words as she shouted 'You fucking lose me all my money. I shouldn't even have a phone. All the money I've spent on you. You piece of shit.'

She stood up at the window and began to wobble. She fell onto the bed. She snuggled up in the spot she had fallen and didn't move for the next 9 hours.

'Oh god' she thought as she woke, cheeks tingling as they do right before you're about to be sick. She ran out of her room to the toilet and threw up repeatedly as her head pounded. She felt awful. This was why she didn't drink. She walked back into her bedroom, picking her phone up from the floor as she did. She laid in bed and squinted again at her phone.

Amy – Hahaha, enjoy your night! Xxx

She felt far too sick right now to stomach a cigarette. She put her phone on charge and tried to go back to sleep. A few minutes later, her cheeks began to tingle again. She tried to ignore it but her body wasn't having it. She was up again to be sick. She flushed the toilet and crawled back into bed. She was absolutely freezing. That weird thing where your body feels hyper thermic after you've been sick. This pattern repeated itself another 4 times.

Leanne popped her head around the door. 'Hahahaha you fucking lightweight! Are you ok?' she asked. 'Did you drink with Amy?'

'Yeah' Steph lied. She didn't want to Leanne to know she'd drank alone. She would know something was wrong.

'Haha you melt' said Leanne as she left Steph's bedroom.

Steph started to get that hungry feeling. This let her know that she was starting to recover from the hangover she'd given herself. She went downstairs and made herself a bowl of coco pops. She took it back to bed and sat there, looking at her phone.

'Haha sorry mate, I was a rate mess x' she replied to Amy.

Steph went onto her banking app. £37.01. She suddenly felt sick again. She'd got her food to buy for the month, her fuel for her car, her phone bill. How was she going to do it? She didn't know. But right now, she needed a cigarette. She got up and went downstairs. Clutching onto herself trying to keep warm as she shivered. Leanne came in from the front room.

'Fucking hell Steph, you're right skinny!' she said as she looked Steph up and down.

Steph's immediate response, that she'd developed in her days of anorexia was 'No I'm not!'.

Leanne looked Steph up and down and gave her a concerned look then carried on up to her room.

Steph hadn't even thought about her weight. She didn't struggle with the mental side of eating now. She just simply couldn't afford to. She grabbed the weighing scales that, for some strange reason, the girls kept on top of the fridge. She stepped onto the grey plastic, which was somewhat warmer than the red tiled floor and the scales read 8st 6lb. This was the lowest she'd weighed in a long time but she was happy about it. Gambling did have some benefits!

She stepped off of the scales and put them back on top of the fridge. She made her way upstairs and cuddled up in the duvet for the warmth. She thought about what the hell she would do this month and it was the same answer as every month. She'd eat nothing. She'd walk when her car was out of fuel. She'd put off her debts for yet another month and she'd lie her way through, pretending everything was ok.

Chapter 26

She'd rejected every suggestion Betty and Amy made to her this month about going out or making plans. She thought up and excuse for everything. 'Sorry, I'm babysitting' or 'I'd promised my mum I'd take her somewhere.' She knew that Betty had had enough of asking her to do anything now because she constantly rejected her. Amy though, was different. Even though she rejected every offer to go out, Amy offered to do other things with her. Walking, watching a film, taking the dogs out and Steph appreciated it. Life was boring and mundane when you had no money and were just counting down every month to the next payday. Steph was so grateful that she had someone else in her life who was as lonely as she was. Steph hid it much better than Amy did, but she was very lonely. Amy and Steph became the best of friends. They spoke every day now and Steph even opened up to her about how hard things were financially, never telling her though, how bad things actually were or the root cause. Amy said things were the same for her since she was living on her own. She had to be careful with money too and so she was glad when Steph rejected Betty's ideas about going out, because she couldn't really afford it either. That's why she always suggested doing things that didn't cost any money.

The pair really did like Betty though. She was a good friend and they felt bad for not doing things with her. Amy and Steph made an agreement that this payday, they would go on a night out with Betty. Payday was on a Friday this month. Steph had known this since last payday. She always knew exactly when payday was. The date was burned in her brain. Betty was pleased that they'd agreed this payday would be a 'girlie' night out. There was nothing girly about Steph and Amy. Amy only ever wore joggers and a T-shirt and Steph wore the same clothes she had for the last 5 years because she could never afford to buy any more.

Betty though was beautiful. She was insanely tall and had hair down to her bum. It was ginger but not like that horrible bright ginger, it was like an auburn colour. She was slim and loved make up and clothes. She always looked like a model no matter what she was doing.

The days rolled by much slower than the reels of Steph's slots. She wished her life would whizz by as fast as they did. As fast as they drained her bank account. There were 8 days left until payday now. Steph ran out of fuel a few days ago, after doing her usual trick with her bank card at the petrol pump and so, she told everyone that her car was broken and she was getting the bus to work. The truth being, she was setting off at 6.45am to walk to work, because she couldn't afford a bus ticket. She had managed though, to get a lift home off of Amy most days. She was so thankful. It was completely the opposite way so she knew it was putting

Amy out doing it. Steph had booked the next 7 days as holiday so that she wouldn't have to walk anymore but she would be in work on payday. She made sure of it to reduce the risk of her gambling. She was shattered and her weight down to 8 stone now. If she lost anymore, she was under threat of being asked about her anorexia.

Amy and Steph got in Amy's car after work. 'Do you fancy coming to see the dogs for a bit? I could do us some tea?' asked Amy. Steph looked at her and smiled. 'Yeah, go on then' she replied.

Steph kept looking Amy as she was driving. This woman was so kind. She'd helped Steph even when she'd been an absolute bitch. She made sure every day she was ok. She made sure she got home safe and never once, had asked for a single thing from her. She remembered admiring a person who could have such a kind heart. Not like her. She didn't have a heart. She just had a slot machine where her heart should be. Amy must have felt Steph's eyes staring at her. She turned to Steph and asked if she was ok. Steph smiled once more and assured her she was.

They reached Amy's house and the dogs were going mad. Jumping up at Steph and making a huge fuss. Amy asked Steph if she liked Spaghetti Bolognese and she assured her she did. Steph sat in the living room, playing with the dogs whilst Amy cooked. She'd missed this. She used to play with Bo all the time.

'It's ready' said Amy.

Steph dropped the rope she was playing tug of war with and made her way to the table in the kitchen. It was a small kitchen but it was still bigger than hers! The table was next to the French doors that led onto the good sized back garden.

'I love your house' said Steph. 'It's so nice.'

'Thanks' replied Amy.

They tucked into their spaghetti Bolognese. It was amazing! Steph hadn't had a big meal for while so she was really enjoying it. 'Do you want a drink?' asked Amy.

'Just water please' replied Steph as the usual guilt she had told her he shouldn't be so rude as to having anything other. Steph's guilt continued as she ate more. She hadn't eaten much and it looked like nothing but she was so full. She felt too guilty to tell Amy she was full so she carried on eating. After a few more mouthfuls, she had to accept defeat. 'I am so sorry Amy I'm just absolutely stuffed.'

'it's fine! Did you enjoy it?' Asked Amy. 'Absolutely amazing' replied Steph. 'Thank you so much.'

Steph went back and sat on the sofa with the dogs, they'd calmed down now. She was in pain with her stomach from the amount of food she'd eaten. Amy came into the room and sat at the other end of the sofa. It was one of them L shaped sofa's. It was grey and she had orange cushions on it. It was relatively new and really comfortable. 'I could just go to sleep!' said Steph, as she nursed her over full belly.

'Just let me know when you want me to take you home and we'll go. Or you can stay and watch a film if you want?' Steph, who couldn't bare the thought of moving at this moment in time, told Amy to put a film on. 'Have you ever seen white house down?' asked Amy. Steph told her she hadn't. Amy picked up the TV remote for the huge curved TV she had on the opposite wall to the sofa. How much money did Amy actually have? Steph had her old TV and she'd got this huge one!

The film wasn't really Steph's thing. It was an action film with guns and fighting. She did like watching Channing Tatum though. He was fit. After another 10 minutes or so, Steph could feel her eyes closing. She fought and fought, keep changing positions she was sat in in the hope it would wake her up a little. Amy's living room was really warm. It was lovely. It was dark now and the sofa was so comfy.

'Steph. Steph. Steph, do you want me to take you home?'

Amy was lightly shaking Steph's shoulder and whispering. 'Oh my god' Steph thought 'How fucking embarrassing'

She'd fallen asleep on the sofa. Amy had invited her round so she had company and she'd fallen asleep. 'I am so sorry' said Steph to Amy. 'Don't be silly, you're tired! You can stay here if you want you know.'

The thought worried Steph. She didn't like being away from home at night. 'No, I'll go home if that's ok. Thank you so much though and I'm sorry again.'

Amy told Steph to stop worrying. She had nothing to be sorry for. They got in Amy's car and drove to Steph's house. Steph was freezing in the car. That cold you feel when you're extremely tired. She was sat shivering and turned the heater up.

They reached Steph's drive and Steph thanked Amy again. She jumped out of the car and ran into the house as quick as she could into the warm. Leanne was sat on the sofa with the duvet. Steph took off her coat and threw it on the dining room table. She walked into the living room, picked up the duvet and snuggled into Leanne. She was home. Home with her best friend.

The next week went by as slowly as the rest of the month had. Even worse actually, because she wasn't at work. She had no money to gamble to pass the time and no money to be able to go anywhere.

The one thing about not having any money was that she had peace from gambling urges. She didn't have any money and no way of getting any so there really wasn't any point in thinking about it. If she couldn't gamble, she was free from the gambling thoughts.

Steph did love to draw. She'd sold a few pieces and was really happy when people were happy with what she'd drawn them. She was really quite good too. It was something else that silenced her everyday thoughts. Just concentrating on what she was drawing. She did a lot over that week. She didn't sell any though.

She spoke to her mum every day. Her mum had no idea how bad things were. Steph knew that she probably had her suspicions, but her mum didn't know how bad things had gotten. The fact that Steph now couldn't afford to eat again. Steph knew she could always go to her mum. No matter how bad things got, she knew her mum would be there for her but Steph's guilt once more, stopped her from going to her. 'Don't you think she's had a hard enough life without you fucking making it worse.' Were the kind of thoughts that stopped Steph approaching her mum for help.

But she had made it through the month. It was the night before payday and she'd not had to tell anyone about what she'd done the month before. She was scared though. She needed to be strong. She needed to not do the same this month as she had for all the previous months. How she had even got through all these years she had no idea, but she knew it needed to stop. She wouldn't last much more. She went to bed that night and prayed that she would have strength tomorrow. That she would be able to fight the twin that she knew would be waking her up at around 3am, screaming in her ear. She put her phone on charge, and laid her head on her pillow. 'Please lord' were the last words she spoke before going to sleep.

Chapter 27

Steph was woken by her alarm clock. She hadn't woken up at 3am! She could not believe it. What the hell had happened? Her twin had let her rest. It had forgotten that today was payday. She had no idea how this had happened but she was absolutely ecstatic. Was this the start of a change? Was this a sign that her twin was dying? And she didn't even have time to gamble! She needed to get to the petrol station to fill her car so she could finally drive again! She got ready with the biggest, realest smile on her face ever. She put on some makeup she'd stolen from Leanne, jumped into her car and made her way into the petrol station. She filled the car until it did those 3 clicks that lets you know it can't accept anymore.

She drove to the work with the music loud. She had Celine Dion blasting out. She loved Celine. It reminded her of when she was younger and her mum would hoover up to Dolly Parton and Celine. They were happy times. Before she ever knew about gambling, money or had self hating thoughts.

She got out of the car and walked into the office in the best mood. Her boss had commented 'Can't you tell it's payday!' due to the smile on her face.

Steph didn't like her boss much truth be told. She'd only started a few weeks ago and she could tell she didn't like Steph much. She'd always question what she was doing and why she was doing it. She'd make her take her coat off even though she didn't want to. Her old boss didn't make her take it off. Her old boss was Coral and she absolutely loved her. She was always really nervous around her though. Steph loved intelligent people. She wished she'd done better in school. Coral seemed to know everything. She was so knowledgeable and funny. There were a few times that Coral had to work away and Steph went with her. Steph always ended up ridiculously drunk and making an absolute fool of herself which she was completely embarrassed about but Coral seemed easy to talk to and she always made sense. Steph wished she could be more like her. Steph's new boss was called Sam but everyone called her LC. She didn't really know why and she thought it was weird but never questioned it.

Steph sat in her usual spot and whistled in her good mood. 'Can you stop whistling!' said LC. For gods sake, she couldn't even whistle now!

The next person to walk through the office doors was Betty. 'You ready for tonight!' shouted Betty to Steph. 'Cannot wait mate.' replied Steph. She didn't really want to go but Steph and Amy had promised her they would.

Steph logged on and looked at the 634 emails that were in her inbox. She was a team leader now. Through all Steph's faults, work was always a constant for her. She tried her best to keep her job. There were a few times she'd called in sick because of gambling but not many. Even when she had to walk to work, she made sure she went. Her job was hugely important to her. She knew every month, it was her only life line. It was the only way she could pay the guarantor loan too now.

'Shit' thought Steph. The guarantor loan. She'd set it up so that the payment would go out of her account of payday, so there was no chance she could gamble it. She went into the toilet cubicle and checked her online banking. It had gone out. She was so relived she'd not let her best friend down. She messaged her, face beaming with pride. 'It's paid Leanne. I love you so much xxx' was the message she wrote. She went back to banking app to see what else had left her account. All of her direct debits were set up the for the 1st. She knew she needed to change it because being paid on the 28th always gave her a couple of days to gamble everything and leave the direct debits unpaid and all Steph needed was a couple of hours to lose all of her wages.

She looked again at the available balance. £1350. She stared at that balance. She knew this pause. She knew it was the tombola drum going around in her head. 'No!' she thought. She locked her phone and put it in her pocket and walked out of the office back into her seat.

'Ahem. Coat!' said LC. 'For gods sake' thought Steph as she removed her jacket.

Fancy coming to mine for dinner? Was the message that popped up on her screen. It was from Amy.

I can't today mate. I'm going to have to work through. I've got so many emails it's a joke.

Steph started to make her way through her emails. To tell the truth, she didn't action any of them. Since she'd become team leader, she'd become lazy. It wasn't through the promotion, it was through gambling. Gambling made her lose interest in everything she loved and not being on the phones anymore gave her more freedom to walk off when she needed to and procrastinate even more than she usually did. She looked at the clock. 10 past 10. Steph got up and went for a cigarette. She knew full well it wasn't her break time but she never cared. She just went anyway. She came back in and saw LC giving her a look to let her know she knew she'd been on break too early. She quickly sat back down and removed her coat once more. Steph couldn't concentrate today. She was too excited about being paid and not having gambled it all! She pretended to work until it was time for lunch. She had planned on working through but she couldn't. She couldn't stare at that screen anymore. She got up and went out for a cigarette. She scrolled through Facebook as she was stood in the smoking shelter. She didn't pay any attention to anything she saw, she just mindlessly scrolled. She saw someone else walking towards her so she stubbed her cigarette out and went back inside. She hated being in the smoking shelter the same time as some she didn't really know. Having to make awkward conversation like, 'what are you doing at the weekend' when really, she couldn't care less what they were doing.

She walked back inside and went to the toilet. She didn't need the toilet it was just the only place she could ever sit without someone trying to talk to her. She opened her banking app once more and saw again the available balance. 'I can afford to just do £200' she thought. And just like that, a gambling thought had creeped in. She was on a complete high, but it still found its way through.

She chose a new website this time. One she'd not been on before. She'd lost so much on the last one she thought she might have a better chance on a new one. She deposited the money and selected no to any bonuses being applied. She knew this meant they'd give her a fiver and make her spend £1000 before she could withdraw anything. It was disgusting really. Sat on that toilet, still feeling really proud of herself, she gambled away £200. She checked the time on her phone. She'd got 14 minutes left on her lunch break by the time the credit reached £0.

Another £200 was deposited and lost on the site. 'It's ok, I still have money.' The same thought that had driven her to lose way more than she could afford last month, had creeped back into her head. She was 10 minutes late off of her lunch when she walked back into the office. 'Sorry LC.' She said. 'I was on the phone to the doctors.' LC gave her another look she didn't like as she sat down.

'Why doesn't she like me?' she wondered to herself. Never thinking that maybe the fact she missed every deadline, didn't do any work, was late all the time and had 15 cigarette breaks may actually be the reason LC had performance concerns. In Steph's mind, LC just didn't like her.

Steph messaged Betty and Amy all that afternoon and continued to avoid work. At 2.30pm, it was time for another cigarette. Once more, she put on her coat and made her way outside. As she walked to the smoking shelter, she deposited another £200 on the game. She'd often do this. She'd position herself perfectly in the smoking shelter so that, no matter what angle someone joined her in there, they could never see her phone or what she was doing. Her cigarette had completely burned out by this point and she was 4 minutes late but she still had £120 credit. She threw her cigarette end to the floor and walked back towards the office, spinning the reels as she walked. At the very last second, before opening the door to the office, she put her phone back in her pocket. As she sat back down at the desk. The screaming in her head was unbearable. She had credit on a game. She was completely unable to ignore it. It wouldn't let her. It was calling her so loudly it was all she could hear. 8 minutes passed before she walked over to LC. 'I'm really sorry, I know I've just been on break but is it ok if I nip out. I've just missed a call from the doctors. They said this morning they would call me back and I've missed it. Can I go and ring them please?'

'Yes go on.' Said LC.

Steph made her way once more to the ladies toilet. She locked herself in and sat on the toilet seat. Completely enclosed once again and in silence, she resumed her game. It had disconnected from being inactive. She hated it when this happened and she had a theory that every session of a game had to pay out at some point and if you left it, you had to start the process all over again. She'd got £80.00 left now. 'Fuck it' she thought. And went straight to a £20 stake.

4 spins later, her balance was empty. The feeling of pride she'd had all day, the feeling that she'd made a step forward had gone. All that mattered now was she got her money back. She deposited another £200 as she chased her losses, losing that £200 too.

She wanted to cry now. She was back to place where she was silently screaming and punching. Then she heard the toilet door open. She quickly flushed the toilet and washed her hands. She walked out and went back to her desk. LC walked over. Steph really wasn't in any kind of mood to have her speaking to her right now. 'Is everything ok Steph?' asked LC. 'Yeah it's fine thank you. They've just prescribed me some tablets.' She'd lost count of how many lies she'd told today so far. LC walked back to her desk.

Steph brought up the calculator on her computer screen.

1350 – 200 – 200 – 200 – 200 =

550

£550 was all she had left. She went back to the calculator.

550 – 300 – 30 – 450 =

Her heart sunk. She didn't have enough for her any of her car bills. She had to pay her rent which was £300 and her phone bill which was £30 and she had to pay for tonight. She couldn't let them down. Steph held back the tears as best she could. Both fists clenched as she sat at her desk. She thought she'd done it this time. She really thought she'd beaten it.

Chapter 28

She went home that evening, filled with anger and upset as she was every single payday. Why did she even expect anything different? It was always the same. She had a bowl of coco pops and began to get ready for the night out that she really didn't want to go on. She put one of the dresses on she'd had for years. It hung off her now. She was so thin. 'You look fucking disgusting' she told herself as she looked in the mirror. She put her phone and her bank card in her purse and told Leanne she was ready. Leanne was dropping her off in town. They always did it for each other and more often than not, Steph would pick Leanne up too. Steph once again, painted a smile on her face as she stepped out of the car and met Betty and Amy outside one of the pubs in town.

The town they lived in was a small one. There was a strip filled with bars and clubs but it was usually filled with underage drinkers and drug dealers. Steph couldn't feel less attractive. In a bright orange dress, which was clearly too big for her ,and a pair of black heels she couldn't walk in properly.

Steph had been with Adrian for quite a long time and since him, she never looked at anyone else. She didn't have time to look for a partner or even want one at this moment in time. She was so hurt by what Adrian had done that she knew she would never trust anyone again with her secret. Steph also really struggled with sex. She never enjoyed it and thought it a chore. She never got that uncontrollable urge to rip someone's clothes off. She would much rather go to bed and go to sleep. It's also hard to find yourself attractive or feel sexy when you tell yourself a thousand times a day you're a piece of shit that doesn't deserve anyone.

Betty and Amy complemented her on the way she looked. 'I know they're lying' she thought to herself. Betty couldn't believe she was in a dress. 'Well Miss Goodyear! Who knew you owned a dress!'

The three walked into the pub and Amy whispered in Steph's ear 'I want to go home.' Steph laughed. For the first time since she'd gambled today she laughed. The three got to the bar and ordered drinks. Steph ordered 3 shots with hers. She needed something to drown today out. 'You're on it!' said Betty.

The three found a table and chatted and drank. It was the pub that Steph used to come to with Naomi when they were friends. After a few more drinks and shots, Steph found herself actually enjoying it. The music was loud enough now to drown out any bad thoughts in her head. The drinks kept flowing and they moved from bar to bar. The pubs in town were all dirty. Your shoes would stick to the floor as you tried to walk. It was gross. They went into one club that had a basement. The girls made their way down the stairs. Steph was sure she was going to fly head first down the whole lot because she couldn't walk in her heels. She made it to the bottom without falling and it opened up into a huge room. A portion of it was a dance floor, the bar was to the left and the toilets to the right. That's when Steph noticed it. A bandit. A one armed bandit in a night club with an old bloke stood at it. Steph wasn't really a dancer and neither was Amy. Betty loved to dance though. Betty went off to dance with an old guy. There was nothing in it, they were just having fun. Steph and Amy sat on a tall bar stool. Steph positioned it so she had full sight of the bandit and how much the guy was putting in. He was stood there for ages. He must have put £30 in pound coins in and it hadn't dropped yet.

Amy noticed Steph looking at the guy on the machine. 'Can you believe they would put a bandit in here. Getting old guys like him, drunk. Of course he's going to put all of his money in' Amy said.

'I know' replied Steph. 'Disgusting isn't it.'

Betty came over once she'd finished dancing. 'Fag?' she asked Steph. They made their way out to the smoking shelter.

'I think I'm going to get off guys but thank you. I really have enjoyed it.'

'Oh you're not are you?' said Steph, secretly glad she could go home now.

'Yeah I'm way too drunk. I need to go home.'

Amy and Steph helped Betty up the stairs, she was wobbling now and much more drunk than they were. Steph wasn't actually drunk at all. She was disappointed considering how much she'd drunk. The girls put Betty in a taxi and waved her off.

'Do you fancy one more somewhere?' Asked Amy.

Steph really didn't but it was obvious Amy didn't want to go home yet so she agreed to another. They went into one of the quieter bars. Steph knew it had a huge sheltered smoking area so Amy got the drinks and she went to find a space. It was pretty much empty. She got a table that had an electric heater overhead and put it on straight away. Amy came walking through with the drink. 'I got you a double' she said smiling. Steph was already dreading how sick she was going to be the next day.

'Betty was battered wasn't she! ' said Amy.

'Yeah I don't know how, I don't even feel drunk'

The girls talked for a while and Steph did start to feel a little tipsy and it made her want more. She went to the bar and got the pair another drink. It was comfortable where they were. It was warm with the heater and they could hear each other speak.

'Thank you for everything you've done for me Amy. You know I've had a lot of shit recently but so have you. You've been so kind honestly. I'm glad we're friends.'

'It's ok. I want to be there for you. I know how hard it is and you've helped me through it too. Hopefully things will start getting better soon' replied Amy.

Steph found herself looking at Amy again. The kindest person with such a good heart. If only she knew what Steph had done. If she did know, she probably wouldn't want anything to do with her. No one needs an addict as a friend.

'One more?' asked Amy

'Steph drank the last little bit that was in her cup and passed it to her. 'Yeah but then I'm going' said Steph. She watched Amy as she walked away to get the drinks. She got out her phone and as she waited for Amy to come back, she messaged Betty. 'Hope you got home ok mate. Thank you for tonight x' She put the phone back in her purse and Amy came over with the drinks.

Amy had a checked shirt on, some black skinny jeans and a pair of brogues. Steph wished she felt comfortable enough to dress like that on a night out. She much preferred being comfy than suffering in high heels.

'Listen' said Amy as she put the drinks on the table. 'I know things have been tight with Adrian leaving and you definitely could do with some fun so I booked us all in at bowling this Sunday. It's on me so don't worry, but me you and Betty can go and just chill out for a bit.'

Steph was overwhelmed with her act of kindness. She knew that Steph loved bowling.

'You literally are the nicest person in the world Amy. Thank you so much.'

Steph was filled with gratitude and admiration for the kindness of her friend.

'It's only bowling ' said Amy.

At that moment, Steph kissed Amy. She didn't know what had come over her but she knew she wanted to. She knew that this woman had one of the kindest hearts in the world and that was something that attracted Steph. She hadn't had this feeling before. She didn't know what she was feeling but Steph loved being around Amy. She made her feel safe.

Steph had never been with a woman before but she was never against it. Steph had thought for years she was an A sexual. She was never particularly attracted to people. She would think they we're fit and nice to look at but, she never felt any sexual attraction to them. She was just attracted to kind people and even then, not in a sexual way. She was attracted to them in a way which meant she wanted to be near them. She wanted to spend time with them because they made her feel good. And this is exactly what she felt for Amy.

Her heart was racing as she kissed her. But after a moment or too, she realised that Amy was kissing her back. After a few more seconds, the girls looked at each other. They smiled and continued with their drinks. It wasn't awkward in anyway. Steph knew now. Steph knew she liked Amy.

Chapter 29

Steph was sick 5 times the next morning. She felt absolutely awful. Not only had she not had chance to think properly about what she'd gambled away, and how she was going to manage over the next month, she hadn't had chance to think about what happened with Amy. As she had her first cigarette on the day and crawled back into bed, she thought about whether what she'd done was a mistake. But she really did like Amy. When she thought about feeling happy, it was always when she was with Amy. She sent her a message to make sure there was no awkwardness between them.

God I'm rough. Are you ok? Xxxx – The message wrote.

As she was on her phone, she clicked onto her banking app. Her stomach churned as the little blue when span as it loaded. It told her she had £430 in her account. As she was in the app, she transferred the £300 for the rent into Leanne's account. 'As long as the bills are paid.' She told herself once again. She didn't care about herself, not in the slightest. She didn't care if she'd have to walk miles or eat nothing again another month. She didn't deserve to eat.

A message came through, interrupting her thoughts about how much of an evil bitch she was.

Yeah I'm fine. I really enjoyed last night Steph. Xxxx – read the reply.

Steph smiled at the message. It let her know last night hadn't ruined their friendship and that Amy probably felt the same way as she did.

Steph's thoughts quickly went back to money. She went downstairs, made herself a coffee and took it back up to bed with her. She opened up her email. Wow. There were so many from last month that she'd ignored. 'Late payment. 'Default notice' 'Final reminder' She chose to continue to ignore them and not open a single one.

She emailed her car insurance and finance company once more. 'I'm really sorry but I am unable to make payment this month. I am a gambling addict and I've relapsed. Please could I make two payments next month?'

At work, she wrote much better emails than this but she didn't care here. She'd asked the question and let them know of her situation. That was good enough. She was still so angry at herself for what she'd done. She did wish she had someone to talk to about it but she couldn't. The embarrassment and shame of it was too much for her to share.

Steph and Amy quickly entered that awkward relationship stage. Where you're seeing each other but it isn't official and they never spoke to each other about it. They had to be very careful though as they worked together and they didn't want the drama that followed with an office romance, especially as nobody, including Steph herself, knew that she liked girls.

Amy was there for Steph every single day. She would buy her lunch, she'd give her lifts, she'd text her just to make sure she was ok. Still, Amy had no idea about Steph's secret. She knew there was something that Steph was hiding and she found it intriguing. What was this pretty, young girl hiding? What had happened so badly in her life that she needed to hide who she really was? Steph's mood's were so up and down. One day she'd be on an absolute high, texting all day, making people laugh and the next she'd be as low as low could be. She wouldn't speak to anyone, she'd walk around the office with her head down and her hood up, as though she was trying to make herself invisible. Amy often wondered if maybe Steph suffered with Bipolar or something similar. But Amy found herself falling for Steph very quickly. Steph didn't make it easy though. She'd pull Amy in close, spending nights with her and kissing her and then, all of a sudden, it would be like a wall went up. She'd barely speak to Amy and she'd tell her that this was too hard and she wasn't sure if it was the right thing to do. Amy persevered. She knew that, below whatever was bothering Steph, below whatever made her act so strangely and try to shut out the world, there was something worth fighting for.

Steph knew that she liked Amy. She really did but it was too hard. It was too hard to deal with the consequences of her gambling and maintain a relationship where Amy wouldn't get hurt. On the days that Steph couldn't eat, the days when the voices were so loud in her head she sat on the floor and cried begging for some reprieve, she just didn't have the strength to even talk to Amy, never mind show any kind of affection. She wished that Amy would give up on her, would just let her rot in the pit of depression that she was trapped in, but she wouldn't. Even on the days where Steph had been a complete bitch, Amy would still give nice responses. She'd still ask if she was ok. She would still turn up at the door telling her she didn't care what Steph said, she was going out for some fresh air with her. Steph knew though, that Amy would definitely leave if she told her the truth.

The next few months passed and nothing changed. Nothing at all. Steph would gamble everything away on payday, just managing to pay her rent and the loan that Leanne was the guarantor on but they were the only things she paid. She'd actually managed to convince Leanne to top up the loan twice more, gambling it all every time. Steph's debt was so bad now she didn't even a clue how much she owed. She'd got 9 payday loans active at the moment, all without a payment made towards them for at least 4 months. She'd been driving her car, when she could afford to put any fuel at all in it, uninsured. Her finance company had actually been very good with her. They'd agreed reduced payments but she didn't even pay them. She knew that, soon enough, her car would be taken too.

Nothing changed between Steph and Amy either. Steph would push Amy away and Amy would still push her way through every barrier. Amy loved those nights where Steph would let her in. Where she stopped with the clearly fake smile. Where she would cuddle into Amy and kiss her and they'd just sit and watch TV. The nights where Steph was Steph, and not this hard faced, tough bitch she tried to portray herself to be.

Amy wasn't the only person that Steph pushed away. She did it to everyone. She didn't even speak to her mum that much anymore. She'd see Belle occasionally and the kids but that was it. She made a conscious effort to avoid every person in her life. Walking around with a smile, Steph believed she'd hit rock bottom. There was no escape and suicide wasn't an option anymore because she couldn't leave Leanne with that sort of debt. Steph was no longer Steph. The conjoined twin had consumed her and Steph had disappeared completely.

Payday came around once more and this time, she hadn't even saved her rent money. The direct debit for her loan had gone out but she didn't have enough money to keep the roof over the heads of her and her best friend. The usual feelings of worry, panic and fear took over Steph. She sat on the edge of the bed and began to type.

'Bab, Is there anyway you could lend me £300? I've fallen behind on a few payments and I need to get it sorted. £300 will mean I can clear them. It's ok if not don't worry, I do understand you've got bigger bills too.'

This was the first time she'd asked Amy for money. She'd treat so her badly but she knew that Amy wanted to help her. She knew Amy had fallen for Steph and she knew, as much as she loved her, she'd be able to manipulate and lie her way to the cash she needed.

Amy read the message but for a while didn't respond. Steph was upset at the thought of losing Amy through this but to be perfectly honest, she was in a place of such desperation and depression, she thought losing Amy was inevitable anyway and had already accepted it. 'Sooner rather than later' she thought to herself.

'Of course beautiful. Why didn't you tell me you were in trouble? I'll always help you when I can. I've transferred it you.'

The guilt filled Steph immediately. How was she doing this? How was she deceiving this woman who had been so good to her?

'Thank you so much Amy. I promise I'll get it sorted xxx'

She had her rent money now. The thought of keeping Leanne and everyone in the dark about how bad things were wasn't enough to stop her this month. She immediately got herself comfortable in bed, and deposited the full £300 on the website. 'I'm going to be clever about it. I'll start only on a £5 spin and make it last longer so I have more of a chance.' She knew as she thought it, how ridiculous it was. She replied to herself with the thought 'You fucking dickhead. You know full well that you're going to lose it all.'

She began rolling. She started on a £10 stake, immediately ignoring what she'd just told herself. On her first spin, one bonus symbol, a second. 'Not a chance' she thought. 'I'll eat my own arm if it lands on the bonus now.' The reel kept spinning and spinning. She didn't even blink as she stared at the screen. 'Fuck off!' she shouted. It had landed on another bonus symbol. A £10.00 per spin bonus. She was the luckiest girl in the world! 'Please don't let me down like you did last time. I beg you, please.'

The screen loaded with those 12 spins. Those 12 beautiful spins that had the power to change her life. The first two spins rolled past with no win. The third, fourth, fifth and sixth spins were all winners. Half way through her bonus round and she was already up to £4,500. Her heart felt like it had stopped completely. The second half of her bonus round continued.

She screamed. She jumped around her bedroom. She'd done it. All these years of trying and she'd finally done it. She'd won enough money to turn her life around completely. £50,000. She'd hit the jackpot she had chased for so many years. She knew it was possible. She knew it was. She knew she'd spent probably 5X this amount over the years, probably more actually. But here it was. All that heartache. All that trying for so long, all the years of misery had led to this.

After her outburst of excitement, happiness and disbelief. She sent a screenshot to her mum. 'MUM I'VE DONE IT. I'VE DONE IT. I'VE WON £50,000. IT'S ALL OVER MUM.' She followed it with a screenshot of the credit bar. She'd learnt after so many times of sharing her news, and then losing every penny of it, not to tell anyone when she'd won but this time was different. There was absolutely no way she was going to lose all of this. She'd worked for this for too many years. She decided in that moment not to tell anyone until the money was in her account. She went into the website and withdrew £50,000. She screamed again in complete and utter euphoria. She decided immediately to call the company she had won the money from.

She couldn't keep still as she called and heard the hold music. She kept letting out a scream. A scream of relief, a scream of excitement, a scream of, for the first time in as long as she could remember, pure happiness. She got through and didn't even wait for the woman to say hello. 'I've won £50,000!' she screamed at the woman down the phone. The woman laughed and asked her for her username and said she would check the account.

Steph knew all to well how difficult it was actually getting your money from a gambling website. They would take your money without asking you a single question but when it came to withdrawing it, they all of a sudden cared about verifying how old you were, wanting your bank statements, your wage slips. Even when they got them, and could see you'd gambled every single penny you earned, they didn't stop you from doing it again. And the verification process took ages. It could take over a week for them to even look at your documents and when you're relying on that money to be able to buy yourself something to eat, a week seemed like a year.

'Wow Miss Goodyear! Congratulations! I have worked here for 16 years, and I have never seen anyone win this amount of money.'

This took Steph back a bit. She was clearly very lucky. 16 years and no one had done it before? It just goes to show how rarely you can win big. But Steph had!

'So can I withdraw it?' asked Steph impatiently and still full of excitement.

'You're only actually allowed to withdraw £30,000 maximum a month.'

'What? You'll let me deposit all that but will only let me draw it out bit by bit? How is that fair!' she shouted angrily at the woman down the phone.

'I understand Steph and I apologise but I'm afraid it's policy. Would you like me to process the £30,000 for you? And then in 30 days time, you can withdraw the remaining £20,000'

Still angry that they wouldn't let her have the full amount, but also overjoyed at the £30,000 she could withdraw, Steph agreed. She hung up the phone and danced around her bedroom once more. She couldn't believe it. All of her problems were solved now.

Chapter 30

It took between 3 – 5 working days for the withdrawal from the site be processed. Over the next 24 hours, she must have checked her banking app 200 times. Constantly checking if it had gone in yet.

She decided not to tell Amy or Leanne yet about the money, not until it was safe in her account. She did ring her mum over and over again though. She needed to share her good news with someone! She told her mum what she was going to do with the money. She was going to pay all of the finance off her car. She would actually own it! Steph didn't own much at all. Anything she ever had in her life had ended up being sold or pawned.

Steph was a regular at the pawn shop. She'd sold every possession she had. She liked this shop though because they would give you money for your item and give you 28 days to buy it back. Obviously at a price much higher than they'd originally given you cash for. So many times, she sold her phone, gambled the money and actually won and went back to buy her phone. Then returning a couple of days later to sell it again. She would open a catalogue, in the days before her credit score was lower than Basset's Belly, and order a laptop or a phone or something that held any kind of value, then sell it to the pawn shop. She obviously never paid the catalogue back either. That was just added to the pile of unpaid debts. She remembered when she was on her own in the flat above the sandwich shop. Her dad had bought her a snooker queue signed by Mark Selby. She loved it. She would occasionally go and play a game of snooker with her dad. It was there thing. She also had a black guitar that her mum had got her. Just an acoustic guitar but it had 3 white seagulls on it. She loved it so much. It was the prettiest thing she'd ever owned.

When she couldn't afford to eat one day, she sold both to the shop. She didn't quite get £40.00 for both items. All the love she had for them, all the memories they held for her were worth less than £40.00.

Once she'd paid the finance off of her car, she'd planned on selling it and buying a Ford Focus ST in yellow. This was her dream car. She'd already researched and researched them and had found the one she wanted. It was £19,000. It was a lot and a good chunk of her money but she thought, 'I've suffered for so long. I'm getting myself the one thing I really want.' She was going to invest in her mum's business too. For the first time in her mum's life, Steph would make sure she had some money. The rest would go towards making Steph debt free. She had a good job so, if she didn't have to pay all of her money out on bills every month, she knew she could quickly get herself in a position where she would soon have an abundance of money.

Her state also led her to show copious amounts of affection towards Amy. She was messaging her constantly, telling her how happy she was with her and how she was feeling better and things would be good for them. She told her she couldn't wait until they would be able to share their relationship with their friends and with the world. She even told Amy that she loved her.

This made Amy so happy. She didn't know what had happened but it had seemed like Steph had finally let down her walls. She was giving Amy the attention and affection she craved, and had worked so hard for from Steph. The message Steph sent with those three magic words lit Amy's face. Amy had known for a while now that she loved Steph and so to know that Steph felt the same way was the most incredible feeling in the world.

She was going to give some money to all of her sisters. Even though she didn't really have much to do with them, she would help them because she loved them. And Leanne. Leanne who had been through her whole life with her. Leanne who was there for every secret, every bad day if only Steph would have allowed her in. She would change Leanne's life too.

Steph began to get more and more frustrated that the money wasn't in her account yet. How could it take this long? It didn't take this when she was paying them. It was instant.

She tried to carry on working as normal but she couldn't. She couldn't focus at all. LC had already noticed that she wasn't doing any work and wasn't at her desk. Steph knew if she didn't buck her ideas up soon, she'd end up without a job. The job she'd worked so hard to protect for all this time.

Steph drove home that day. She'd been able to do the fuel station trick but she'd never have to do that again soon. She'd never have to have coco pops for tea. She'd be living the life she was supposed to.

She got home and immediately checked her account again. Still nothing. She was getting really irritable now. As the feelings of anger and frustration grew, so did her twin. The thoughts of gambling getting stronger. She had literally nothing in her bank at this point and knew Leanne would be asking for the rent money. She knew now though that the Jackpot was a thing. And although she was the first person in 16 years of that woman's career to hit it, it could be done.

As she smoked, she went to the website that had changed her life for the better. She looked at the £20,000 sat in her credit bar. She looked and smiled. Still in complete amazement at what she'd achieved. 'Even if I just do £5000, I'll have more than enough money and I might do it again!'

This was the thought that fell out of the tombola drum this time. Leanne was out again tonight as she often was. Steph made her way up to her bedroom once more. She got herself comfortable as though she was about to watch a movie. Rearranged her pillows, coffee ready, a couple of cigarette's ready to smoke. And so, the show began.

'I can do another £5000 it's fine'

'I can do another £5000 it's fine'

'I can do another £5000 it's fine'

3 hours and 12 minutes later, Steph had a credit of £0.00. She'd lost all concept of money and the value it held. £5000 was nothing. Absolutely

nothing. Steph came out of the autopilot state she'd been in, still sat in the position she was in when she started. She was frozen. Her phone on the bed, still open on the game she'd just rolled £20,000 away on. She stared without blinking at the wall. How? How had it honestly got this bad? How could a girl who couldn't even afford to eat, think it was ok to spend £20,000? How had the site that had told her she couldn't withdraw more than £30,000 in a month let her gamble away £20,000 in 2 hours?

Steph ran to toilet. She was retching but her empty stomach brought up nothing other than dregs of the half cup of coffee she managed to sip as she gambled. She knew what was coming next. The panic attack. She was petrified of losing consciousness again as she had previously and so, she closed her eyes and began to talk to herself.

'You've still got £30,000. You've got £30,000 coming Steph. You can still pay everything you want to. Come on, you're going to be fine. £30,000 is huge!' These thoughts did seem to calm Steph. She was going to be ok. She did have that money coming back and thankfully, she couldn't withdraw the reversal because it had already been processed. She hurriedly ran to the bedroom and grabbed her phone, which had locked itself now, and went to her banking app.

She prayed that the money hadn't gone into her account. You see when you're in a gambling frenzy, the only thing that can stop you is running out of money or, having a significant amount of time where you can't do it. For example, had the money gone into Steph's account, she was still in a state of frenzy and would have continued her session whereas, if the money wasn't in there, it would mean in the absence of being able to get any money, there would be no way for her to continue gambling. It would mean that she had time to come down from the heightened frenzy state she was in and the urge to gamble would ease. It would allow her thinking time and she could take a breath and the need to continue would, eventually, leave her.

'Thank god.' She sighed. Her bank account showed it was empty. Steph continued to try and bring herself down from the level 100 state she was in. She had a cigarette and continued to tell herself, she was still richer than most people. Luckily, there was only her mum she'd told about the

£50,000. She wouldn't find it too hard to lie her way through the missing £20,000.

As Steph was gambling, she did have a number of messages come through on her phone. She didn't look or read any of them. She couldn't whilst she was gambling or there was a threat that her connection from the session she was in would be lost. Also, there was nothing anyone could have to say that was important enough to drag her away from the reels.

As she continued to try and calm herself down, she read the messages. Two were from Amy.

The first read: 'You've made me so happy today Steph. I feel like you're finally opening up to me. I've known for while I feel this way about you but I was scared you didn't so I never said anything. I'd love for us to be able to tell people but I know work makes it difficult. But I'm here for you. I really do love you and I'm so glad you feel the same way.'

The second: 'Are you ok? I'm sorry if that came off a bit strong.'

She knew Amy would have been sat at home now for the last hour or so, thinking that she'd upset Steph. Regretting that she'd opened up and thinking Steph didn't mean what she'd said earlier.

She replied: 'I'm sorry bab, I fell asleep. I feel the exact same way don't worry. I feel a bit shit though, I've got an awful headache so I'm going to go back to sleep.'

Steph wanted Amy to know that she did mean what she said but also, needed to push her away tonight. She didn't have the headspace to think about messaging her and keeping her happy right now. She'd rather pretend she was asleep than give her half hearted responses because her mind was on other things.

The third message was from her mum. 'I'm so pleased things are sorted for you Steph I really am but you really must stop. You'd told me you'd stopped gambling and obviously you haven't. Please Steph, keep your money safe. Please don't gamble it. This is everything you've wanted. You're very lucky and it will never happen again.'

Steph replied 'I wont don't worry mum. I would never ruin it'

Nobody, absolutely nobody must ever find out what she'd done. 'Imagine what they will think about me' she thought.

Steph's belief of what other people would think of her was a driving force, as well as the guilt, for a lot of the things she did. 'They'll think I'm a bitch.' 'They'll think I'm crazy' 'They'll think I'm dirty' It was these kinds of thoughts that led her to yes to almost everything, when she really wanted to say no.

Having successfully calmed herself down now, convincing herself that the £20,000 loss wasn't as bad as she thought, she went through again what she would do with the money.

£2,000 – Natasha

£2,000 – Lillie

£2,000 – Belle

£2,000 - Leanne

£5,000 – Mum

£7,000 – Car

£14,000 - Debts

£32,000 – Total.

She didn't have enough to do everything she wanted to now but it was ok. She would just not pay all of her debts completely and share the rest out as she had planned. She also needed to forfeit her Focus ST but she didn't deserve to have it anyway. Losing the car she'd wanted so much, she felt, would be an appropriate punishment for her actions that evening.

Steph poured herself a bowl of coco pops and went up to bed. She was sure the £30,000 would be in her account tomorrow morning.

She woke up 5 times during the night. Each time checking her banking app to see if the money had gone in. After each disappointing check of her phone, it took her between 30 – 45 minutes to get back to sleep. She was too excited, nervous and her brain working way too hard telling her all the things she would do with the money and pushing the thoughts of how much she'd lost to the back of her brain.

A shattered Steph was woken by her alarm. She got ready for work as normal, checking again whether the money had gone in. It hadn't. She walked into the office, visibly tired and made her way to her desk.

'Steph' shouted a voice from a few seats away. 'Coat!'

She really didn't have the time of day for LC at all now. What the hell did it matter if she had her coat on or not. It's not like her customers could see it or it would have an impact on filling in the spreadsheet she needed to. She complied begrudgingly and removed the Parker.

She wanted so much for Coral to come back and be her manager but she'd moved onto marketing now. A strange noise came from her computer and she looked at the appointment reminder. '121 '

'Fuck' she thought. She'd got a 121 with LC. She knew this wasn't going to end well. She knew how lazy she'd been and how many things she'd let slip since she'd fallen further and further into the black hole of gambling. It had crossed her mind on a few occasions to tell work but she always quickly decided against it. She didn't need the people at work judging her.

She'd done no prep at all for this 121. She'd forgotten it was even happening. She had a look at where the meeting was. It was in meeting room 6. She thought it strange that it was in there. No-one ever used that room. As the 15 minutes passed, she made her way to the room that was in the adjacent building. She took the opportunity to check her account as she made her way there. Still no money. It was starting to worry her now as to why it was taking so long. When she'd withdrew from the other site a few months ago, it was in the same day.

She sat at the table that was the length of the room. She thought it ridiculous that LC had booked this huge room just for the two of them. A few moments later, LC walked through the door with a folder and a cup of coffee in hand. Steph began to feel nervous.

'How are you Steph? You look a bit peaky.' Said LC.

'I'm ok thank you, I'm just tired. I didn't sleep very well.' Replied Steph.

'Ok, I'm just going to dive straight into this Steph. I have real concerns about your performance. You've missed a number of deadlines. You don't interact with your team at all. They lead you when it's supposed to be the other way around. You don't respond to emails and you have dropped the ball on a number of customer accounts which has really caused us some issues. You're attitude too Steph, is completely unacceptable. You go for more breaks than you know you can. You're late back from them. You whistle when people have customers on the phone and continue to do so even when I tell you to stop. And your coat. I ask you everyday without fail to take off your coat. You don't dress like you're ready to work Steph. You wear jeans when you know it isn't allowed and t-shirt. The dress code, as far as I am aware, has always been office wear and you simply do not adhere to it. Is there something going on Steph you need to tell me about?'

Steph sat for a moment in silence, trying to take in everything LC had just said to her. She ran over the comments in her head. There was two ways that Steph could respond to this. She could tell LC that she'd been struggling and that she knew she was slacking and she wanted to get better or she could retaliate. It was another tombola drum moment...

'How the hell can you comment on my performance?'

The tombola drum had spun and retaliate was what was drawn.

'You've not even been here long enough to know the projects I've been working on. Who's giving you this information? Is it your boss because you can get him in here and I'll tell him he's a dickhead to his face!' Steph was stood up at this point shouting.

Steph didn't like LC's boss. He was never there. He never spoke to her and never knew anything she was working on but he somehow felt that he was able to deliver her performance reviews. She could have had weeks off and he wouldn't even notice she was gone.

'And as for my attitude LC. Do you have any idea how many times I asked for help? Any idea how many times I went to that useless twat and asked him to help me with stuff and he never did. There's only so many times you can ask people to help you before you give up. So you know what, yeah. I probably haven't put my everything into work because my work doesn't put all it can into me. It doesn't support me, it doesn't tell me when I'm going wrong. I didn't even ask for this job, it just got put on me and I didn't even receive a minutes training. I got expected to do a job I'd never done before and now you're sitting here telling me I'm not good enough at it. '

She could see LC was stunned. Steph was crying at this point. She'd let all her frustration of the night before, of the months before all out on LC. She didn't really deserve it but she was in the firing line.

'I'm going for a fag' cried Steph.

'Steph do not leave this office' said LC.

'No!' she replied hysterically. 'When this company made me go on that shit course, they told me if you find yourself in a situation where it's overwhelming, you have the right to walk out and return when things have calmed down so that's what I'm doing' Steph walked out of the door and headed straight for the smoking shelter.

She was furious as she smoked 2 cigarettes, one after another. How dare she? How fucking dare she make any comment about Steph when she didn't even know her? She tried to calm herself down. Even with £30,000 on the way, she still needed her job. She checked her bank once more. It was there! £30,000! Steph mood immediately changed. All of a sudden she was ecstatic. It was finally there. The company hadn't tried to cheat her out of any it, they hadn't asked for anymore documents. Sure, they took the £20,000 last night but they really had put the £30,000 in her account.

She stubbed her cigarette out and made her way back to the office. She was still nervous about how this conversation was going to end but she felt a whole lot better knowing she had £30,000 in her bank! She walked through the door and LC was sat in the same seat she was when Steph left the room. Steph made her way back to the seat around the other side of the table.

'I'm sorry. I shouldn't have shouted like that but I'm sure you can understand my frustration.' Said Steph.

'I want to help you' said LC. 'I think that you can do this job well. I think you are capable but we need to change your attitude. I need you to have your head in the game. Be dressed for going to work. People look to you for leadership so set an example. I can help you with the bits you don't know. I'll give you the support and training you feel you've missed.'

Feel. Steph hated that. She didn't feel she'd missed it. She knew had. Although she looked up to Coral, she was never around. When she got the job as team leader, Coral actually moved 3 buildings away so Steph just had to muddle her way through.

'Ok LC. I'm sorry again. I'll make more of an effort I promise.'

The tension in the room had relaxed and Steph accepted the offer of help from LC. She would do what she needed because she really couldn't afford to lose her job.

'Please can I go for another cigarette LC? I don't want the team to know I've been upset and I could do with calming down still.'

LC agreed and Steph went once again to the smoking shelter.

The thoughts of her conversation with LC had already left her mind. She looked again at the beautiful sight on her phone screen. £30,000. Who would have ever thought Steph Goodyear would have £30,000 in her account.

Chapter 31

'How does it feel to have a rich girlfriend?' she messaged Amy that night.

'What?' replied Amy.

'I've won £30,000!'

Amy did know that occasionally, Steph would gamble. She of course never knew how much and how often but Steph told her that from her days of working in the bookies, she knew that sometimes it was worth a gamble.

'You jammy bitch! As if! Have they paid it you yet? Well done bab. I love you'

Steph stared at the message full of happiness. She decided not to tell Amy that the money was in her account now. Only because she wanted to call her finance company tomorrow and pay off her car and know exactly how much she had left.

'Not yet, it takes 3 days. I'm so happy. I love you too'

Steph was going to help her family and help herself! She would own her car, have a chunk of debt cleared and have so much worry and distraught lifted from her.

'Mum, I want to invest in your dresses. You have helped me so much over the years I want to repay you. I know how much you love your dresses mum and, for the first time in my life, I'm in a position to help you. I want to give you £3000 put to put into the dresses and the shop. Buy the stock you need. I really want to do this for you mum, just to go some way to thank you for everything you have done for me.' Was the message she typed out to her mum. She had never been so proud in all her life. Her mum meant so much to her. She'd lied to her so many times and deceived her into giving her money. She was so pleased she could help out her mum. She went straight onto her banking app and transferred her mum the £3000 promised. It was the best feeling ever. Maybe even better than winning it in the first place. It felt so good, she wanted to do it again.

'Mum I've put another £2000 in. I want you to buy all of your stock and then keep that so I know you will be secure. I want to know that you will never have to worry about money mum so please don't give it anyone. Keep it in your bank and keep it safe.'

'Oh Steph. You don't need to do that darling. It's your money, I just want you to be happy and not to gamble anymore.'

'I wont mum, please just accept it. I love you so much and I want you to have it.'

£25,000 in her account, an unbelievable girlfriend, a best friend, and no more worries, Steph sept soundly that night. 'It's over.' She whispered as she fell to sleep.

'Hi, Can you tell me how much it is to pay off my finance please?' Steph asked the man on the phone.

He was quiet for a moment as he checked her account.

'To bring your account to day Miss Goodyear, it'll be £1079'

'Ok thanks, but how much is it to clear it completely?'

'Oh apologies! Let me check.' Replied the guy.

'To clear completely Miss Goodyear it will be £8,212'

This was more than she thought! For gods sake, the car was only actually worth £4500! 'Ok, can I just bring the account up to date please.'

Steph gave the guy the 16 digits off of the front of her card and the three on the back. She couldn't warrant spending £8000, no way. As he confirmed the transaction had gone through, Steph was filled with a sense of achievement. She no longer had any arrears on her car. The next thing, was to get it insured.

She was on her lunch break at work but really wanted to get it sorted. She quickly inputted the details of her and her car into the comparison website. She'd toyed with the idea of lying of the question where it asks you if you've ever had a policy cancelled before. She had but it was through missed payments, not through any kind of bad driving. She decided against it though as it told her failure to answer correctly could void her policy and they wouldn't pay out if ever she had a crash. She was looking between the time and the results as they loaded. She'd only got 2 minutes before she was due to be back off her lunch and after yesterday's performance, she really couldn't afford to piss LC off again.

She stubbed out her cigarette and the gross old ash tray the company had installed years ago in the smoking shelter. She walked towards the doors of her office and the results popped up.

Cheapest offer - £212 a month.

'Fucking hell.' She thought to herself. She could never understand why things were more expensive the worse your credit was. Surely if you were bad at paying, you were more likely not to pay if the bill was higher than lower?

Steph put her phone away and kept running through the calculations on her computer of what money she had left. She still needed to get up to date on all of her payday loans but she had paid her car finance, her mum and her rent and to Steph that was a huge achievement. At the end of her shift, Steph went ahead and paid the first instalment. Now driving legally, Steph was once again proud of herself.

She'd arranged to spend that night at Amy's. She'd spent a few nights there and it always made her feel nervous. She didn't know why because she loved Amy, the house and the dogs but she'd picked up lots of weird thoughts and feelings throughout her addiction. She wanted to give Amy a lovely evening and show how much she meant to her. Steph got the pair their favourite takeaway and two desserts. It was an expensive takeaway but money wasn't an issue anymore and Amy was worth it. They watched a film and Steph made a conscious effort all night, to not look at her phone at all. She would give Amy her full, undivided attention. Steph stayed snuggled up to Amy the whole night and would randomly kiss her.

'I love this version of you' Amy said to Steph.

Steph didn't need to question Amy on what she meant because she knew. She meant she loved the version of Steph that wasn't constantly nervous. The version that wasn't riddled with anxiety and who's mind was quite obviously somewhere else when you tried to have a conversation with her. The version that loved Amy back. Both Steph and Amy felt blissfully happy as they made their way to bed.

The next morning, Steph lay in bed with Amy and they were looking at Focus ST's. Amy knew it was something that Steph wanted and she'd asked her if the money had gone in.

'Not yet, they're being ridiculous.' lied Steph. She didn't even know why she'd lied this time but it was too late to take it back now.

The girls continued to look at the ST's. Amy was showing Steph ones for over £20,000.

'I can't afford one for that much. I'm thinking about getting an older one and maybe sticking a personalised plate on it'

'You can afford it! Even if you spend £20,000 you'll still have £10,000 left!'

Steph's brain went into panic mode. 'No because I've got loads of stuff I need to pay off still' came spilling out of her mouth. What had she done? That wasn't a lie, it was the truth! 'Because obviously all my bills went up when Adrian left, I told you I'd fallen behind on a few bills so I want to use this to get it sorted. Don't get me wrong there's not £10,000's worth but I want to save some for a rainy day.'

Steph felt sick as there was a moment's pause.

'Yeah that's fair enough. Can you give me my £300 back?' asked Amy.

'Of course I will, I'll transfer it you as soon as the payment hits my account'

Steph was so relieved that Amy hadn't asked anymore questions. When you tell as many lies as Steph did, it's easy to forget what lies you've already told and get tangled.

The girls spent the morning together, happy in each others company. Amy made them brunch and they walked the dogs around the big pond which was a 5 minute walk from Amy's house. They got back and Steph had a cup of coffee whilst Amy had a beer whilst they watched a film.

As Steph was at the door, getting ready to leave she said 'Thank you Amy. I do love you.' Amy had a beaming smile and said 'I love you too' They kissed and Steph climbed into her car. She sat for a moment before she drove off, thinking about what a lovely time she'd had and how much she really did love Amy. She never thought she'd be with a woman, let alone in love with one.

On the way home, Steph had the radio on. 2 gambling adverts came on. One offered 5 spins, and the other a £5 free bet. Why is it they were allowed to do this? Promote something widely known as addictive and harmful yet advertise it as though it was a great giveaway? They don't say buy 20 cigarettes get 10 free so how could they do it with gambling. It made her so mad when she heard the adverts. What she didn't realise at the time, was they also triggered her. It was almost like the adverts woke up her twin. And so, Steph wasn't alone in the car anymore. Her conjoined twin was driving with her.

Steph didn't make it home. She'd found an industrial between town, which was where she was at when she'd heard the advert, and her house. It was the perfect place. She was in a spot where she could get good signal and there was nobody around. She turned off the engine of her car, rolled herself a cigarette and then proceeded to gamble.

The words of that woman on the phone stuck with her as she chose the best site. She was the first that woman had known in 16 years to hit the jackpot so she definitely wasn't going to win it again on that site. She selected a new one, one she hadn't played before and started depositing.

Steph and her car were hidden in the darkness of the night now. It was freezing. Steph's whole body was shaking and she could see her rapid exhales of breath in the car because of how low the temperature had dropped. She diverted, for a second, her eyes from the spot on the road her line of sight was pointed in to look at the clock on her phone. It was 8pm. She'd been sat on this industrial estate, the secluded road where only 2 lorries and one other car had past her, for 4 hours. Without a sip of water or a bite to eat. Without speaking to a soul. Without any understanding of time, Steph had escaped the world, and reality, for 4 hours.

Steph turned on the engine, lowered the handbrake and began to drive. Lord knows how she managed to get home in one piece. Her eyes never moved from directly forwards. She couldn't even remember the drive. She stepped out of the car and into the house. She went straight up to her bedroom and lay in her bed looking at the ceiling. Not once that night did Steph look at her phone again. She just lay, looking straight up until at some point, her body gave way to sleep.

'Why do you do this? We have a really nice night and day, you tell me you love me and let me say it back and then you ignore me for the whole night. You make me feel like an idiot Steph and I'm getting a bit sick of it now to be honest. I've tried to be there for you. Tried to make sure you're ok but you're so hot and cold I don't know where I stand.' This was the last message she'd got from Amy. She read it in her bed the next morning. She'd not meant to hurt Amy. She didn't respond to anyone yesterday.

'Amy I'm really sorry. I'm so sorry. I had some really bad news and I just sat and cried most of the night. I didn't want to ruin the lovely time we'd had with it. I did mean it when I said I love you and I really did enjoy it too. Please don't hate me Amy. Please.' She responded. Not a complete lie but still, far enough from the truth that she could continue to protect her secret.

Steph had gambled £10,000 whilst in that car yesterday. £10,000 down the drain and with it, any sense of pride or achievement she had gained from paying her mum and her car finance.

'What's happened? Why didn't you just tell me instead of letting me feel like it was me? I've not slept all night worrying it was too much yesterday. Are you ok?'

Again, even though Steph had neglected her and given her a sleepless night, Amy was asking if she was ok.

'I had an email from the company I won the money from. They said, because I'd accepted a bonus and the maximum winnings from the bonus were £10,000, I was only entitled to that. I complained obviously and told them I'd rung and a woman told me I had won £30,000 and there were no catches but it didn't matter. They've given me an extra £5000 as compensation but yeah, I've gone from thinking I had £30,000, to having £15,000.'

When Steph woke up in the night, she was thinking and thinking about the astronomical lie she was going to have to tell people to explain the missing £15,000. She remembered now, why she didn't tell people she'd won anymore. Because this is what happened. She'd gamble it all and have to lie her way through the reasons as to why she had no money. She was relieved that she was only having to explain a £15,000 difference rather than £30,000 that she'd actually lost. She was glad she'd only ever told Amy she won £30,000.

But she'd remembered when this actually had happened to her once. Not on this scale obviously but she'd won and tried to withdraw. They told her though, she could only withdraw £100 because she'd opted into a bonus and that was the maximum she could win when it was applied. She was furious. All the money she'd spent with these companies and they wouldn't even let her have all of her winnings. She was completely disgusted. But this gave her the idea of using this to lie her way through the missing money.

'What the fuck!!!! They cannot do that, surely?? I'm so sorry babe I had no idea. I can imagine how gutted you must be. I'm sorry I kicked off I was just worried. Want me to come and pick you up?' Amy messaged.

Steph couldn't face it today. It was a Sunday and Sunday was the one day she could hide in her room all day and not be bothered. Sunday's were her favourite days.

'No I don't feel up to it bab. I'm gutted and tired because I didn't sleep well through it all. I've transferred you your £300 back. Thank you so much.'

Chapter 32

5 days all in all. It took 5 days for Steph to gamble her way through £47,000 on just 5 different websites. She contested with all of the sites as to why the hell they had let her gamble this much. How could they let a

person gamble that many thousands of pounds in one sitting? All but one refused her request for her money back completely. The other, asking her sign a form to confirm she wouldn't gamble with them again and could take no further action against them, in order for her to receive £500 compensation. £500 out of the more than £10,000 she'd spent with them.

She'd even asked her mum for £2000 of the money back she'd given her. She lied that she'd purchased her car. She gave her the same lies she'd given anyone else told about her win. That she didn't ended up getting as much as they told her.

It's hard to describe what Steph felt. Initially, it was anger and hatred for both herself and the gambling sites. Followed by panic. She'd got so desperate at one point, she asked her work to lend her money. They didn't as 'it was against policy'. Once Steph accepted what she'd done, once she realised there was no getting it back, Steph felt nothing. She was lower than suicidal. She was so depressed, so traumatised that honestly, she felt nothing. Nothing at all. She didn't care anymore whether she lived or died. There wasn't enough energy in her body to try and end it all. She was completely and absolutely numb. If she stepped out into the road, she didn't hope for a bus to hit her. She didn't hope for a bus to swerve her. She didn't hope for anything at all. She was now a zombie. The walking dead. Steph was incapable of feeling.

When a person wins on the lottery, and they don't claim their ticket and miss out on the deadline, it is mandatory for them to be offered counselling. Steph not only had won a huge amount of money, she'd lost a huge amount of money. All within a week. And she didn't share this with a single person. This would go to the grave with her.

She'd told Amy that she'd made the decision to completely clear her debt management plan, in which was £12,000 worth of debt. She had to open up slightly, and tell her lies about how she'd racked up this much debt. Amy agreed with Steph that it was the best thing to do and told her she was proud of her. Steph didn't even feel guilt anymore either. She didn't feel shame when she told her how much debt she was in, even though she'd lied about the total amount because it was about 4 times this. Steph didn't feel anything.

She was unable to hold a conversation at all. With Amy, with her mum, with anyone. Steph was no longer able to paint on the smile that she had for so many years. The world could now see that Steph was not only sad, but she was ill.

Amy knew that Steph was ill too. She worried about her, everyday just wishing she could help. She would often ask Steph 'what's wrong?' to which she received the same, cold response. 'Nothing.' But still, Amy stayed by her side. Refusing to give up on the girl that she loved so much.

Steph's work got even worse too. She turned up, looking gaunt and ill and would do absolutely nothing as she sat at her desk. She'd occasionally reply to an email to let people think she was there and working, but she wasn't. Not in any way other than in body.

The numbness didn't stop Steph gambling. Even when she could feel nothing at all, when her life was in absolute tatters, when a young girl had lost her soul to gambling addiction, the addiction continued to rule her.

Months and months went by of Steph being in this state. She continued to gamble on every payday but the difference now was, she didn't care. She didn't care if she won or lost because it didn't matter how much she won, she knew she was never going withdraw it.

Another difference was the fact that she'd stopped paying any bills at all. She'd stopped leaving enough money in her account now to pay the loan Leanne was a guarantor for. Very luckily, she'd always found a way to pay it before they took the money from Leanne. She managed to lie or manipulate someone every month to pay it for her. Her mum, Belle, Amy. It didn't really matter, as long as it was paid.

During this time, the worst time of Steph's entire life, her and Leanne made a move to a small flat in an effort to reduce their outgoings. The flat was disgusting and it was owned by the council. There was so much work to do on it. The walls had blood stains on them and everywhere was covered in that bumpy wallpaper everyone seemed to have in the 90's or early noughties. Everywhere was painted in either bright green or pale pink. Steph thought to herself 'well this is more like what I deserve'. But Leanne was excited. She was excited about the thought of getting herself back on track with money and the reduced bill amounts would let her do this. For Steph of course, it made no impact really. She'd just be borrowing a different amount from someone every month to pay her bills and still gambling every other penny of it.

The move was hard. They spent weeks getting the place ready to move in. As they stripped the wallpaper off the walls, they found there were 4 layers of it. The previous tenants just papered over the other layers. Underneath the layers of rotten, vile wallpaper was a layer of paint and because the girls had used a steamer to try and tease the layers and layers of paper off of the walls, it had melted the paint. It had turned into an almost glue. Like when you used to put PVA glue on your hand in school so you could peel it off. They worked every day and every night on that place. Stripping, painting, glossing until finally it was ready to move in. Amy borrowed her dads work van to help them with the move and Belle did help one night too, but it was stressful. As if there wasn't enough going on, enough to think about, they had a move on top of everything else and it pushed the girls to the edge. They began to fight more, argue more. Both Leanne and Steph had volatile mood swings and they took it out on each other until one day, Steph had had enough.

The girls had always been together. Always. They'd always promised each other they would be together. But the pressure of her gambling, the lies she was telling, the depression she was so badly suffering with, pushed Steph to do the unthinkable. The thing that no matter what happened on this earth, she thought would never happen. The thing that none of her family ever thought would happen! Steph left Leanne. She left her in that flat to pay all of her own bills with no help from Steph at all. She left her, even though she knew Leanne had poor mental health, to manage on her own. Gambling had finally taken the most long lasting relationship and the only friendship Steph had. Gambling took Leanne from Steph.

Chapter 33

Steph moved into Amy's house. Amy was happy that Steph was coming to live with her but was also worried. Worried that Steph would never pull herself out of this state she was in. That she would be depressed forever.

Steph told Amy that she had already paid the bill money to Leanne this month and so she would be unable to pay her this month but would start from payday. Amy reassured her it was fine.

As Steph sat on the sofa in her new house, she looked around. The perfectly painted walls, the beautiful, orange check curtains, the two dogs happily playing on the big, green back garden. She was happy to be here. She was hurt by the fallout with Leanne but she was happy that she had somewhere safe to stay. She couldn't mess this up though. She couldn't live with her mum now, since she'd moved into her nans house to look after her. She'd broken basically all communication with her sisters now so that wasn't an option. She couldn't go back with Leanne. Steph had no-where in the world to go if she gambled away the last relationship in her life.

Steph really made an effort to try and paint a smile on around Amy. She didn't want to hurt her and she really did love her. Where would she be if this woman hadn't have come into her life? Constantly checking in on her, making sure she was ok. Feeding her when she couldn't afford to feed herself. She wanted to make her happy and still, after all these months, Steph tried to protect Amy from her secret. The two liked living with each other. There were no arguments, no fights. It was chilled at Amy's house and Steph was able to relax, however, the trauma of the £50,000 would enter Steph's head at any point. Any random moment during the day Steph would think about what she'd done and it would immediately lower her mood. It would make her incapable once again of conversation, affection and feeling. Steph knew this would haunt her for the rest of her life.

It was on payday, at 3.13am and, after gambling every penny of her wages yet again, she decided to tell Amy the truth. After knowing full well that she couldn't afford to give her any rent money, any of the money she already owed her and knowing this month her car would be repossessed, she decided it was time. She'd already lost everything by now. She'd lost every relationship she ever had. Everything she ever owned. Her home. Her car. Her best friend. Her family. It was inevitable she would lose Amy too so it might as well be today.

Steph's heart pounded as she made her way up from the downstairs toilet which had become her gambling place whilst Amy slept upstairs. She tip toed her way through the living room, trying not to disturb the two dogs that were sleeping on the living room floor. She opened the door from the living room to the stairs, trying not to let it make that horrific high pitched squeak. She made her way up the stairs, every step her heart pounding faster and faster with the thought of what was about to happen. It was the first time in so long, Steph had actually felt something so strongly. Fear.

She stood in the doorway to the bedroom for a second. She tried to make out the position Amy was laid in through the darkness that filled the room. She took a deep breath and made her way to her side of the bed.

'Amy' she whispered.

'Amy' she said a little louder, tears now filling her eyes. Amy murmured and mumbled 'yeah?'

'Amy, I need to tell you something.' Amy rubbed her eyes. She could sense from Steph's tone it was something serious but needed to wait a moment before the connection between her eyes and her brain had woken up properly.

'Amy, I do love you. I do. Please don't ever doubt that. But I have a problem and I have for 10 years now. I'm a gambling addict Amy.' Steph let it all out in that sentence in an attempt to rip the plaster off as quickly as she could to reveal the huge wound that was her addiction.

'Do you think I'm surprised?' asked Amy.

What? Did Amy know!? How? Steph had spent so many years hiding this from anyone. Had she known all this time?

'What?' replied Steph in absolute shock.

'Steph. You never have any money ever. Like ever. Every month I can see the lies you tell to try and hide it. You're a manager in a company who can't afford dinner sometimes. Plus, you've said that you gamble sometimes. I've always known that you gamble more than you tell me you do.'

Steph was shocked and relieved. Amy had some idea about what was happening. Not to the extent that it was but she knew she gambled more than she could afford to on occasion. The next bit was the hard part though. Telling Amy she'd gambled her whole wage and for another month, couldn't afford to pay her.

'I've gambled all my wage Amy.' She sobbed.

'What we got paid today?' Asked Amy.

Steph just looked at Amy, She wouldn't have been able to see the tears falling down her face because of how dark the room was. Steph just nodded. For a moment, it was silent. Suddenly, both of Amy's arms were wrapped around Steph as tightly as they could be. She pulled Steph down into the bed and spooned her. 'We'll sort it, don't worry' whispered Steph in Amy's ear. Steph sobbed and sobbed. Amy was even more amazing they she already knew she was.

The girls didn't talk about it anymore that night. When Steph woke up, Amy was already downstairs. Steph was nervous. She didn't want to go downstairs and have to talk about it again. She didn't want to have to tell Steph the numbers of what she owed and how much she'd gambled.

Steph hated it when people did that. When she'd told them she'd gambled, they'd always ask 'how much?' Why did it matter how much? Why did they need to drag out her shame and embarrassment by making her give them the usually 4 figure number?

She made her way downstairs, feeling physically sick with every step closer to the living room she got. What if Amy hadn't been thinking properly last night because she was asleep? What if she'd only just processed what Steph had told her and she was not in that angry stage? She opened the door to the living room. Both dogs came to her and made a fuss as they always did. Amy wasn't in the room. She must have been in the kitchen. Swallowing her own salvia as it filled her mouth, Steph stepped into the kitchen.

'Here you go beautiful.' Amy handed Steph a cup of coffee. Steph wanted to cry again. Amy didn't hate her! She'd made her a coffee as she did every morning. 'Go and sit down' instructed Amy.

Steph took her coffee into the living room and sat in the corner of the L shaped sofa. A few minutes later, Amy followed. 'Let's not let it be awkward bab. What help do you need to get through this month?'

All the saliva she'd had a moment a go had now gone. Her mouth dry as she was faced with telling Amy just how much trouble she was in. She took a sip of her coffee.

'I need to just pay you and Leanne's loan. I can't let her down with that.'

'Right.' Said Amy.

'I will help you. But this is the third time now Steph that I'm paying that loan on my credit card. I really cannot afford to it again, honestly. It's starting to impact me now and I'm struggling to get through month on month. I'll pay the loan again but I really need it back next payday towards my mortgage. Please don't let me down.'

Steph hated it when people tried to guilt her. She wanted to kick off and say 'I'm not asking you for anything am I? I'll sort it out myself.' But she knew she had no other way of paying this loan and even though her and Leanne had fallen out, she didn't want to leave her with that debt.

'I know' said Steph. 'Thank you so much. I have tried to get better Amy, so many times. I've had counselling, been to gamblers anonymous and all sorts but nothing works. It's literally killing me Amy.'

'I know but it has to stop now. I will be taking your bank card off you from now on.'

Steph knew the digits of her card. These had been imprinted on her brain as soon as she got her card. She didn't tell Amy that though. 'Yeah of course' she replied.

Steph had tried these methods before too. Putting her wages in someone else's account. Someone having her card. But she always managed to find a way around it. Always. Whether it was lying as to reasons why she desperately needed money transferring, not transferring all of her wages but pretending she had or linking her account to another payment method so she didn't actually need a card. She'd always found a way around it. The thing about gambling addicts is they're good with problem solving and good with numbers. They tend to be able to manipulate situations, calculate something perfectly or find another way because they focused their minds were solely on doing so.

Steph wanted to get better, of course she did. But 10 years in, hundreds of thousands of pounds later and knowing every trick in the book, she believed that it was too late for her. She, with all her heart, believed there was nothing that would stop her gambling and nothing any company, any charity or any person in the world could for her that would make her better.

'There's one other thing.' Said Steph. 'The finance people are taking my car off of me at the end of this month.'

Whilst Steph had been walking around in her zombie like state, she'd had a number of emails from her finance company. Looking at the amount she owed and knowing, even if she managed to get the money together to pay them what she needed to save her car, she'd only gamble it anyway. And so Steph arranged for them to collect her car. She'd told them the reason she couldn't pay was the had been made redundant.

'Oh.' Said Amy.

'Well how much do you need to pay to save it?'

Steph immediately lied. It was her go to. She didn't even know anymore what was the truth and what wasn't. '£700'

It was actually more than this. She didn't know how they'd let her get that far behind at all.

'I'm sorry Steph but I don't have it. I'll add you to my insurance though so you can carry on driving.'

Yet again, Amy didn't look to punish Steph for what she'd done. She was still looking for ways to help her and make sure she wasn't too deprived even though Steph herself believed, she deserved to be punished.

Without a penny to her name, no friends in the world and suffering with a 10 year old addiction, Steph knew just how lucky she truly was.

'Yeah I was made redundant so I just can't afford it anymore' said Steph to the guy who was loading her car onto the back of his tow truck. He didn't show her any sympathy, he just put the car on the truck, got Steph to sign and left. She watched the car being taken away from her as it drove down the road, getting smaller and smaller as it finally escaped her vision. Just as so many other things in her life had slipped away now, the car that she loved, that she was so proud she'd been able to get had now too been snatched away through her addiction. Other than Amy and her mum, Steph simply had nothing left that her addiction could steal.

Steph did everything Amy asked of her that month. If she found a pound on the floor, she would give it Amy. Amy had financed her life completely now. She'd paid for her rent, her food, her loans even though she knew the reason she couldn't do it herself. Amy even told Steph that she could continue to live there rent free whilst she got on top of some of her debts but she really would need that loan money back. She truly was an angel.

It was the day before payday and Steph's twin would not let her forget it. She fought and fought though. Everything Amy had done for her, she couldn't throw it in her face by gambling. What kind of evil would that make her? They enjoyed their evening meal and the pair went up to bed. As Steph put her phone on charge at the side of her, she waited for Amy to tell her that she was taking it from her. She waited for her to say that she wouldn't be having the phone on her side of the bed. But she didn't. How? Steph knew full well how. You see for some reason, if they were due to be paid on a Monday, the money would be in her bank account on the Saturday. She didn't tell Amy this. She needed to leave an option open for her to gamble.

Steph begged herself to tell Amy that she'd have money tomorrow. She begged herself to just make the move and give Amy her phone. Steph laid awake, petrified. She knew she wasn't strong enough to fight the screaming that the twin was doing in her ear. She knew as much as she appreciated what Amy had done for her, it wouldn't be enough to stop her from doing it again. Addiction was the strongest force in the universe and a person within its grasp has absolutely no chance of fighting it alone. Steph was about to lose again.

Chapter 34

'Please help me Belle, Please.' Steph begged as she was at her sisters house. She'd been to Belle quite a few times now, begging her to bail her out. Belle had recently started earning quite a bit of money through selling photo's of herself online. Now you might judge this but, Belle had to feed her kids. She didn't gamble all her money like Steph did and leave herself with nothing. She simply didn't get any help or support. She made a decision that she would make a better life for herself and her children and this was a way to do it. She was making more money than Steph at this point so it was doing really well. She no longer needed to use a food bank and her children we're happy. 'I can't Steph, not again. You really need to tell Amy what you've done.' Steph screamed immediately in desperation and anger at the suggestion. 'I can't! Do you realise I'll be homeless? That I will lose the last thing I have in my life?' Steph was looking for enough cash to give Amy to cover at least the food shopping, and pay Leanne's loan. Amy had already warned her she wouldn't pay it again. 'I really can't Steph. I'm sorry.' Said Belle once more.

Steph tried everything that day to get money. She messaged her uncle who she'd only seen once in 20 years, when she went to south Africa. He was insanely rich. It broke her heart when she saw he'd read her message but ignored her. She asked her mum, Natasha and Lillie and she was so desperate, so unbelievably out of options, she asked LC. All of who were unable to help her. She stayed out of the house all of that day. She hid at her mum's shop. She'd told Amy that she had arranged to spend the day with her mum. Amy believed her too, completely oblivious to the fact that once again, Steph had no money to live on this month.

Nobody helped Steph. Either they couldn't or they knew by now that giving Steph money was the worst possible thing they could do. Steph went home and acted as though nothing had happened. It was hard but she had a lot of practice. As she sat on the sofa with Amy, she could feel her phone vibrating. Someone was calling her. She hated her phone going off when she was near Amy because it could be someone saying something about gambling, or they would mention money. Steph looked and it was Belle. 'Is your phone ringing?' asked Amy. Shit. She'd heard it.

She needed to answer it now. She answered the phone and turned down the volume as much as she could on the side of her phone that Amy wouldn't be able hear her. 'Hey Belle, you ok?' she asked, petrified of her response. 'Yeah are you? Did you sort it?'

'Yeah I'm fine' answered Steph, avoiding a direct answer to Belle's question.

'Have you told Amy?'

For fucks sake. She stood up and went into the kitchen to roll a cigarette, out of earshot of Amy. 'No, it's fine. I sorted it' she lied, saying as little as she could to avoid the questions Amy was going to ask her afterward.

'Oh right.' Said Belle. 'Natasha wants to go out tonight. Is there any chance you could babysit?'

Steph was happy with the suggestion. If she was babysitting, she could stop having to pretend everything was fine. She could have some space to think about what the hell she was going to do. So, she agreed and told Belle she would be there in an hour. She apologised to Amy but she felt like she needed to. Amy was looking forward to spending her Saturday night with Steph but did know how much Steph loved her nieces and so told her to go and enjoy it.

Amy dropped Steph at Belle's house and as Steph walked through the door into her sisters house, she broke down. Crying hysterically like she was when she'd told Adrian, but worse. She couldn't breathe, she couldn't talk, she just sobbed. Steph sat at the dining room table and continued to cry uncontrollably. The kids were in bed thankfully, so they wouldn't see their auntie in this state. Natasha and Belle both kept trying to ask Steph what was wrong but she couldn't talk. She simply couldn't do anything other than cry. 15 minutes passed and she was still sobbing. She didn't know what was happening to her but she continued to cry.

'I feel bad for leaving you.' Said Belle and she sipped on her drink.

Steph's guilt made an appearance for a moment. Driven by her guilt, she managed to string a sentence together. ' I'll be fine I promise. Just go and enjoy your night.' Doing her best to put a smile on her face, Natasha and Belle left for a night on the town.

Steph felt very left out of her sisters. They would do things together all the time. She'd see in the group chat that they'd go to the park or a play centre or they'd go round town. The only invite Steph ever got, was to babysit whilst they went out. It really did hurt her.

As soon as they walked through that door, Steph sobbed once more. It was more than an hour later that she'd managed to stop herself. She really thought she must be having a breakdown. 10 years of addiction now had broken her. Steph, picked up her phone and typed 'I've done it again.'

'What?' replied Amy.

Steph, trying to strain her eyes to see the keypad on her phone, knew what she had to do.

'Amy I think we should split up. I'm not well enough to be with you. I will drag you down further and further into debt and I don't want that. You are kindest, most loving generous person I have ever met and I know what I've lost. But I lose everything in my life Amy. I've gambled that loan money that I know you needed back towards your mortgage. My money goes into my bank early when we get paid on a Monday and I've lost the lot again. Amy I truly am sorry. You're too good for me and I don't deserve you. I am so sorry. I'll love you for as long as I live but I can't have you with me, sinking further into this addiction. Look after yourself Amy. I love you and I know you'll find someone who treats you how you should be treated. Like the angel you are. Bye Amy. Xxxxx'

Amy didn't respond. Steph checked all night and although she could see Amy had read it, she didn't reply. Her twin had been successful. It had taken Amy too.

Steph woke the next morning and immediately started sobbing as she had the night before, with no control over it what so ever. Her sobbing woke

Belle who came downstairs, clearly hungover. The sisters started arguing. Steph didn't even know what they were arguing about but it ended in them screaming at each other at the top of their voices. 'You're nothing but a fucking gambling addict. All you care about is paying Leanne's loan. Why is it not ok to hurt her but it's ok to let everyone else in your family down? You're disgusting. You won £50,000 and you didn't even give any of your family a penny. You don't deserve a family!'

How did Belle know? How did Belle know about the £50,000? It must have been her mum. She hadn't told anyone else. Steph stormed out of the door and began to march up the street. She didn't have anywhere to go now, after gambling away every relationship she had. She was furious and heart broken. How could her mum have told Belle? Her mum had always promised she'd never breath a word of her gambling to anyone. She knew how important it was to Steph that it be a secret. She called her mum and screamed 'How could you? How fucking could you! I didn't even get £50,000 I told you that, and I did help someone. I helped you!' she put the phone down before her mum had chance to respond.

Steph had found herself exactly where one day, she knew she would end up. Alone. Without enough money to buy herself a drink, nowhere to go and without any one in the world she could reach out to.

Steph started to think about where she would sleep that night. Her life had gone so horribly wrong that tonight, she would be homeless like the people she'd previously felt so sorry for. She remembered a subway that was close to her dad's old flat. It'd be dry at least in there. Steph thought about the options and where would be the driest, warmest place to sleep as she wandered the streets aimlessly. At that moment, her phone buzzed.

'I'm hugely hurt Steph that you've done this to me. I've tried and tried to help you but I do understand you're ill. I don't want to lose you but you're right, we can't carry on like this. I'm sorry I didn't message back but I needed to sort my own financial mess out. I don't want to lose you Steph, where are you?'

Steph couldn't believe it. Even after what she'd done, Amy still wanted her.

Steph told Amy where she was and Amy arranged to pick her up. Steph was nervous as she saw the black Peugeot driving towards her on the road she was on. Amy had a personalised number plate so she knew it was her. Amy pulled up and Steph got in.

'Hey' said Steph.

'Hi' replied Amy.

The girls were silent all the way home. It was awful. Steph would rather Amy scream at her as loud as she could than do this.

They got home and Steph fussed the dogs, being careful to do nothing at all that could piss Amy off. Not even breathing too loudly. Steph sat on the sofa. Amy stayed in the Kitchen for ages. She was sure that she was just staying in there to avoid her. Then, Amy walked into the room. Steph got a lump in her throat the size of grapefruit.

Amy knelt on the floor in front of Steph.

'Steph I need you to listen to me. Unfortunately, I am completely in love with you. To be honest, I wish I wasn't but I am. You've hurt me Steph. You've hurt me more than if you'd have cheated on me but I know you have an illness. Steph, this is the last chance I will give us, it really is. If me saying this to you isn't enough for you to stop gambling, I have to walk away. I'm in a worse situation financially than I have ever been in my life and that's because of you Steph. I know that's not nice to hear but it's true. Steph, do you think you can do it? Do you think you can find a tiny bit of fight anywhere in you to beat this?'

Wow. Amy's words cut through her like a knife. She also didn't know how to answer because to be completely honest, Steph didn't have anything left. She had no fight left at all. She was exhausted in every sense of the word. In every way a person could be truly exhausted, Steph was. But Amy was worth fighting for. She knew she'd said the same about Adrian but Amy was different. She wanted to save her.

'I know I can't do it on my own Amy. I'm broken but yes. I want more than anything in the world to have a life with you. So yes, I promise you. I will fight.'

And Steph meant every word. It was a pivotal moment. She knew it would be hard and she didn't believe honestly, that it was possible after all these years, but she would at least try.

Chapter 35

Steph had made up with her mum. She'd apologised that she'd spoken so rudely to her. Her mum was always there for Steph. Always. She often forgot how badly her addiction affected other people. Steph's mum was watching her daughter waste away. Watching her die and Steph didn't even tell her half of it. She would do everything she possibly could. Her mum had tried and tried to help her but Steph never wanted to listen. If she had, she would have heard some of the advice her mum had given her that may have given her a shot of getting better. Steph's mum hadn't told Belle. Belle had seen a message on her phone when Steph was in that state of excitement, repeatedly telling her mum about what she'd won.

Steph was sat on her phone. She'd googled 'help for gambling addicts.' So many of the things she'd already tried came up. Gamblers anonymous, different counselling companies, NHS. She'd tried all the major things before and nothing had worked and the treatments just didn't agree with her. Steph needed facts, figures, research to be able to engage in something. Colouring and talking to 50 – 60 year old men wasn't going to help her. She changed her search. 'Residential rehab for gambling.' She'd often thought that the only way she could get better would be to be taken away. Maybe shock therapy or something. She looked at a few sites but they charged for their services. Really? Do you think if I could afford to pay to go into rehab for gambling, I'd need to go into rehab for gambling? She clicked off of the page and selected the next search result down.

'Gordon Moody.' It read.

Steph continued to read. Women's therapy. She liked the thought of it just being women. She thought it might be easier to talk in a group of women than it had been with mainly older men. Steph continued to read. The charity did help both men and women but they separated the treatments. The women's retreat was in total, 5 nights. 3 in the first session then 2 nights, 2 months later. Steph was hugely sceptical. 5 nights would never be able to change an addiction 10 years old, but she continued to read. The articles intrigued her. It sounded different. They did have facts and figures. They explained they could offer a different type of treatment which looked into the areas of addiction that she hadn't explored before. She looked at the images and it was a beautiful old house where the retreat was. Steph had a good feeling about this charity. She'd tried all the rest and she was willing to do whatever it took to not have to sleep in that subway. She filled out the short application form.

They didn't ask for too much information but it let her know the full application process. That she would be contacted for an assessment and based on that, they would decide what the best treatment for her would be. It could be that she go back to her GP, that sessions are arranged or that she be selected for a place on the retreat. It explained they had a large number of applicants. Steph wondered how many women were struggling just as much as she was. It also told her the next retreat was in May. It was only Feb now! She was pleased with herself that she'd made the first step though.

The next thing to sort was work. Steph was dangerously close to losing her job and Steph and Amy both knew it. The next morning, Steph was physically shaking in the car. Amy grabbed her hand to steady her shaking and told her 'You'll be ok.' Steph was petrified.

People knowing about her addiction was her worst nightmare. The shame of it. The guilt. What people would think of her. Steph had spent all of her adult life hiding this from people and so telling anyone made Steph go into a physical panic attack. They pulled up in the car park of their work and Steph continued to shake. 'Come on Steph. You can do it. You have to.' Said Amy.

Steph looked at Amy. The woman who was trying to help her. She knew she needed to undo a lot of hurt and broken trust and she could only do with honesty. Her twin now though wasn't telling her to gamble, it was telling her what people would think of her if they knew. Screaming in her ear that she needed to lie. Just tell Amy you've done it, she wont know you haven't!

She found in herself, the strength to fight those thoughts. Steph walked up to LC and said 'Can I have a word please.' Her voice shaking along with her body. LC looked concerned. She could tell something bad had happened. She led Steph up the stairs to the offices in the IT department. They were generally quiet and didn't have too many people around. Steph sat opposite the tiny table facing LC. Her twin screaming at her even more, telling her to make something up and not tell her the truth. 'I'm a gambling addict LC. I'm in so much trouble.' Steph started crying as she sat shaking in the chair, not even able to lift the tissue to her eye.

LC was brilliant with Steph. Absolutely brilliant. She'd seen a completely different side to her. She offered Steph help. She explained how someone in her family had a similar issue so she knew how hard it was. She talked to Steph for ages and she could not have been more supportive. 'I do need to have a chat with HR though Steph.' Explained LC. The thought petrified Steph but, in keeping with the promise she had made to Amy, to do everything she could this time, Steph just replied 'Ok.'

Steph explained to LC that she had a doctor's appointment that afternoon, which she genuinely did, and would she be ok to attend. LC told her it was fine. She would borrow Amy's car and Betty would take Amy home that night. LC gave Steph a hug before she left the office, and thanked her for telling the truth.

That afternoon, Steph went to the doctor once again. She explained to the fat, middle aged doctor that she'd got a gambling addiction and how badly it had affected her. He continued to stare at his screen just asking her generic questions. Steph explained, for the first time ever, every bit of detail she could in the 10 minute slot she had with guy. When she got to the suicidal feelings and everything she'd lost, his attention was fully on Steph. He was no longer looking at his screen. Once Steph had finished, leaving out the only £50,000 that she still swore to secrecy, the doctor she could see, truly empathised. 'Well Steph. What a time you've had of it! I'm so sorry. I don't think though that this can get better for you. I think first and foremost though Steph, your body needs to rest. You are right, you are exhausted and it's not something a good night's sleep is going to fix. Your body needs time to repair itself and so Steph, I'd like to sign you off of work. I'm actually going to sign you off for 3 months. You must rest Steph. You need to find some reprieve from these thoughts. I'd like to prescribe you some anti-depressants, just to help you stabilise your mood a little. ' Steph agreed with everything the doctor said. She'd promised herself that from now on, she would listen to people and do whatever they said that would help her get better. After all, nothing she'd tried had worked. He also gave her the details to refer herself for counselling.

Steph walked out of the doctors and up the road to her mum's house. She told her mum everything she'd done that day and that she really wanted to get better. Her mum was beaming with pride. 'I just want my old Steph back.' She said.

'Mum, I don't have the money to buy these tablets...'

Steph's mum walked with Steph to chemist and they picked up the prescription. Steph's mum paid for it. The chemist was next door to the doctors where Steph was parked. That small building that smelt like alcohol and Steph had always found completely useless. But this time would be different. She would get better.

Amy was hugely proud of Steph. She'd done as she'd promised she would and made some good steps towards getting better. Another thing that Steph needed to sort was her debt. She didn't even know where to start with it. Hundreds of unopened letters, hundreds of emails she'd ignored and she'd even changed her mobile number again so that nobody could get in touch with her anymore about the debts she owed. She'd decided that today, she'd done enough. She was going to give herself a week or so to try and relax and calm her anxieties before she put anymore pressure on herself. She told Amy this was her plan and Amy agreed that was ok.

6 weeks passed, including one payday and Steph had done it. She transferred all of her money to her mum. Amy would be sat downstairs on the morning of payday with Steph's phone. She would make her open her banking app and transfer her the money she needed and then the rest to her mum. Steph wanted her money to go to her mum because it was actually her idea. She also knew it was safe with her mum. It wasn't that she didn't trust Amy because she did. It was just that her mum was her safe place and it comforted her to know the money would be with her now. It was working. Everything she'd done, all the help her mum and Amy were giving her was helping. For the first payday in so long, Steph didn't gamble. It didn't stop the thoughts though. It didn't stop her brain

trying to search for ways she could feed her addiction. Like a heroin addict, she believed that just one last hit would make her feel normal again. But after she spent hours thinking about it and coming to no possible way it could be done, her brain began to relax.

Amy was a huge football fan. It would be on all day and Steph hated it. Every players T-Shirt displaying yet another betting site. The posters around the edges of the field, sharing in huge letters another site and another offer and the adverts. For goodness sake the adverts. Every half time or full time there would be no less than 3 betting adverts on. She didn't understand it. The players would never wear a tobacco brand on their shirt so why were they promoting something that had literally nearly killed Steph. It was hard to ignore but she knew the industry didn't care. She knew the government didn't care. She had to learn to live with it and try to ignore them.

Steph needed to try and find things to fill the days whilst Amy was at work and she couldn't gamble. The boredom would drive her crazy. She'd walk the dogs or draw but she still wasn't able to properly concentrate on anything, so she did little bits of everything without ever finishing it. She'd just wait every day, for Amy to get home.

Steph started to download games on her phone. Candy Crush, Pool, Uno. She found herself ridiculously obsessed with them and she'd even spend money on them. Spent money to buy fake coins that essentially, she would fake gamble so it really wasn't a good substitute. She'd only ever have a couple of pounds in her account because she'd transfer it all to her mum but say she had £1312, she'd transfer £1310. It gave her a similar buzz to gambling and the same frustrated feeling when she lost. She knew she probably shouldn't be playing them but it wasn't costing her a lot and it was filling up her time whilst Amy was at work.

It was on the following Tuesday that Steph got an email.

Subject – Gordon Moody application

'Good afternoon Steph,

I would like to arrange a suitable time with you to go through your application to be a participant of the women's retreat with Gordon Moody and go through an assessment. '

The email gave a list of dates that she could do the assessment. Steph replied immediately, requesting the first date they had available for the assessment which was the following Monday. She'd wished it was sooner but she knew she'd be available, given her sick note. Steph really wanted to go now. She was scared that they'd tell her she didn't meet the criteria and refer her to her doctors. This was Steph's last chance.

That night, Amy told Steph they were going to meet her friend Abigail at the pub. She wouldn't take no for an answer because she knew Steph was getting cabin fever. Steph had met Abigail a couple of times. She seemed really nice but she always thought she didn't like her much. She didn't know why, it was just a vibe she got from her.

They went to the pub that Amy was always in. Steph hated it there. It was split into two sections and it was always the same faces. Amy knew all of them but it made Steph feel really uncomfortable. Betty and Amy would often meet for a drink here too and they knew a lot of the same people.

Steph and Amy walked up to door and Abigail walked out. She was clearly drunk. She put her arm around Steph and said 'Listen. I know it's been hard but I'm really glad you're trying to get into rehab.' Steph's stomach felt like it had fallen straight out of her. She was frozen on the spot. How the hell did this woman she barely knew, know about her secret? She couldn't even walk into a pub without people knowing her whole life and that she was an addict? Everything she'd hidden for 10 years was now public knowledge?

'Steph, I need to talk to you. Steph!' shouted Amy, tugging on her shirt. Steph, still completely stunned turned to look to Amy. She followed Amy into the toilet.

'I'm so sorry Steph. I'm so sorry. I told Betty about it. I needed someone to talk to Steph so I told her and she told Coral then Coral told Abigail's mate and he told Abigail. I didn't mean for it to happen Steph I'm so sorry.'

Steph, still speechless and absolutely gutted replied 'You swore. You swore that you hadn't told anyone. I've done everything you asked me to. You know how important it is for me to keep this secret and now half of my work know and everyone in this fucking pub!'

How could Amy have done this? How could she have told anybody when she knew how depressed she was about it all. When she knew how hard she'd worked to keep this a secret. She was so hurt. She just wanted to run away. But instead, she marched out of the door and over to where Abigail was sat. 'What did Amy say to you Abigail?' she asked.

Abigail, in her intoxicated state, wasn't capable of saying anything but the truth.

'Well she had to borrow money from me once because you'd gambled again so I lent it her. She told me that you have an addiction and that you're getting help for it and trying to get into rehab. To be honest, Andy told me as well. He'd been talking to Coral, you know your old boss? Well anyway, she'd found out you're an addict and she told Andy that you're toxic and you wont last long in your job and it made Andy worry because he's mates with Amy so he asked me if she was ok.'

Steph's world as she knew it fell apart as Abigail told her the truth about what people had been saying about her.

She thought Amy would never share her secret. She didn't believe she would every betray her trust. Why had she told people?

She also thought Betty was a friend but not once after learning about how Steph was struggling, did Betty ask Steph if she was ok. She actually hadn't even messaged to see if she was ok since being signed off sick. This, exactly what addicts are afraid will happen, is what Betty and Coral had done. Talked badly about her and cut her off. As for Coral, she looked up to this woman. She'd often thought how she wished she could be more like her. She'd often gone to Coral for advice on things because she genuinely had a huge amount of respect for her and all the time, she didn't even like Steph. She was sat in a pub talking to her friends about how toxic she was. Again, never asking her if she was ok after learning how much she'd been struggling.

Steph knew the truth now and it cemented what she'd thought all her life. That people would think bad of her and talk about her if she ever let anybody know she was an addict.

'Thanks Abigail, I appreciate your honesty.' Steph said, as she walked out of the doors. She heard, as she walked, Amy shouted 'Thanks mate' in a sarcastic tone. Steph walked to the car, trying to hold back her tears and she could hear Amy's footsteps running behind her to catch her up. 'Take me home' said Steph. Amy did as she wished and jumped into the car and drove Steph home.

'I'm sorry Steph.' Said Amy 4 times on that car ride home, never once getting a response from Steph.

They pulled up on the drive and Steph went into the house and sat on the sofa, looking at her phone to ensure at no point did she make eye contact with Amy. All that was running through her mind was 'How could she? How could she do this to her?'

Amy went upstairs to avoid any awkwardness but soon came back down. She was crying. 'I'm sorry Steph.' She said. 'I didn't know how to deal with it. It's new to me and I didn't have anyone to talk to about it.'

Steph felt a certain degree of sympathy for Amy but why the hell would she tell people at work? Steph managed these people. How the hell could she ever show her face again there now?

'You do know Amy, that I can never go back there now. You do know that the only thing enabling me to pay anything back, you've ruined.'

Amy sobbed and went back upstairs.

Steph sat and contemplated what had happened. She felt embarrassed. Embarrassed that these people, people who she thought were friends knew about her addiction. And worse than that, didn't even care that she was struggling as badly as she was. Instead of reaching out to Steph, they sat and bad mouthed her in the local pub.

Her thoughts went back to what Amy had said. She knew it would have been hard for her and it is a big thing to deal with but not her colleagues.

Why, out of all of her friends, did she choose to tell the people Steph worked with?

A couple of hours passed and Steph calmed down. She kept reminding herself of everything Amy had done for her. Paid her bills, fed her, stood by her. It didn't change how hurt she was but she could understand that she'd needed someone to talk to. And so, she made her way upstairs. Amy was sobbing on the bed. She climbed into the bed next to her and put her arm over her. 'It's ok' Steph said in her ear. 'I know you just needed someone to speak to. I just need you to promise Amy, that if you need anyone to talk to about it, speak to someone not connected to work. Talk to my mum. Talk to any of your friends but please, don't involve my work. It's so hard to deal with people knowing.' Amy rolled over to face Steph, mascara all the way down her face where her tears had stripped it from her eyelashes. 'I really am sorry Steph, I love you.' Cried Amy.

'I love you too.' Replied Steph.

Chapter 36

Steph was watching her phone intently, waiting for it to ring. She was pacing the carpet of yet another house! She wanted to go and roll a cigarette but she didn't dare move into the kitchen in case she lost signal. And then it happened. Her phone lit up and begin to vibrate. Private number displayed on the screen. She let it ring a couple of times before she answered.

'Hello?' said Steph who was more nervous now than she was waiting for a third bonus symbol.

'Hi, It's Helen from Gordon Moody. We have an appointment to run through your application and complete your assessment. Is now still a good time to talk?'

'Yes, yes of course.' Replied Steph.

The woman at the end of the phone confirmed all of her details and proceeded to ask about Steph's gambling. This was completely unnatural to Steph. Speaking so openly and honestly about how much and how often she gambled. She felt the shame and guilt fill her as she answered the questions the woman asked of her but, she answered them all with nothing but the truth. This was Steph's last chance. She needed to get onto this retreat. The thought that they would say her doctors would be the best option still petrified her because she knew, she knew the services they offered her didn't help. They weren't enough to stop her gambling. What would she do if she didn't get in?

The woman on the end of this phone now knew more about her addiction than anyone in her life. In 45 minutes, this stranger knew the extent of her gambling and how badly her life had been affected from it. 'Thank you Steph, I've got everything I need. We will inform you of the decision within the next 4 weeks.' Is what the stranger ended the call with.

Steph was exhausted after the call. She'd given her a 10 year story in 45 minutes. Now it was time for Steph to wait. She was doing that thing that you always do after an interview, analysing everything the woman had said to see if there was anything she could extract and determine whether it was swinging one way or another, but there was nothing. Steph rang her mum and told her about the conversation, hiding the details she still wasn't ready for her to know. 'Oh Steph. I'll keep everything crossed for you.' Steph's mum went on to tell her how proud she was and how much she loved her. Steph was proud to. She wasn't excited to gamble anymore. She was excited to be gamble free.

Another payday, another success. Steph sat and transferred every penny, under the eagle eye of Amy. It made her proud once again that she'd done it. It wasn't like she had much choice in the matter but still, it was an achievement to her. 'I've sent it, mum' was the message she sent.

'Well done Steph! I'm so proud!'

'I'm proud too' said Amy, as she kissed her on the forehead.

Things had started to get a little easier for Steph. She still had the voices and the urges but, having no way at all to gamble, they didn't last as long as they had previously. Perhaps it wasn't too late for her?

Steph waited and waited for a response from Gordon Moody. Although she wasn't gambling any money, she knew from previous experience how easy it was to fall back into it and she really couldn't afford it this time. Unable to hold in her want and desire any longer, she emailed the lady who had confirmed her assessment appointment. She just politely asked if there was any update and if she knew when she would find out. 3 of the 4 weeks she needed to wait had passed so she knew she was being slightly premature but she just needed to know. She checked her emails every 10 minutes or so over the next few days. Praying and praying for an email that said accepted. She couldn't see 'unfortunately' again. She just couldn't.

During her time off work, Steph promised herself she would try and see her family more. It was hard because Amy needed the car for work but she didn't mind walking. She was walking to Belle's house when her phone buzzed. She reached into her pocket and the little envelope symbol was on her front screen, letting her know there was an unread email.

She stopped walking. She leant against the fence she'd been walking along that protected the old, run down factory on the other side of it. She put the passcode into her phone but in the excitement, she did it wrong. She did put it in again and prayed. Prayed that it was Gordon Moody. She scrolled down notification bar. It was! It was them. Filled now with anxiety once again, she clicked on the email. 'Please, please.' She whispered. 'Please don't let me see 'unfortunately'. She read the email, hands sweating, heart racing. It reminded her of that day at the bookmakers, on that cold leather stool. 'We're delighted to be able to offer you a place on the upcoming retreat in May.' Steph let out a shout in excitement. 'Yes!' She began walking faster to get Belle's house so she could read the email properly. She was practically jogging at this point. She reached her sister's house and burst through the front door. 'Hello!' she shouted. Nobody was there yet. She'd spoken to her mum earlier who'd said they were nipping to the shop down the road and they would leave the front door open for her. She knew they wouldn't be long.

Steph made herself comfortable on the sofa and brought up the email once more. She read every single word without skimming even once sentence. The email told her the details of the stay. It would be on the 4th

May and would be for 3 nights. The second would be a 2 night stay in July. Steph had to agree to a number of terms before the placement was confirmed. She needed to agree to attend on the dates they'd offered, agree to engage fully with programme and agree to hand over her mobile phone upon arrival which she would be allowed for two hours per day. Steph of course, agreed to all the terms immediately. There was a deadline on the response before they offered someone else the placement. She wasn't prepared to let this happen. This was her place and her turn to get the help she needed. As sceptical as she was about its success, she knew she needed to be there.

Her mum and Belle came through the door with Amelie and Hettie. 'I've been accepted!' Steph shouted. 'Into rehab! I've been accepted!' Rehab probably wasn't the right terminology but it her mind, that's what it was.

Her mum immediately ran over and gave Steph a hug. 'Oh well done Steph, I am so proud of you.'

She sat and told her mum about the retreat. What they offered, when she'd be going etc. She was so excited. She couldn't wait to get home and tell Amy the good news. This was it. This was the start of recovery for the girl gambler.

Chapter 37

Steph felt sick as she made the journey to work. 3 months had passed now. And within that 3 months, she didn't gamble a penny. The plan that her and the ones she loved made, to become gamble free was working. She went to work, wearing the size 4 shirt that was too baggy for her. She needed to start gaining weight, she knew that and she was eating much better now but she found it difficult to gain weight. Stress often makes you lose weight, and Steph had a lifetime of it.

'You ok?' asked Amy as they pulled into the car park of their workplace.

'No!' said Steph. This was a huge thing too. Not pretending she was ok. Not painting a smile on. Not brushing off the enormity of the anxiety she felt in this moment, having to walk into work. Amy grabbed Steph's hand. 'I'm proud of you Steph. You can do this.'

Steph stepped out of the car and made her way into the office. She was so dreading the questions. The false sympathy from people acting like they gave a toss as to why she was off. None of them had messaged her whilst she was off to find out if she was ok, so why did they care now? And the fact that she would have to lie her way through it. She hadn't decided yet what she would tell people when they asked why she'd been off. She figured though, she could avoid any detail and hopefully, her absence would be old news by the end of the day.

She walked into the office, through the big blue doors and waited for people to notice it was her. And it happened, immediately. 'Oh my god Steph, are you ok?' 'It's so nice to see you back!' 'Are you feeling better?' She was like a rabbit in the headlights. How was she supposed to answer? There were so many thoughts filling the tombola drum that was her brain now, that it was too jam packed for anything to fall out! But then, finally it did.

'Yeah I'm fine thank you. Just had some stuff going on that I needed some headspace to sort.'

Steph surprised herself with the response. It was more honest than she realised when searching in her brain for the most suitable lie. It did stop people though, from trying to get any more information out of her. They seemed to accept the response and usually replied with 'Ahh, well I'm glad you're feeling better.'

Steph found her way to her desk. She was shaking as she turned on the tower and monitor. Luckily, Steph sat on her own so there was no one around her immediately that would see. Over 3000 emails were in her inbox. She couldn't manage her inbox when she was at work everyday so how the hell was she going to manage this?

As she stared at the screen in despair, she felt a hand touch her shoulder. She looked up and there was LC, smiling at Steph. She didn't look angry or disappointed. She looked proud. It comforted Steph. 'Let's go have a chat.' Said LC. Steph followed LC to the room where she had told her before about her addiction.

'You look smart Steph. I'm very proud.' Said LC.

Steph had purposely made an effort to look smart following the advice LC had given her about looking like she was going to work. 'So, how are things?' she asked.

Steph told LC the truth. She had been so good to her when she found what Steph was really going through that it was the least she owed her, and, she was really trying with the promise she'd made herself about being more honest. She told LC about how well she'd done over the last few paydays. She even told LC about her and Amy which was a huge step. No-one at work knew. LC actually listened. She listened to every word without letting anything distract her. She'd not look at her phone, even though it must have had 12 emails come through. She gave Steph her full attention. Steph told her about the retreat she would be going on to and LC told her it wasn't a problem. She would need to use her holiday days for it but she didn't mind, as long as she could go. Steph couldn't thank LC enough. She made her feel safe and like she wouldn't be judged by anyone which was something she feared hugely. She promised to keep her secret. And Steph would repay her by actually working hard. By doing things on time and putting effort into her work. Steph's job was a lifeline. It was her ticket to getting back on track.

The weeks passed by and today was the day. It was time for her to make her way to the retreat. Steph's stomach swirled and swirled. It was a 4 hour drive away from where she lived. Amy had booked the day off to take Steph. Amy had some breakfast before they set off but Steph couldn't stomach it. She was far too nervous. Steph suffered from horrendous travel sickness so they agreed that she would drive there. She double checked that everything was in her bag, ready for the retreat. Toothbrush, pants, jeans, phone charger. She must have checked a million times. Amy kept reassuring her that she had everything she needed and that they needed to go. 'Steph, stop it now. You're just procrastinating.' Said Amy.

Steph climbed into the car and began to drive. 'Did we lock the door? Did I pack my toothbrush? Did we leave the dogs some water?' she asked Amy.

'Yes!' she replied, knowing it was just the nervousness that was leading her to do this.

Amy had made a playlist for the girls for the drive. A playlist full of her favourite songs and songs she knew she found calming. Amy was going to miss Steph so much. Since Steph had moved in, they hadn't really spent much time apart. She didn't like the thought of going to bed without her.

They were over half way there now. Steph struggled the calm her nerves and concentrate on driving but she knew she had to. On that long motorway, Steph focused her eyes forward. This was the motorway that was going to take her to new life. To the light, at the end of the tunnel.

They arrived in the town where the retreat was based. They took a sharp left turn off of the dual carriageway. Steph had never seen a road like this before. As they continued to follow the instruction of the SatNav, they arrived at a long dirt road. She wasn't even sure that her car would fit down it! 'This is wrong Amy, it wouldn't be down here!' Steph exclaimed. 'It say's were 10 minutes away so just keep going.

Steph was petrified. What had she signed up to? Why was it in the middle of no where? Maybe this was actually a group of murderers, luring young vulnerable women in and they didn't offer gambling therapy at all. It was after this thought, Steph pulled up. Having a full blown panic attack at the wheel, Amy tried to calm her down. It wasn't working though. Steph rang her mum through the Bluetooth in the car. 'Hello?' said her mum.

'I can't do it mum. I can't go here. There is nothing here it's in the middle of nowhere. I can't do it mum, please don't make me go. I promise I wont gamble anymore I promise. Please.' It was ironic that Steph was asking her mum to not to make her go. This wasn't a choice her mum had made for her. This is something she wanted to do on her own.

'Steph. Listen to me. Take some deep breaths and calm down.' Steph's mum had obviously heard the state of panic Steph was in and was trying to help. 'Steph. Of course it isn't going to be in the middle of a town. This is a retreat Steph, to give you a rest from the thoughts you have. Being in the middle of a town where there are shops all over selling scratch cards and bookies isn't going to help you is it. It will be a beautiful place. A quiet place so that you can escape for a while and forget for a few days and get better.'

Her mum's words helped to calm her down. She was right. It wouldn't be much good her going to an office where she could walk over the road and place a bet. Steph took control back of her breathing. Amy was rubbing her back the whole time. A few minutes passed and she thanked her mum. She told her how much she loved her and explained again that she would be in touch with her when she could because she wasn't allowed her phone when she was there. Her mum told her again how proud she was and how much she loved Steph. Steph lowered the handbrake, and continued following the dirt road.

They drove down a drive that must have been a mile long. It was stunning. There was a beautiful old house, surrounded by fields full of flowers. There were two beautiful horses in the field to the left of the house and a pond running alongside the house. 'That's where they put your body when they murder you' joked Steph to Amy. They reached the front of the house where they pulled up. Steph looked up at the house. It was huge. It looked really old. It must have been a listed building, she was sure. It had really old windows and frames. It had concrete steps leading up to a pair of glass door which had another paid of solid wooden doors behind them. There were no other cars here yet. She must have been the only one. What if there was no one else coming? What if she would be here alone? She began to panic again. 'I can't do it Amy. Please. Please just take me home. I'll get better on my own I promise.'

'Come on bab. You're going to be fine. I am so proud of you. It's only 4 days. I promise you you're going to be fine.' Replied Amy, doing her best to comfort Steph. It didn't work though. All Steph wanted to do was go home. She felt like a child going to school for the first time.

'I need a fag.' Said Steph.

She rolled herself a cigarette, hands shaking, and told Amy she wanted to walk. She started to walk up the long driveway, knowing in her head she wanted to reach the gate a mile ahead. She looked around and it was so tranquil. It was absolutely stunning. She'd have loved to come here any other time, but not under these circumstances.

'We need to go back now Steph.' Said Amy as they walked further up the drive.

'Hello!' shouted a male voice suddenly. Steph's heart skipped a beat. She turned around and there was a tall man walking up towards them. He had a friendly face. He was wearing a pair on chinos and a jumper. He wasn't dressed really smartly like he was at work but this made Steph feel more comfortable. 'I'm Dean, what's your name?' he asked politely.

'Steph' said Steph in a shaky voice. 'Ok Steph, and you're here for the retreat?'

She nodded her head, unable to get a word out now. 'It's normal to be nervous Steph so don't worry. Have you travelled far?' He turned and started to walk back towards the house slowly. Steph knew what he was doing, he was trying to get her to stop walking further away and entice her in. She didn't answer any of his questions. When Amy realised she wasn't going to talk, she answered them for her. 'Yeah, about 4 hours!' said Amy to the man. He kept asking questions, stepping closer and closer to the house as he did, whilst Amy answered them. 'The other counsellors will be here soon and the residents of the retreat. You're the early birds!' joked the man. They were now back at the car. 'We're here to help you Steph. It can be petrifying, facing your gambling head on but we're here to help you. ' Steph was shocked that he'd already mentioned gambling. She was so used to never speaking about it, that it felt like it was wrong to be this open about gambling. 'Would you like to come inside?' he asked Steph.

'No.' she replied. 'I need a cigarette first if that's ok.'

'Of course it is' replied the kind man. 'There's an ashtray there for you. Whenever you're ready, just pop inside.'

Steph rolled yet another cigarette sat in the car with Amy. As she smoked, another car pulled up beside her. A woman got out of the car and took her suitcase out of the boot. She walked immediately up the concrete steps into the house. 'How can she be so confident?' thought Steph. 'Just walk in, knowing that everyone knows she's an addict, and not even be bothered.'

The girls were in the car 45 minutes before Amy said 'Bab. It's time.' Steph looked at her, eyes welling up. Amy took her bag from the boot of the car. She gave Steph the biggest hug and kiss ever. Steph clinged on a lot longer than normal, hoping that Amy would just say 'Come on, I'll take you home.' But she didn't. She gave Steph one last kiss, told her how immensely proud she was and reassured her, that she would be back in 4 days time to pick her up. Steph watched Amy drive away, back down the long road. And here she was. Stood on her own, miles and miles away from home, about to face her conjoined twin head on.

Chapter 38

Steph walked through the doors into a hall way. It was absolutely huge. It had that smell that all old houses have. The floor was dark wood and there was a huge rug covering a section of it. The rug was tatty and stained. Immediately to the left, just through the doors was a bench. It looked like a church pew and underneath it were shoes. She'd remembered in the paperwork she'd received that they told her she needed 'indoor shoes.' She'd interpreted this as slippers. She sat on the bench, looking up at the old ceilings and the beautiful beams. She put on the slippers her mum had bought her and placed her trainers neatly, in line with the other pairs under the bench. The kind looking man who was stood in the hallway told Steph to take a seat in the room which was behind the first door on the right. She walked through, still incredibly nervous. The room was massive. It had about 6 sofas in there and 6 chairs. They were all against the edges on the room so that the back wall was what everyone was focused. There were 4 other women at this point in the room. Steph quickly scanned the room to find the most appropriate place to sit. She saw a chair that was as near to the corner as she could get. She didn't want to have to share a sofa with anyone.

She perched herself in the chair and said hi to the women. She could see they were all nervous, apart from the woman she watched walk in, she still looked quite confident. It was a few moments later that Steph realised the woman worked for the charity and she wasn't a resident.

Steph pulled out her phone and looked at anything she could to avoid contact and hide how petrified she was. There was no phone signal at all so she was looking through ridiculous things like her calendar and a shopping list she'd written. Over the next hour or so, the group got bigger. More women walked sheepishly through the door and found a seat. Nobody spoke though. There was a huge elephant in the room, and that elephant was gambling.

Once everyone was there, the counsellors walked in. There were four of them. 3 women and the kind man. The counsellors introduced themselves and explained who they were. Jamie was the leader it seemed. She did most of the talking. She was sat in the chair directly opposite Steph which made her feel a little uncomfortable. The woman, who had long dark hair and wore all black clothes was sat on her bent leg and was tilted in the chair. Like you do when you're watching something on TV or just doing something completely normal. This was anything but normal to Steph. Then there was Dean, Kirsty and Kelly. Kelly was the woman who Steph had originally thought was a resident and Kirsty was a tall thin woman who had the most softly spoken voice Steph had ever heard. She thought she must have been putting it on. No-one could speak the softly all of the time.

The counsellors broke the ice. They confirmed the reason everyone was here. They were all there because they all had a problem with gambling. After that, people seemed to chat more. The elephant had gone and they could speak. Steph didn't though, she was still crippled by nerves. Then the part she hated. An around the room introduction where they we're going to make her say 'I'm Steph Goodyear and I'm a gambling addict'

They didn't. They said you could say as much or as little as you want. Steph had already counted and she was 5th to speak. She was trying to think what she would say before it was her turn. The women explained who they were. Some said a lot, some said barely anything. But they all said how much they struggled and how they wanted so much to get better. It was Steph's turn. Her mouth now completely dry she said in a croaky voice 'Hi I'm Steph. I've gambled for about 10 years now, since I was 18. I'm not much of a talker to be honest but I really hope this course can help me.'

'Thank you Steph.' Said Jamie and she moved onto the next person. Steph was sweating ridiculously as her turn passed. The next women told who they were and their stories. Steph was amazed at the diversity of the group. So many different ages, different backgrounds, it made her feel like she wasn't alone.

The team then went on to explain the house rules. They took everyone's mobile phones off them and they assigned duties to everyone. They explained that having a responsibility could help people feel more settled in the house. Steph was allocated the job of collecting the phones at the end of the 2 hour period they were allowed it for each day. She would rather have done the pots to be honest, than be the person who took away the contact from their loved ones. But she knew she had to it and the women here understood that.

Jamie let everyone go for a break. Steph rushed to the bench outside of the room and put on her shoes. She'd noticed a bench under a tree a few steps away from the house. It was far enough that she wouldn't have to congregate and speak to the women and that she would be alone. She still wanted to go home at this point. A car pulled into the car park. A big Land Rover and out of it, another woman stepped. She noticed Steph on the bench and made her way straight over. 'Oh my god are you here for the group? I'm bloody late! It's taken me 6 hours to get here!' Steph told the woman she was a resident and that they'd just split up for a break. 'Oh good, I'll have a fag then.' Said the woman as she sat herself next to Steph.

'God this is scary isn't it. Is everyone alright? I was dreading coming here. I was made to by the police. I bloody stole some money to gamble with and this is part of my probation. To be honest, I wanted to anyway. I can tell you this can't I?' as she looked at Steph. 'We're all the same here aren't we.'

This woman had no idea what she had done for Steph in this moment. In her frantic talking, her smoking, her honesty, she'd let Steph know she was going to be ok. That she wasn't going to be judged. Steph knew in that second, that this woman was going to be her best friend here. Steph loved how down to earth she was and how open and honest. Steph suddenly felt as though she could do this. With Filipa here, Steph could find the strength she needed.

Filipa and Steph sat for the 15 minutes Jamie had said she could break for and chatted. About anything and everything. About how they thought the retreat would go, about how they felt, about how worried they were the others would be stuck up.

'We'd better go in.' explained Steph. She walked in with her new friend and sat in the room with the sofa's. Filipa introduced herself and apologised for the fact she was late. The group spent the afternoon just taking about their lives and about the charity and what they could expect over the next few days. It was like a huge weight had been lifted. Steph was in a place now where people did understand, where every single person here knew what she was feeling. Where they all had their own stories. Their own shame. Their own guilt. And where, not one single person in that room, no matter what they'd done, judged them or their actions.

The counsellors left the group at 6pm. They went upstairs into a different section of the house where the residents weren't allowed up. It was their space and everyone respected that. Steph spent all of her time with Filipa. She was so easy to talk to. All of the group though, not even being encouraged to by the counsellors, talked about their gambling. They told each other what they felt and every single of them had felt that exact feeling. Had felt what Steph had felt. They talked for hours and hours. It was absolute heaven. They were all in a place where they didn't need to hide who they really were. They didn't have to paint smiles on or hide anything at all.

Steph went to bed that night and thought to herself how amazing it was. How lucky she was to be with a group of women just like her. Her bedroom was on the top of the stairs to the left. There must have been 12 bedrooms in this place. It was like a maze! Filled with hope and a sense of freedom, Steph went to sleep.

The group were asked to be ready and in the room with the sofa's at 9am the next morning. Steph was up way before this. She knew they'd said the breakfast would be ready from 7.30am. She made sure she was the first one there. From Steph's anorexia days, she still had a huge phobia of eating in front of people. She got ready and quickly made herself a slice of toast before anyone saw her. She ate it as fast as she could and made her way to the bench with the shoes. She sat on the concrete steps and looked over the fields. The sun was rising. It was absolutely stunning. Tree's and fields for as far as you could possible see. This was what her mum had meant. It was this calming, beautiful view that made it the perfect place for a retreat.

She heard the glass door open behind her. 'That's bloody beautiful isn't it.' She knew without looking it was Filipa. She sat on the steps with Steph and they didn't even speak. Both of them took in the beautiful view. As people started to wake up and get themselves some breakfast, Steph sat back in the room with the sofa's. There was a huge bookcase against one of the walls so she looked through the books on it. They weren't all about gambling, they were about everything. They books were so old she didn't dare turn the page in case they fell to bits.

It was just before 9 and all of the women were in the room now. They were chatting about what they thought the day might bring and how beautiful this place was. Steph didn't say anything but felt happy as the women chatted. There were women twice her age there who had gambled for much longer than she had. There were women almost the same age and a few who were a few years older. Steph thought she had the worst addiction in the world, and hers had lasted longer than anyone else's on the planet. She couldn't have been more wrong.

The counsellors were there at 9am sharp. It was Kirsty who started the conversation this time. She explained that she did a lot of work with mindfulness and mediation. Steph thought this was perfect for Kelly because her voice was so soft. Kirsty asked everyone to close their eyes and join her in a mindfulness exercise. Steph was dreading it. She hated stuff like this. She could never stay still for long enough and always wanted to laugh with stuff like this. But these people were offering to help her and she was willing to try whatever they told her. Kirsty started talking and telling the group to focus on their breathing. Focus on the what they could hear and their bodies as a whole. Steph actually really enjoyed it. She was so sceptical, knowing she hated these kind of things but she was able to completely relax with the exercise they were doing. Kirsty told everyone to open their eyes. That was brilliant!

Next was to go around the room and ask people how they felt. Some of the women said they were still a bit nervous about what was to come on the course. Others felt happy. Some sad because they missed their families. It was Steph's turn. Oh god! She'd been listening so intently to the other women, she'd forgotten that she would need to speak too. 'I feel ok.' Said Steph. 'You fucking idiot' she thought to herself. 'You've made yourself look a right twat!'

'Thank you Steph' said Kirsty, and she moved onto the next woman. The team told everyone what they would be going through that day. There was a paper chart in front of them. Like the ones in school that stand on 3 legs and you flip the paper over. They talked about how gambling made them feel. Everyone was really engaged in the conversation. Everyone said what they felt, not having to hide anything and being completely open and honest about it. Before they knew it, was time for a break. Just before they finished for lunch though, they looked at the chart.

Sad, angry, guilty, ashamed, bad, suicidal, depressed, hurt, worried, anxious, scared, hopeless, restless, uneasy.

These were just a few of the feelings the group had written. No-where, no-where within the page of feelings was a single positive one. Everyone felt the same. Why did they continue doing an action that made them feel these things? It was a really powerful statement.

The team came back in and they started again with the mindfulness exercise. They all spoke about what the first session had made them feel. The afternoon was spent talking about what they had gained and lost from gambling. They were split into teams to work it out together. Steph wasn't in a team with Filipa which she didn't like but she was happy to speak to any of the women here, they'd all been through the same. Once the group had done, they presented their piece of paper.

Gained	Lost
Anxiety	Jobs
Depression	Family
A criminal record	Friends
Debt	Partners
Bankruptcy	Money
Divorce	Self
respect	
Suicidal thoughts	
Belongings	
	Identity
	Love for anything
	Concentration
	Health
	Security
	Credit score
	Sex
	Motivation
	Career
	Self-control

Everyone looked again at their results. And there were even more than this from other teams. Things that Steph and her team hadn't even thought of. Again, there wasn't a single positive thing gambling had brought into their lives. It made Steph really think. Really think about every gambling had taken away from her and that it gave absolutely nothing in return. She had a sense of true understanding.

At lunch time, they ate in the next room along. It was a big room with 6 tables in it that sat 4 people at each table. The food was laid out on tables which ran the length of the room. There was all sorts! It looked delicious. With Filipa by her side, Steph felt a little braver. She got herself a bowl of soup, a slice of bread and some pasta for main. She had a rule though, that she was never allowed to go back for seconds. Steph and Filipa ate at a table where Bally and Katie joined her. The other two women were nice. They were easy to speak to, as was everyone in the group. Steph finished her food quickly and told Filipa she was going for a cigarette. She sat on the concrete steps once again and admired the view.

They got an hour for lunch but everyone was back in the room before they needed to be. They all genuinely enjoyed speaking to each other.

The day was filled, cram packed with talks within the group about their experiences and how gambling had affected them. The coaches were amazing. You wouldn't even think they were coaches. They joined in the conversation and were able to give the people there understanding as to why. Why these thoughts creeped into their heads, why their bodies reacted the way they did. It all started making sense to Steph and she couldn't be happier.

The team were so engaged in listening to each others stories. Some had broken the law, some had stolen, some had lied, some had cheated. That's when Steph realised. She realised she wasn't an evil person. She wasn't out to hurt everyone she loved just as none of the people here were.

At 6pm, when the day had ended, it was Gem's job to hand out the phones. The signal was absolutely terrible here so there wasn't much point. Steph got her phone and turned it on. She walked around and around the house trying to find anywhere she could get a signal. She walked out into the beautiful field where the two horses were. She lost herself for a moment, taking in the stunning views. But then, her phone began to vibrate in her hand. Message after message came flooding through. Most were from Amy but there were messages from her sisters, her mum, even LC, all telling them how proud they were and how much they loved her. Steph felt overwhelmed. She rang Amy, being sure not to move from the spot she was on so that she wouldn't lose signal. 'I miss you babe!' she shouted as soon as she answered the phone. The girls talked for the full 2 hours Steph had. She told Amy about how amazing this place was. How it wasn't like the other things she'd tried and how she knew it would work this time.

Steph told Amy again how much she loved her and hung up the phone. She took a deep breath and looked at the view one last time. Steph thought she'd felt happy before. When she won all that money but in this moment, right now, she knew she wasn't happy when she won. This was happiness. This feeling of freedom, relief and without a twin putting any thoughts of self-loathing or gambling, this was happiness.

Steph turned off her phone and walked back into the house. She walked around the women and collected their phones. No-one told her 'just 5 more minutes' or I'm not done yet.' They all handed it straight over. A lot of the women had actually turned their phones off before the 2 hours was done. They found so much peace without their phone's, they didn't actually want them at all. Steph, hands full of phones, walked up the stairway to where the coaches stayed. She was nervous! She knocked on the huge wooden door and Jamie answered. 'Come on in' said Jamie. Steph felt like she'd been invited into the staff room at school. It was a big living room with a few sofa's. They had a TV in there as well. The residents didn't have TV's. Steph knew though this would be to encourage the women to talk and also, to avoid the copious number of adverts that were on the TV all the time about gambling. Steph dropped the phones on the counter top, thanked Jamie and walked out of the door.

The women once again spent the evening speaking to each other. Talking about how helpful this was. They talked about the different things they'd tried before to get better and how this was so much different. Steph noticed though, that Filipa wasn't here tonight. She immediately jumped up and went to Filipa's room. 'Is that My Steph?' asked Filipa as Steph pushed open her bedroom door. 'It is.' Replied Steph. It was crazy how close the pair had come in 2 days. Filipa knew more about Steph in 2 days than her own partner did. Steph and Filipa stayed up that night until 2am, talking about everything. Their home lives, their families, everything. Steph slept in Filipa's room that night. In the room that she had found her new best friend.

Chapter 39

Steph had found a shower she liked. It was at the other end of the house so the chances of her getting disturbed were minimal. She didn't spend long in there though as she didn't want to hog it. She knew the women would be waking up soon too and they would want to use it. Once she was ready, she went downstairs. There were already 2 women there eating their breakfast but they welcomed Steph to join them. It made feel Steph feel easier about eating. Steph took her coffee out to the concrete steps to once again enjoy the view before the day started. 'You alright baby girl?' asked Filipa. 'Yeah' she replied smiling. 'I wish I could see this everyday.'

The pair finished their cigarettes and headed into the room where the rest of the women were congregated now. Filipa though, didn't seem herself this morning. The coaches joined them and Kirsty guided them through the meditation process. Steph loved it now. It really did clear her mind. Jamie went around the room again and asked people to tell the group how they felt. Steph was determined that she would give a better response than she had yesterday.

'Steph' said Jamie 'How do you feel today?'

'I feel lucky Jamie. I feel like my place here is the best thing that's ever happened to me and I'm so lucky to be here.' Jamie smiled at her. 'Thank you Steph' she said and moved onto the next woman.

When it got to Filipa, she left the room upset. What was wrong? Steph wanted to follow her but the coaches had said before that if someone does get upset, they were not to fuss or hug. Steph was worried for her friend. A few minutes later, Filipa came back. She apologised to everyone and explained she just felt emotional today. She was missing her children. She came back with a smile though that made Steph feel better.

Dean lead this mornings session. He got everyone to tell each other who their hero's were and what they found inspirational in a person. Steph knew straight away who hers were. Her nanna and her strength. Her nanna who, despite all that heartbreak, continued to help people and be so kind to everyone. Her nan still loved her husband so much. She held his hanky in her hand every night as she slept and before she went to sleep, she would kiss it and say 'I love you darling' she still did this 10 years after he passed.

She wrote Leanne, Amy and her mum next, all for the same reasons – For their perseverance, patience and strength. They were the only reasons that Steph was here today.

And finally – Stephen Hawking for his intelligence – A man who had to overcome so many barriers. A man who quite rightly, could have chosen to be miserable and trapped in his condition but he didn't. She used his incredible intelligence to teach the world what he knew.

Steph was excited to share with the group her hero's. She was surprised when they weren't asked to. Instead, the group explained to each other how they themselves held everything they looked up to and found inspiring. How every one of them were strong and intelligent. So why didn't they look up to themselves. It was so moving and a few of the girls cried.

After a short break, it was Jamie who took the lead. Jamie was talking to the group about what addiction does physically to a person. About how, a chemical is released when we gamble and that is what you're addicted to. And to keep producing that chemical, you have to gamble more and more and more. She explained the stats around it and the things your body and mind will do to ensure you gamble. And then Jamie said, 'You go into auto pilot mode. Sometimes, a person can have no memory of what they're doing. Your body is just reacting to an urge and you have no control over it. It sometimes can feel like it's another person doing these things and making you gamble. And so, we named this person Rita.'

It was her twin! She was talking about her twin! Rita! It felt good to give her twin a name at last. Steph wanted to cry at the relief that she wasn't crazy. That other people had the same feeling. That it wasn't them doing these awful, horrible things. It was Rita!

Jamie got the group to write a letter to Rita. Steph always enjoyed writing so this was right up her street. She wrote her letter, telling Rita how much she hated her. How she'd done nothing but bring her misery and sadness. How she was sick of her holding guns to her head and screaming in her and that she wouldn't listen anymore. She would kill Rita and she would win. She told Rita what she'd lost through her and that, no matter how loud she screamed, Steph would win.

Jamie asked the group to read out their letters. They didn't have to if they didn't want to but Steph did want to. With no shame or embarrassment to worry about, she wanted to verbalise her letter so that she knew Rita could hear. She actually felt emotional as she was reading it.

Next, Jamie asked everyone to grab their coats and head over to the fire pit. The group were all to throw their letters onto the fire and the letter, along with Rita, would no longer exist. Steph remembered thinking how often she thought Rita would attend her funeral, but it was the other way around now. She'd killed her.

The group went once again for lunch and returned into the room an hour later. Steph was completely inspired by every single minute of this retreat. It all made sense. It was so different and she was so happy to be here. The afternoon was to talk about how to resist the urges to gamble. This was the part Steph needed the most. She'd acknowledged her gambling, understood the effects mentally, physically and emotionally and now would learn how to not give into them. Jamie showed them so much. She showed them how the brain worked and how they ended up gambling, even without realising. They explained that every urge to gamble, comes from a trigger. This could be absolutely anything. It could be an advert, it could be a song, it could be the sound of a lighter clicking. If your brain could make a connection from your trigger to gambling, it would. Steph was fascinated. She knew quite obviously what her trigger was. It was payday and having money in her account. Steph knew that this made her urges to gamble uncontrollable.

Jamie went on to explain what the women could, and needed to do to control these. There were so many tips and tricks, all that Steph had never been taught before! How had she been so many places for help and not been told immediately about these tools and tricks which she knew would make sure she was successful! One of the things that really resonated with Steph was the triangle. Jamie drew it up on the paper chart. In it's three corners, were the three things that Steph needed to remember for the rest of her life.

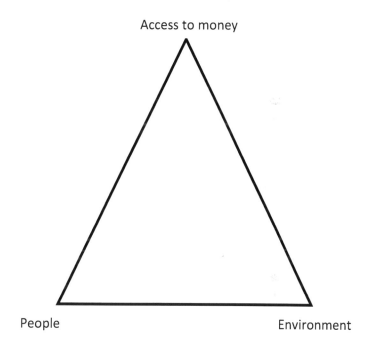

Access to money

People

Environment

You see, if even one of these things isn't in place, the triangle would fall, the triangle being Steph. If Steph made sure, in every situation she was in, she had no access to money, she was with other people and she wasn't in an environment where she could, or it may be acceptable to gamble, she simply couldn't do it. This is the triangle that Steph would carry with her throughout her life.

Jamie even talked through with the group, any situations where they thought it may be hard to resist the urge. She told everyone every that, as long as the three things were in place, it couldn't happen. Jamie also explained to the group about trap doors. How even when you were making a plan to get better, Rita would make sure you left a trap door open you could fall down. It could be anything at all but it would be one avenue you would leave yourself to make sure, should you get the urge, you could still gamble.

Steph thought back to when she didn't tell Amy she knew the digits on her card, even though she took it away from her and when she didn't tell Amy that she got paid early if she was being paid on a Monday. Jamie was so right. Everything she said was right.

The group broke up and went for another break. They all went outside this time. They were all absorbing what they'd just been told and agreed that, these methods were so different to what she'd been told before. Everyone was amazed and you could see in each and every person's face, they had believed they could stop gambling.

They went back in and it was Kirsty's turn to lead. Kirsty was talking about the psychological side of gambling and how your brain reacts rather than responds. It's like fight or flight. Your brain, on so many occasions, has given way to the gambling urges that it was a standard reaction now. Kirsty told everyone how, if you put some time between you and your gambling urge, you were able to respond instead of reacting. If, instead of getting the urge to gamble and running straight towards relieving it and gambling, if you gave it a few moments, acknowledge that 'ok, my body and brain are looking to gamble now, let me actually think about this. Let me think about what I should do' , you can avoid going into that auto pilot state and actually make a decision. She also explained how your body, if you'd just listen, will tell you what it needs. If you think about the state you get in before you gamble, the elevated heart rate, the sweating, the restlessness, there is no other situation in the world where you would think this was ok. Kirsty taught the group how to manage their thoughts and give them the best chance possible of getting back control of the urges.

6pm came around before they knew it. The women were absolutely exhausted. So much information, so much to take in but every single bit of it useful and would help them in their recovery. The coaches had arranged yoga for tonight. Steph didn't know how she felt about it. Bending and stretching in front of people but, in the spirit of doing everything they asked of her, she did it. She actually really enjoyed it too! It was calming. The woman leading the yoga had asked them all to close their eyes and concentrate on the ground they were laid on. How it was supporting them. How the world was supporting them. It was ironic as Steph had never felt so supported in her entire life whilst at this retreat. All of a sudden, she heard a snore. Bally had fallen asleep! She saw Filipa in the corner of her eye laughing and Steph couldn't hold it in anymore. She burst out laughing and the group followed. Steph, in that moment, thought this was the happiest she had ever been in her life.

The group got their phones and she returned to the exact spot she knew she'd managed to get a signal the day before. She called her mum to let her know she was ok and how much she was enjoying it here. Next she rang Amy. She told her how happy she was. She also told her she didn't need to make the 4 hour car journey tomorrow afternoon because Filipa lived only a few junctions down and had agreed to take her home. She told Amy again how much she loved her and that she was excited to see her tomorrow before ending the call. Steph sat on that patch of grass, staring at those two beautiful horses in the sunset. In all her happiness, Steph did miss one thing. She missed Leanne. She remembered how Leanne had always been there for her and how silly it was the things they fell out over.

'Leanne I miss you. I love you so much and I don't want a life without you in it. I'm in rehab so I can't message back, should you chose to reply to me, and I wouldn't blame you if you didn't! I wont be able to read in until tomorrow. I love you Leanne and I'm sorry.'

Steph sent the message. She made her way back to the house and collected the phones from all of her now, friends. The group sat together again that night. They were all nervous about going home tomorrow. They we're safe here. There were no triggers, no adverts here. There was no hiding who they were. They were safe here and nobody wanted leave.

Steph spent the night in Filipa's room again but they didn't speak much tonight. They we're both absolutely exhausted. At 2.30am, Steph heard the loudest bang she'd ever in her life. It made her jump in her bed. She could hear through the old, thin walls, it had woken some of the other women up too. Then it happened again, followed by lightening so bright, the room filled with light. Steph listened to the rain batter the ground beneath them. It was amazing. Steph had never seen a storm like this, not even when she went abroad. She jumped out of bed and grabbed her tobacco from the bedside side table. She ran down the carpeted, spiral staircase and quickly put on her shoes. She stepped outside under the safety of the ledge that covered the step. 'Wow' she thought as she watched the rain bounce off of the ground. Steph sat for half an hour and watched the storm as it moved further and further away into the distance. Because the sky was so clear, she could see the lightening even when it was miles away. Steph imagined it was her twin. Rita. She imagined it was Rita, letting her anger out that Steph had won the battle. She imagined it was finally leaving her body.

The next morning, Steph enjoyed her coffee as usual on the step. The sky was perfectly clear and blue now. You would never have known the huge storm that had passed in the night. The birds were singing and it was picture perfect. She finished her coffee and went into the big room that the women gathered in everyday. Everyone seemed a little down and subdued. She knew it was because today was they day they went home. It was scary, to go back into the big wide world. But at least this time they'd know. They knew the trap doors, they knew their triggers, they knew how to beat an urge. They would go back into the big wide world, gamble free women.

It was Kelly who led this morning. She'd always been really quiet so it was nice to hear her talk. Kelly told the group about her own battle with gambling addiction. About how bad it had been and how she recovered using the methods that the coaches had shared with the team. Kelly was living proof it could be done.

The final exercise the women did was a silent walk. Steph didn't think much to the idea but she went on anyway. She was looking forward to venturing into the fields she'd spent so long admiring. The walk took them through the field into another. There were children learning to horse ride in this field. It was like a scene from a book. Children laughing and smiling as the trainers led the horses. They continued to walk and got to a little church. It was stunning. They went inside and sat down in the pews. Still completely silent, Steph took in the surroundings. She'd always liked churches. She often thought that humans now would never build such grand buildings with intricate details. It was all about doing small buildings packed as tightly as they could be. The group continued to walk. They past other walkers and Steph found it really difficult not to say hello, but she did as she'd promised and didn't say a word. The next thing on their walk a beautiful brook. It was almost like a tiny beach. There were children paddling and their parents playing football on the bright green grass just next to it. This was so calming. Not a single worry entered Steph's mind. Not a single thought other than how beautiful this was. Not a single peep from Rita. They made their way back to old house. Steph saw it in the distance. This was it. It was time for her to face the world alone now. She was dreading it a little but was looking forward to seeing Amy. As they all gathered in the room for the final time, Kirsty once more, asked them to meditate. Everyone was so relaxed, they could have stayed there forever.

Jamie led the conversation once more. She handed out some packs including a 12 week journal. It would be 12 weeks before the group would gather again. She gave the women a number of links that she made them all confirm they would log onto and install or register as soon as they could. There was a link to software that would block your phone from letting you on any website. This was fantastic! How did Steph not know about this? She could have done with this years ago! She also told them about the services you could sign up to that would inform the gambling companies you were not to be allowed to gamble. There was GamStop, sense, Gamban, all sorts! Steph had never heard of this either. The group said goodbye to each other. Everyone was quite emotional, even the coaches. Steph grabbed her bag, hugged everyone in the group and climbed into the Land Rover her now new best friend had arrived in.

Filipa started the car, and they made their way down that drive. That mile long drive that had scared Steph so much to go down when she got here, she was now leaving a new woman.

Chapter 40

Steph noticed everything on the way home. She noticed the birds, the wind turbines. She noticed the bingo halls and the adverts on the busses promoting gambling. She recognised how these were triggers.

Amy had agreed to meet Steph at the junction of the M1 that was her town. As she got closer, Steph felt more nervous. Nervous of leaving her best friend and going back to fighting this on her own. Steph wasn't on her own though. Armed with the knowledge she now had, the tools Gordon Moody had given her and 12 weeks of counselling with Kirsty, Steph felt stronger than she had in the last 10 years.

Steph gave Filipa the biggest hug of her life when she got out of that. 'Thank you Filipa. I love you.'

'I love you too mate.'

The girls agreed that they would go back to the retreat when it was time together. They would meet up back here and Filipa would drive them. Steph had made it all the way home without feeling sick once. She was impressed with herself!

Steph ran up to Amy and gave her a huge kiss and a hug. Amy squeezed her and span her around. 'I've missed you so much' said Amy.

The girls got in the car and made their way home. The dogs were super excited to see Steph and she was them. It felt strange though. Even though she'd only been away for a few days, it felt strange that she was back here. Away from the safety of the retreat.

The next few weeks passed and Steph was a completely different person. She did every single tip the coaches had taught her. She ordered a new bank card to Leanne's house and got Leanne to scratch off the three numbers on the back before she gave it her so that Steph could never know them and would never be able to use it online. She downloaded the gambling therapy app and continued with the meditation. She downloaded the software on her phone and she made sure, always, she did not have access to money.

She dived into her work, doing the best she possibly could and it was noticed by LC. LC was so supportive. Steph thought ' She gave me a chance. She was within her right to sack me when I was ill but she didn't. She believed in me' and for this she would be forever grateful.

She also did get a reply from Leanne. The reply said how much Leanne had missed her too and how proud she was of Steph. Everything in Steph's life changed for the better. She started to put on weight and looked healthier. Her relationship with Amy was stronger than ever and she'd even got an apology from Betty, explaining she just didn't know what to say.

She kept up with every counselling session with Kirsty. Her voice really was like that all the time but it was so calming and soothing. Steph looked forward to these counselling sessions, they were different to any she'd had before.

Kirsty helped her realise what her triggers were and they were more than just payday. Steph had told Kirsty about how she used to gamble just to escape and Kirsty helped Steph realise that, not having time to herself, not having any space and not having peace and quiet was a trigger for Steph too. Steph had never thought about it this way but it made sense. Steph started having a bath some days rather than a shower. This gave her just 1 hour of complete silence. 1 hour of being alone with her thoughts. She would often listen to a meditation recording as she was in the bath and she would come out completely refreshed.

Payday after payday passed and Steph grew stronger and stronger. She still had urges to gamble but she fought them. She didn't react anymore, she responded. And, through listening to her body and giving herself time to think, she decided she did not want to look for a way to gamble and the urge passed.

Amy and Steph were closer than ever too. No lies, no secrets, complete transparency and Steph loved it. Steph loved her life.

Steph stayed in touch with Filipa and even visited her house. The women were close and they were both doing so well.

It was the following week when Steph was sat in Amy's car, at that junction, waiting for her friend to pick her up to take her to that place that she felt so safe. As Filipa pulled up, Steph gave Amy a kiss and a hug and jumped into the car her friend was driving. She waved to Amy as they set back off to the house that had changed Steph's life. On the way there, Steph and Filipa talked about how they'd coped and how they thought the others will have coped. They genuinely hoped everyone had done well. The drive didn't seem as long this time. Maybe Filipa's car was faster than Amy's. This time though, as they drove down that long, beautiful driveway, Steph felt excitement instead of fear.

Steph and Filipa sat on the bench they had met on that first day, and smoked a cigarette. Steph made a promise to herself that if she beat gambling, she'd work on beating smoking next. The others started arriving as they sat there. They all approached Steph and Filipa and every one was hugging and smiling. Everyone had a huge smile on their face. Steph felt as though she was home.

Jamie, Dean, Kirsty and Kelly were already in the room with the sofa's. Steph ran to the chair she had spent all of her time in during the sessions in her last visit. Some of the women were sat in different places to the last time they'd come but Steph had become fond of her little chair. She sat in this chair a completely different woman to the one she was she was when she first sat in it last time. She was a happy, healthy, gamble free woman this time.

They started the sessions as they always did, with Kirsty guiding them through the meditation. Steph loved it now and it was nice to have Kirsty's actual voice, rather than a recording, guiding her through it. And now, it was time for the around the room. It was so different. Polar opposites from what had previously happened. Last time, people spoke of their entrapment, of their depression and helplessness but this time, this time they talked about their freedom, their happiness and how far they'd come. It really was beautiful. It was Steph's turn to talk once more. 'I am simply, the happiest I have ever been in my life. I'm doing well at work; I'm paying my debts and I do not gamble.' Everyone congratulated Steph, as they had everyone. It was pure joy.

It was time for a break. Steph made her way to the concrete steps that she loved so much. The fields were as beautiful as ever and Steph's soul seemed at peace. All of the women joined her. Not all smoking but just around to the steps. Steph just sat and watched. Watched the faces of these women, all beaming and thought how unbelievable it was that 4 days, 4 days of being taught the right methods, in the right way, just 4 days was enough to help these women who have struggled, some, their entire lives.

The women regrouped and the afternoon was spent talking about how they had managed some of their urges, what they'd done and any advice they had for anyone else. No-body here was under any illusion that they couldn't fall back into the trap. The retreat wasn't a magical fix in that it took every single urge you ever had away. It was about teaching you how to recognise them and manage them so you had the best chance possible of fighting them in the right way.

Steph explained what she had done with the bank card and that Amy still watched her, every payday, transfer her money to her mum. Some of the other women had done some really clever tricks too. Bev, who was hilarious, told the group that she'd got a 'billy basic' phone. A phone that did no more than text and call. She was a lot older Steph and had struggled for a lot longer. But a 'billy basic' worked for her and had stopped a lifetime of the same cycle. Steph remembered feeling so incredibly proud of Bev.

It was Yoga again that night. Everyone laughed about the time Bally had fallen asleep. They completed the yoga and all returned to the room. It was already time for the coaches to go upstairs. Everyone got their phone but nobody really even used them! They were all too engrossed in conversation with each other. Steph felt like she was back with her family. Steph collected the phones back in but she bumped into Kelly on the way. She handed them over to Kelly for her to take up the 'staff room' as Steph thought of it.

After hours of talking with her recovery family, they went to bed. Steph slept with Filipa of course but they were shattered from the journey, so it wasn't long before both were sound asleep. Protected by the walls, the ceiling, the roof where these women had found freedom.

It was a 9am start the next morning. Steph had missed so much starting her day sat on these steps, drinking her coffee. She went into the room with the sofa's once more, and joined her family. At everyone's usual seat, was an envelope with their names on it. Steph knew what it was straight away. The last time they were there, before they left, they had to write a letter to themselves. It had to say what they wanted, what they needed and what they promised their selves they would do. Jamie confirmed what it was and asked the group, one by one, to open the letters and read them out. The promises people had made to themselves were promises of happiness. Promises to try. Promises that they would not gamble again and if they struggled with an urge, they would reach out for help. Steph read hers out. She'd promised herself 8 weeks earlier, that she would look forward to payday. That it wouldn't be a day of dread anymore. That she would love Amy the way she deserved to be loved and that she would kill her twin. She had an immense feeling of pride and she realised, in 8 weeks, she hadn't lied to herself, she hadn't lied to anyone. Steph was now Steph again, for the first time in 10 years.

As another woman read her letter, she began to cry. It was Gina. 'I can't do this' she sobbed. 'I gambled.' Steph remembered not feeling disappointed, not feeling angry, not having any judgement about what Gina had done. She just felt empathy. The group reassured her it was ok and the coaches quickly took over. 'Thank you for your honesty Gina. Who in this group can say that they've never hidden that they've gambled?' Nobody could, of course they couldn't. They were all there because that's all their life was. It was to reassure Gina that, even though most hadn't gambled, it was ok and everyone knew how she felt. Recovery is hard! The coaches got Gina to talk them through what had happened. Gina explained she had received a letter with some really bad news. The coaches explained to everyone there that this was Gina's trigger. Bad news, stress and worry was a trigger on its own. Gina went onto explain that she had installed the software on her phone but hadn't installed it on her daughters IPad. And there was the trap door. Explaining these made it so easy for everyone to understand how important it was to close these trap doors. Things you didn't even realise we're trap doors! They continued to talk through it and explained the relapse and how we could all make sure it didn't happen. Gina was absolutely gutted. You could see that she felt like she'd let the group down. But she hadn't. Not one person thought that of her. She was in their family and they were there for her no matter what.

It was lunch time before they'd talked through everything! Steph was so engaged with what was happening, she hadn't even noticed she'd skipped a cigarette! The girls all offered Gina as much support as possible, reassuring her they were all there for and proud of her.

In the afternoon, the group recapped over everything they had learnt, making sure it all stayed fresh in their brains. This time when they left, they wouldn't be coming back. They spent the last evening they had together talking and arranging ways they could stay in contact with each other. For the last time as a group, they laughed, they cried and they shared their stories without any attempt to hide any bit of it. Steph was going to miss them.

The next day, the women went through the normal meditation and said what they were feeling. They then moved into the next room where they'd done yoga. They all sat in a circle on the floor and told each other that they deserved to be happy and gamble free and reminded each other, no matter the thoughts that may ever tell them otherwise, they were good people.

The women were invited to speak to the group and say their goodbyes along with any comments. It was so emotional. Something like this before, Steph would have found completely cringe worthy but not now. She was sharing her gratitude for her coaches, the help they'd given her and for making things make sense in her mind. And to her friends, for making her feel so comfortable, for not judging her for what she'd done, for letting her release Rita and the guilt she carried for so long.

The girls, for the final time, hugged each other and said their goodbyes. Even Steph cried this time. She thanked directly and personally, Jamie, Dean, Kirsty and Kelly. These for people had taught her how to live again and she owed everything to them.

Once again, Steph made her way to Filipa's car and drove, for the final time, down that mile long driveway she had once hated. Steph was no longer, the girl gambler.

Chapter 41

6 months passed and Steph was completely unrecognisable. A healthy strong young woman who was now a manager within her company. A woman who had money. Not in her account of course but with her mum. A woman who had a brilliant relationship with her partner, and was once again was in regular contact with her childhood best friend. She'd finished her sessions with Kirsty and she had Kelly to reach out to whenever she needed to. She didn't find herself ever needing to. She was never bothered enough by the urges now. She would still get them of course but she was strong enough to fight them. The shouting wasn't nearly as loud and she controlled her thoughts with the tricks that Gordon Moody had taught her.

There were some really big obstacles put in her path. The fact that her sister won a large amount of money online was one. She had also become hugely successful in her picture selling business. She was now earning thousands and thousands of pounds in a week and she was proud of it, so of course she would share it with Steph. Steph recognised quickly that this was a trigger for her. She found herself in huge arguments Belle every time she saw her and she knew really, it was just the frustration that being triggered caused her. She wasn't responding to the triggers, she was reacting. Both Steph and Belle made the decision that it was best they had nothing to do with each other. Steph would still see the kids but that would be it. It might get better one day but, right now, they both gave each other bad vibes and it wasn't right, as they were both trying to find their way in life, to be together.

Steph continued to thrive. Christmas was coming up and she was excited that, for the first time in years, she could afford to buy the ones she loved gifts. She enjoyed Christmas shopping and absolutely spoiled Amy. She knew Amy would have thought it was too much but she didn't care, she wanted to spoil her. She deserved it after all.

It was on the way to work when Steph got the news. Her phone rang and it was mum. 'Steph, I've got some bad news I'm afraid.' Said her mum. For the first time in months and months, Steph's heart dropped. 'Your dads had a stroke, he's in the hospital.' Steph immediately burst into tears. Amy kept trying to ask her what was wrong but Steph couldn't answer. As they got closer to the car park at work, Steph told Amy what had happened. 'Can I borrow the car?' sobbed Steph.

Steph called LC as she was sat in the car park outside her office. Sobbing down the phone, Steph told her about her dad. 'Wait there' said LC. A moment later, she came bursting out of the office doors and ran to Steph. LC squeezed Steph and told her everything would be ok. 'Now go and be with him' instructed LC. Steph dried her eyes and drove the 5 minute journey to the hospital. She ran onto the ward they'd put her father on but they were still giving him treatment. She wasn't particularly close to her dad but she still loved him, and didn't want him to die. Her Auntie was sat in the waiting room. 'He's still in the treatment room' she sobbed to Steph. The pair waited anxiously for someone to come and give them an update. It was half an hour before a doctor knocked on the door and told them that they needed Steph's auntie to sign a form so that they could give her dad an injection. It would break up the clot on his brain but there was a risk of death.

When you're put in that situation, of course you would sign it. And that's exactly what they did. They explained that they needed to get her dad to a specialist hospital in Sheffield as they may need to operate to remove the clot. The morning went by so quickly, Steph didn't have time to process anything at all. She just went where she needed to go. Her Auntie was able to go with her dad in the ambulance and Steph reassured her she would meet them in Sheffield. But she was too frantic, in too much of a state to drive. She rang Amy who got a taxi to the hospital and drove Steph to Sheffield. Steph was praying all the way that her dad would survive. As they reached the front of the Hallamshire hospital, Steph thanked Amy, gave her a kiss and went into the huge, multi storey to find her dad.

Her dad had survived but it was big stroke. For weeks and weeks he was unable to feed himself or even get out of bed. He was on the intensive care unit in the stroke ward of the hospital. Steph was doing 2 trips a day to the Hallamshire which took her about an hour to do from her house. She would pick her Auntie up in the morning, take her home for dinner and then they would return in the evening. Steph was exhausted. She wasn't eating properly or looking after herself. They were grabbing what food they could at the hospital but that was it.

Amy was fantastic with her. She was using Amy's car more than Amy was by now. She hardly saw her for weeks and weeks but Amy just supported Steph in any way she could, as she always did. It was getting closer to payday and Steph was struggling to pay for fuel, food out and parking. Her Auntie did give her money towards it but not having any of her own money meant she couldn't even get herself a drink and it not like it was a 5 minute trip home to get a couple of pounds.

'Mum, I need my bank card. I need to be able to get fuel and tobacco and stuff whilst I'm out. I can't keep going all this time without things because I don't have a card.'

Kirsty had warned over and over again about complacency. How this was the biggest thing that led to relapse. Convincing yourself you'll be ok if you have your card or telling yourself just one scratch card is fine.

'Ok Steph. Are you sure?' replied her mum.

'Yeah I'll be fine, honest.'

Steph collected her card from her mum that night and filled her car with fuel. She went home to Amy and not once, did the fact she have her card back bother her.

The next day, Steph followed her usual routine. She was so tired though. She'd had to go back to work now so she was going to the Hallamshire straight after a full day of work. She picked her Auntie up and they made their way there. Her dad was getting a bit better now. He was awake more and was trying to feed himself. He was like a child though with yoghurt all over his mouth. It really upset Steph. Although she didn't see her dad lot, she always had good conversations with him. And that was impossible now.

Steph went home that day more upset than usual. Her dad didn't seem to be making any significant progress. What if he was never going to get well enough for her to talk to him again? Steph pulled up on her drive and wiped the tears from her eyes before making her way inside. 'You ok babe?' asked Amy. 'Yeah' replied Steph. She didn't have the energy to tell her about the day.

Amy had started playing for her local football team again and they'd arranged a night out tonight. Amy was going to get a taxi home after because she knew how tired Steph was so didn't want to drag her out to pick her up. Amy had cooked Steph some tea and left in in the microwave for her. 'Abigail's here Steph so I have to go. Get your tea and some sleep!' Amy kissed Steph as she walked out of the door. Completely exhausted, Steph fell to sleep.

It was 00:18 when Steph woke up. She squinted at her phone to check the time and there, just underneath, was the date. The 28th.

By 00:45, Steph had gambled. All those months' gamble free, all that hard work. All for nothing.

Steph climbed into bed heart broken. Completely distraught at what she'd done. She thought over everything Gordon Moody had told her and asked herself over and over again how she'd managed to do it.

Her mind went back to that triangle.

People – There was no one around to stop her!

Access to money – She had her bank card!

Environment – She was at home, alone!

Steph thought about trap doors. She'd dropped her phone in the bath a few weeks earlier. Amy gave her the old phone she had and Steph hadn't downloaded the gambling software. She'd recently created a new email address and hadn't updated this with the GamStop that blocked her gambling on websites. Without realising it, Steph had become completely complacent. She was also in a really low place, full of worry and stress as well as being physically exhausted because of her dad's stroke.

Steph knew exactly how and why it happened. These little steps. These little areas in which she'd become complacent had allowed her to undo all those months of work.

She begged and begged Belle for the money to replace it but she wouldn't. Belle was helping her really. She'd already helped Steph so many times in the past. When Steph was so desperate, she would ruin Belle's entire day trying to extract money from her. She knew she couldn't help her anymore.

And Steph was secretly glad she didn't. She had to face what she'd done and get back on track.

On the evening of payday, having managed to slip out before Steph woke up due to her hangover, avoiding having Amy watch her transfer the money, Steph confessed to Amy. She hadn't had these feelings for a long time. The sweating hands, the heart rate, the classic signs that her body was in distress. She explained to Amy why it had happened and everything she'd learned from it.

Amy was disappointed but she did understand the stress Steph was under at the moment. It didn't make it better but she could understand. And so, the girls stuck together through this once more.

Steph reached out to Kelly too. She told her what had happened and what she'd learned from it. Kelly was fantastic. She supported Steph in putting back the measures she needed to in order to be safe again. They rebuilt the triangle. With the software on her phone now, all email addresses signed up and a new bank card on the way that she would never have sight of, Steph felt happy and safe once more. Steph had found her strength. She knew she had a lot of trust she needed to earn back and that it would take a long time before she ever trusted herself. But Steph knew, she was ready.

Chapter 42

Two years on with just one slip, Steph was strong. She had knowledge about how the addiction worked and how it would try to trick her mind, so she could fight it. She had the best of friends who knew what it meant to struggle with gambling addiction and on hand support whenever she felt she needed it. Steph's dad's condition improved a bit and he was allowed home. She would never have one of those deep conversations again, but it was enough to have him safe at home.

Steph was still doing well in her job and her and LC we're actually friends too now which was lovely. Steph's mum was now a life coach too. Seeing the devastation addiction had caused her daughter made her want to help anyone she could so they wouldn't have to go through what Steph had.

Leanne and Steph were also the best of friends once more. A bond so strong, nothing could break it.

And Steph and Amy we're stronger than ever. They'd had a roller coaster of a ride but they'd made it through.

Steph had defeated her evil twin. With the help of Gordon Moody, her family, her friends and her boss, at long last, Rita was dead. Steph had freedom from the guilt, the shame the noises that constantly filled her head. She had freedom from the debt and anxiety that had crippled her for so long.

Steph knew though, that there was always a pothole somewhere. There would be things thrown in her way that she'd need to dodge, swerve, or fight head on that would try and rise Rita from the dead once more. Steph wasn't naive though. She knew the very real danger that she could fall back into gambling and that Rita could rise from the dead. She knew that for the rest of her life, she would be looking out for triggers and trap doors. She'd be making sure there were no other potholes she could fall down. But Steph was ready. She was no longer that weak girl who suffered so much, who wanted to die, who didn't know how to fight the powers of addiction. Steph was happy, strong and intelligent, all the things she'd admired in others. Steph loved her life, and finally, after ten years of hell, Steph was free from gambling addiction.

Printed in Great Britain
by Amazon